THE RED DOVE

BY GERRY HILLIER

to touch the world

© Copyright - 2015 - Gerry Hillier

FOREWORD

When I first began writing The Red Dove, it was a two page legend for a class of pre-adolescent young people and something happened. I couldn't stop writing. I chose the name Teilo for the main character because it had been in my mind for many years. I first saw the name over twenty years ago in a book of names. For some reason it stayed with me. Often when I would sit to write it would jump into my thoughts. It seemed only natural that Teilo would become the warrior in this story.

While writing The Red Dove I discovered Teilo seemed to have a mind of his own and I often felt as if the words were not mine. Sometimes I even argued with 'someone' saying there was no way I would write what was coming to life on the pages because it didn't fit with how I wanted the story to go. In the end, I always acquiesced.

Some time after the completion of the book, I was talking to my son who was awaiting the birth of his second child and searching the internet for babies' names. I asked him to look up Teilo while he was browsing and that's when I discovered St. Teilo of Wales.

After doing some research of my own, I discovered similarities between the two Teilos. Both left their communities for foreign communities and planted groves of fruit trees. Both stayed in their foreign community for seven years and seven months. My curiosity got the better of me and so I went to Wales.

I cannot begin to describe the experience I had in Wales but it was almost like standing between two worlds. As I walked through the woodlands where the historical Teilo would have walked it all felt so gloriously familiar. I half expected the characters of The Red Dove to step out of the trees to greet me.

I have no explanation. I found more amazing coincidences and similarities as I wandered the countryside. My active imagination some might say but it seemed much more. I felt as if somewhere within me was the imprint of a memory – be it genetic, cellular, past life – none of that is important –

but this memory in some way was prompted to surface and expand and create a new beginning. I began to ask myself – what is real and what is imagined? I began to think about the stories we create and the ones that tell of our own experiences. Does it matter that a story is fact or fiction? Teilo is more real to me than many factual stories from my own life.

Creativity is about trust. It is there – a current – an energy, waiting to be downloaded. When we plug into it, we have to trust it and be guided by it. Everything exists – everything has a story waiting to be told.

The power of stories is what they open inside of us rather than their qualifications. And the writing of this story made something in me start to sing.

"May everything be smooth between Heaven and Earth"
Chew Chi Leng (1925 – 2015)

ACKNOWLEDGEMENTS

It is always difficult to acknowledge everyone who contributes and assists in any creative work. Inspiration has its source in many places – beauty, generosity, kindness, belief – all come to us from those who touch us in some way. Nature offers us an abundance.

Those who are blessed with a loving partner, family and friends who offer inspiration, encouragement and support have much for which to be grateful. I am one of those. My heartfelt thanks to you all.

PART ONE

THE LAND OF ROMARRAH

1

"Teilo!" The voice held the brittle edge of fear. Teilo turned. Amis had stopped. He was looking at the forest – his dark, luminous eyes darting from one direction to another. It was, to him, as if the forest had closed itself around him. He had become its prey. He felt the first flutter of panic.

Romarrah stood on the balcony overlooking the main courtyard in Imoshtan. There was little movement in the square below him. Against the west wall several young warriors were discussing their patrols for the following day. Romarrah could not hear their conversation but the occasional word reached him and left him in no doubt as to the subject of their talk. He smiled fondly at their youthful yet earnest discourse recalling his own time of training as he made the journey from boy to man – a golden time of excitement, tempered with education and discipline – a time when an entire new world opened up within him.

The sun was sinking beyond the distant hills and he watched the stillness of evening gradually settle. The land before him lost its colours to the gathering shadows. The young warriors left for their quarters. Another emerged from the south wing and quietly, almost reverently, went about the courtyard lighting the lamps. The soft light illuminated the buildings and the stone floor, and posed there a tranquillity that was unequalled. This was Romarrah's world and it lived in him like a song.

He was in his thirty-fifth year and had only just assumed the title of Romarrah, the Great Master. His training had prepared him well for this time and yet, now as he acknowledged the perfection of his surroundings, he wondered if he was ready for such a daunting responsibility. That he had readily accepted his role with the typical humility of a chief warrior, in awe of the honour bestowed on him, gave credit to his intent to serve his people and protect the Land. But the title also required that he settle disputes and grievances between people or villages, train hundreds of warriors with wisdom, compassion and understanding and, when the time came, ensure the line of Romarrah would be continued after his death – to choose his successor in the same way in which he had been chosen. Certainly he possessed the powers of a chief warrior. He understood the Great Wisdom and was at peace with his understanding. He knew from where his power came and he stood without fear. Yet there was the smallest prickling of doubt in his knowing and this troubled him. It was like a minute tremor in the stillness of his peace.

The dark of night gathered around him and still he stood, observing these feelings – letting them come, watching them go.

"There is nothing to fear, Amis – there is no threat – see – there – through the trees – that is the path that will take us home."
Amis looked to where Teilo pointed. He could see no such path. He made a face. Teilo laughed and at once the forest lost all sense of menace.

Two nights past, after the retiring Great Master had named him as his successor, Romarrah had the strangest dream. It left him with a sense of unease he had not experienced before. In this dream he had been standing on the side of a bare mountain, looking up at its peak, and there appeared a laughing boy child, climbing to the summit, unaware of the danger of his daring. The boy moved with amazing grace and agility as if sure of each step, but suddenly he stopped and, sensing he was not alone, looked at Romarrah. For a moment he appeared hesitant. Then he touched Romarrah's hand.

The Great Master stared at the open, innocent face before him – the soft blonde curls damp with sweat against the forehead and cheeks.

"You are a very beautiful child," he said gently, but when he looked into the boy's eyes, he felt as if his soul had been torn in two.

"Do not be sad, Master," the child spoke. "I will not hurt you – I will only destroy the mountain – it is too old and inside itself it is cracking. Do you not feel it?"

When he awoke, Romarrah could still feel the touch of the child's hand. The following day the dream had walked with him – it shadowed his every step. Even now it still hovered in his thoughts. Was it a warning – a prophecy perhaps? He had sat for a long time recalling every detail, as he had been trained to do, and yet nothing revealed itself. The Great Wisdom told him he was not yet meant to know its meaning. Nothing would be achieved by holding it. He slowly released it into the night before turning his thoughts to the coming day.

As was the tradition, the child who would be his daughter would be brought to the compound to live with him. Syrath had not yet reached her third year. When the time came, he would train her to be a warrior, just as the previous Romarrah had trained his own daughter, Tharease. On the eleventh full moon he and Tharease would be wed – a union sanctioned by the old Romarrah to ensure the Land was ruled fairly – by man and woman as was the custom. Their marriage would be founded on respect for they had both trained and fought side by side and they knew each other well.

As the air began to grow colder the Great Master sighed, almost reluctant to leave the balcony and return indoors. On the morrow he would commence his journey through the land accompanied by a small army of warriors. He would travel to each village that they may see his face and know him as the new Romarrah.

"How is it you always know such things, Teilo?" Amis brushed the dark curls from his forehead. *"I have no feeling of direction – nor do I see any path."* The voice was lighter now.

Teilo shrugged. He was only seven years of age – too young yet to know his difference.

♋

Vulone watched the warriors as they passed through his village. They were always an impressive sight – both male and female. They were quiet as they walked – they did not speak and although their feet touched the earth lightly they stepped with strength and assurance. Their ease of movement intrigued him – a uniformity that was not orchestrated but arose from an awareness of each other. He walked parallel to the army, striding purposefully like a man at one with his intent. When he came level with Romarrah, he bowed respectfully. He had heard that the new Romarrah had come.

The Great Master glanced at Vulone and acknowledged the bow with a nod of his head. He was impressed with what he saw, for Vulone was a giant of a young man – tall and muscular with a rugged look that seemed at once familiar and likeable. He appeared a man completely at ease with himself. There was about him an air of joyful but impatient expectation. Romarrah continued to watch him as he went on his way.

"Do you know that man?" he asked a young boy playing with his friends by the side of the road.

"I do, Master," replied the boy. "He is Vulone, Keeper of the Fires."

Romarrah smiled and nodded to the boy. That would explain the man's ease and confidence. Fire Keepers held a place of honour in the villages. Theirs was the task of providing fire wood for each dwelling but, most importantly, they kept the village fires burning and they had the gift.

The fires, one at the north end of the village and one to the south, smouldered continuously in deep pits. They served several purposes. Clay pipes running from a nearby spring through the pits fed hot water into the communal village baths. The villagers also used the fires to harden their clay bowls and pots but it was the smoke from the fires that brought the most comfort. It told their story and sent messages to neighbouring villages. Soft white or pink smoke indicated all was well. Green smoke was an invitation to all and marked a festivity or celebration. Yellow smoke honoured a birth, purple a death. Orange summoned the villagers to their gatherings. If the village was threatened, plumes of grey smoke streaked with red could be seen rising high into the sky.

The Fire Keepers had the gift of fire knowledge. They understood the fire – they spoke its language and could make the colours reach up through the smoke.

Vulone was a man content with his life and yet Romarrah had a feeling their paths were linked in some way. Perhaps they would meet one day. There was something almost compelling about the Fire Keeper but there was also a shadow – a slight, depressive moodiness. He holds his dissatisfaction in check, thought the Great Master as he moved on to the next village.

Amis knew the difference between himself and Teilo. Even if he did not understand what separated them. He heard the elders speak of Teilo. His own father forbade him to play 'with the fair-haired one – the son of Shimmera'. Yet he was drawn to this forbidden child – his magic and enthusiasm – the one who could take away fear, as he did now, with a look, a touch, but especially his laughter.

♋

Shimmera saw the warriors coming. She had sensed them long before they came into view. The day had not yet reached its full warmth and she was working in the village garden – her hands sifting through the soil –

feeling the rhythm of the season – knowing the songs of the earth spirits. It was like a dance in her heart weaving invisible threads of music that moved between the heavens and the earth.

As the warriors came closer, she held herself busy in her work. She did not need to see the new Romarrah – she already knew of his play in their lives. Apheilio, the man to whom she had given herself, would this day ask Romarrah to accept him as a warrior and their separation would begin. Apheilio would go away for long periods – he would not be there as her companion or offer her respite from the other villagers – those who held her outcast. Shimmera was not of their tribe and she had long ago grown accustomed to distrust in the eyes of others and being outside their circle of belonging. That she had come here to love this man and bear his child was enough. She needed no other testimony.

Romarrah missed nothing as he walked. He saw the woman in the garden and that she purposefully did not look at him. In a glance he recognized her beauty and grace – the gentleness of her hands. She caressed the plants, the soil – it was as if those hands spoke a language he could not understand. Beguiling she is, he thought, but why does she avoid me – what could be her reason. Her manner does not speak of shyness – there is a strength in her that few others possess.

A man stepped onto the road ahead and Romarrah saw him look briefly at the woman in the garden. It was the look between a man and wife – the look that tells the other everything they need to know. Holding up his hand to halt the warriors, Romarrah stepped forward to greet this man. "What is it you want, my friend?" he asked.

The other bowed. "Great Master," he replied, "I am Apheilio. It is my wish to become a warrior – to offer my service."

Romarrah smiled – perhaps this explained the woman's reluctance to greet him. "I am always ready to accept such an offer, Apheilio, but you must know that the time spent in training as a warrior will take you away from your family and your village – sometimes for many months. Will they be willing for this separation – will it leave them disadvantaged?"

He watched Apheilio carefully. The man before him was tall – his features strong yet neat, but it was the fire in him – the passion – that made his physical presence more powerful. This man was alive – no part of him was sleeping and his eyes held Romarrah's with a certainty that would not waste time with pretence. Whatever his answer, it would tell Romarrah the measure of this man.

"Master," Aphelio began slowly, "I feel that I have left the confines of this village a long time ago – it is as if my heart knows my destiny is not here. When my training is complete, my wife and son will follow me. My wife will then have a freedom that respects her difference, rather than excludes it. My son also will have an expanded vision of his own future."

"Well spoken, Apheilio," Romarrah responded, "but I fear you yet need to leave with your wife's blessing for it is her choice also. Only then will you leave openly without seeds of discontent within you. When that is so, I will gladly accept you as a warrior of Romarrah."

"My gratitude, Master," Apheilio bowed again and stood back to watch the warriors pass.

A small group of village elders had gathered to observe the proceedings.

"It is perhaps better Apheilio will be leaving us," one of the older men announced.

"He is the only one who seeks that life," spoke another whose name was Emanis. "There is no cause to leave our village and become a warrior. We must respect our own ways above all else – even those of Romarrah."

"Apheilio leaves because she wills it," another elder interjected, nodding in Shimmera's direction. "There are spells she weaves in the earth. He was wrong to bring her here. She is not our kin nor does she belong to our land."

They stopped talking as the warriors came closer but Romarrah had already sensed their resentment. He had also been aware of the way in which they had looked at the woman who was still intent on tending the garden. Perhaps all does not bide well in this seemingly peaceful village of Athanan, he noted.

"Close your eyes, Amis," Teilo was still watching him.

Amis did as he was bid – waiting. Teilo stepped closer and nearly laughed again at the serious expression on his friend's face. Amis could often be sullen and brooding. Teilo delighted in causing him to erupt into childish laughter and melt into joy.

Standing very close, Teilo whispered in his friend's ear – the same words Shimmera whispered to him.

"While you look so hard, you cannot see."

Amis giggled and made to pull away.

"Ssh, Amis!" Teilo placed his hand on the other boy's arm and waited until he became still again before he continued.

"*My eyes are watching – not afraid to close – eyelids touch unnoticed – in this moment, I cease and the world in me steps forward and becomes known.*"

Amis opened his eyes. "That makes no sense," he giggled again.

"You didn't wait long enough, Amis," Teilo admonished. "You didn't take the time to listen."

"What is it that I am meant to hear?" Amis frowned.

"The way home," his friend insisted.

"But I know that already, Teilo," Amis teased then laughed. "You just this moment told me."

Bravely he ran off in the direction Teilo had pointed – all fear banished and the adventure resumed.

♋

As he and the warriors moved beyond the village and into the wood, the Great Master glimpsed between the trees two young boys fighting playfully with their wooden swords. Their voices rang out in the stillness of the forest.

"I am a chief warrior of Romarrah, Teilo," spoke one, thrusting out his chest and holding his sword aloft. "Who are you?"

"I am Romarrah himself," said the other child who was hidden from view by the undergrowth.

Romarrah laughed quietly to himself as the boys went running and yelling through the trees, unaware that they had missed seeing the real Romarrah. He watched their retreat – one dark and one fair. Like darkness and light, he mused – but it is all light, is it not – there is no darkness, only shadows.

He smiled again, recalling the name he had just heard – Teilo. Surely that would be Apheilio's son and he certainly possessed his mother's fairness. Perhaps his father did not yet realize his son's vision of the future was already well expanded.

The wood was cool and he was enjoying the freshness, the peaceful colours. It stirred in him a great joy and he let it claim him for a moment. Above all, he knew his first duty was to protect this land – to hold it sacred.

The land of Romarrah was known far and wide. Many armies had sought to lay claim on it, desiring its riches and beauty, for it was known as paradise. But any who sought to destroy this paradise with their greed, would first have to defeat the warriors, and there was none who could come even close.

All these thoughts and feelings Romarrah savoured as he walked. The privilege of being the Great Master was only beginning to arise within him. The daunting prospect of his new responsibilities began to soften. To his right, he saw through the thinning trees, the edge of the land and the white curtain of Avarinsa – the land shrouded in mist – the land of mystery. What lay beyond that mist was unknown for none came forth from that place and none ventured beyond the curtain. It was like an unspoken law that would not be broken.

The ancients had said it was the land of light – there were no shadows there – it was the place of immortality.

Romarrah experienced a sudden flutter of unease and although he let it pass, he became wary. Motioning to his warriors to stop he closed his eyes and absorbed all that was around him. There was no danger – of that he was certain. Satisfied, he continued on his way, leaving Athanan and Avarinsa far behind him.

Vulone the Fire Keeper had only one thought in his mind – that of his love for Tharease. Now he had seen the new Romarrah he began to feel unsettled. He had heard of the decree – the betrothal of Tharease to the new Master. This he did not understand. A man or woman was free to choose their own path of love and companionship It was not something that was dictated. Tharease had chosen him, Vulone. They had pledged their love – they had lain together – offered themselves without pretence, without disguise – withholding nothing, leaving no part of themselves closed to the other. This was the highest knowing of another and it was sacred.

A small ache of fear tightened in his stomach and he hastened his step.

Tharease was waiting for him by the river – patiently watching. He knew she had sensed his approach long before he came into view and that he need not speak of his feelings – these too she already knew. He bowed to her and sat by her side. They were still and quiet, waiting - each appreciating the presence of the other. Finally she spoke.

"Vulone – you are fearful – give me your fear." She held out her hand. He took it in his own and felt a deep groan of sadness leave his body.

"I will speak with Romarrah, Vulone – do not fear what is yet unknown. There are things I do not yet understand about myself, and my place in the land, but I trust my father's wisdom and that of the new Romarrah. There is only goodness between us and I will hear their words. If my father's decree is bound by the law of the land, if perchance I must accept it with honour, my love for you will remain. Romarrah will understand that we, you and I, are still at liberty to be together. What then is there to fear?"

Vulone did not speak for a moment. He wanted to tell Tharease that this would not be enough – to be together for the pleasure of each other but not to share their daily life. She smiled at his silence.

"I am not like you, Tharease," he said at last. "I have not your understanding, but I know the fire that is within me – that longs to burn freely for as long as I am of this earth. This fire needs to breathe – not to be smothered or dampened. It needs to speak to the heavens – to rise above the earth and declare its existence. This is what I understand – this is my law."

Again they sat in silence. Tharease looked into the forest behind them. A soft afternoon sunlight filtered through the trees. She knew better than to lose her peace by becoming lost in thoughts and feelings that were baseless – existing only through fear and possessiveness.

"Come," again she smiled at him, "let us refresh our bodies in the river."

But he shook his head, preferring to stay within himself. He watched her walk to the water's edge, undress and quietly slip beneath the shimmering surface. How empty his life would be without her. Did she not feel the power of his passion? Her head appeared above the surface again – so serene that face, he thought. Then he frowned in irritation – these damned warriors – how could they be so calm amid turmoil and discontent? Perhaps he too should train as a warrior that he might match her peace with his own. It was not that he did not know peace within himself. When he worked with the fire he understood that place of quiet in him – where all else ceased and he became as one with the flames, the smoke, the warmth. He felt the same peace when he was with Tharease.

Suddenly he leapt to his feet and without taking the time to undress, dived into the water.

Later, as the sunlight was fading, she sat silently, watching him make a small fire to stave off the chill of evening. How he plays with the fire, she thought as she saw him urge the flames to life, then soothe them into a constant, flickering rhythm.

"Will you stay?" he asked, looking at her with quiet expectation. She was silent for a moment, pretending to consider the invitation, while in her heart she sang with the feeling of warmth and utter belonging that spread through her body.

Vulone did not wait for a response – he knew she teased him. From his sack he took a blanket and spread it on the leafy ground. Together they would lie beside the fire and allow its warmth and the cool of night to play between their bodies while the darkness wrapped them in its sleepy secret.

2

Shimmera drew her cloak closer to her. It was cool at the forest's edge. She did not worry for the child. His destiny was strong within him. Without turning to look behind her, she became aware of the other woman who had come to stand beside the path. It was Lornaya – waiting also for her son, Amis. Shimmera felt the woman's fluttering anxiety.

"I know it is late," she said soothingly, "but they are safe – do not fear. They have wandered too far but now return in haste."

"My gratitude," Lornaya bowed and not knowing what else to say, she walked slowly towards the village. Although her husband had forbidden Amis to play with Teilo, the bond between the pair was strong. She had relented and it became a secret between the two women and their sons.

Shimmera waited. After a time she could make out the two shapes moving swiftly through the dark. The pair parted with one final clash of their swords and Teilo ran to her.

"You have wandered far, Teilo," she spoke, placing her hand upon his head. "I fear your friend Amis will suffer for his lateness. Spare him that next time will you not?"

The boy nodded, still out of breath from his homeward flight.

"What did you see on your wanderings?" Shimmera smiled at him. The adventures of his day still danced in his eyes.

"We climbed to the top of the Mother Mountain," he replied. "Amis found a cave but it was not safe to go all the way into it and I told him we had to stop." His words came out in a rush.

"How did you know it was not safe?" his mother asked.

"The voice told me," he responded.

No other explanation was needed and Shimmera asked no more questions. "Come Teilo – your father is waiting and wishes to speak with us."

Apheilio watched the woman and the child as they came towards him. He had made a small fire and prepared food for them. The sight of their soft, happy faces both delighted and pained him. Could he really leave them to train as a warrior? It was not their safety that concerned him, it was their exclusion.

Five years it would be. He might come home three, perhaps four times a year. Would it be enough? Yet was this not the best he could do? He must make a life away from Athanan. Here Shimmera was treated with suspicion and by some, loathing. It angered him that the other villagers could not see the goodness of her heart. Her gifts only served the land. He had watched those hands heal – indeed he himself had felt their healing. Could the others not see that she would do them no harm? Their distrust was founded on suspicion – they clung fast to age-old fears.

He had never revealed to anyone Shimmera's origins. To do so would be to make her life unbearable. Theirs was a union that should never have been and yet she had come to him. He had first seen her in the forest, standing still – like a beautiful vision. When she sensed his presence she was gone in an instant – melting into the undergrowth.

For weeks he had thought of little else but saw not even a glimpse of the mysterious woman. Perhaps indeed it had all been a dream. Then one day, quite unexpectedly, she returned. This time he saw her dance and it was as if the trees and every part of the earth danced with her. He witnessed the rhythm of all life move through her body. Her long, graceful hands spoke the story that all creation loves to hear – its own mystery revealed. Her long fair hair flowed like a waterfall about her and her body mimicked the play of life.

Again, when she felt his presence, she turned to flee.

"I beg you – do not go," he called after her. "Let me speak with you."

There were tears on his cheeks. When she came towards him she stared at his tears as if she read in them a story he did not know. Neither spoke but the words played between them – seeking a voice. He reached out his hand. Only briefly did it touch her.

"I am not meant to be here," she said turning away. "I will cause you pain."

Then she was gone.

He had touched something that was endless – bottomless – boundless. Already her colours gathered around him.

They met time and time again.

"Know that I love you, Apheilio, but I will also bring you tragedy," she warned him sadly.

"Then I will gladly suffer tragedy," he laughed. He was young and there was recklessness about him. Shimmera had seen beyond his untamed spirit when she had first seen his tears. In this man there was a deep aching to know that which is unknown – the core of existence, the essence of life. He would not be satisfied with less, even if it cost him dearly. It was the reason he had called her to him.

Shimmera sought counsel with the five Noble Seeds of creation. They had no form and their voices filled her being as she lay upon the ancient blessing rock.

"This love of fire and passion steals the freedom of your song and yet it is as holy as all other. Within you lies the life of your earthly wandering. So shall the boy child be born that this love fulfils itself and he walks upon this earth. Let one drop of blood be shed in your name and you will return, knowing fully the pain of earthly death."

Apheilio rejoiced in his good fortune – that this exquisite creature he had found would stay and bear his child was an indescribable joy. He felt vividly alive. He had not known her power then – nor did she use it – she tried to live the life of his land. Nevertheless, he had not expected the strong reaction within the village to her arrival. Even his own parents, who were then still living and whom he respected above all others, turned away from this union.

Instead of sharing their home, as was the custom, Apheilio built a small dwelling on the edge of the forest – close to the mist of Avarinsa.

For a time they lived contentedly but it was within Apheilio that a restlessness began to stir. Frustrated that although he could walk freely through his own village – work with the men – engage with members of his family, his wife and son were excluded. He gradually released all ties to those of Athanan. He began to conceive a different life away from the traditions that felt like chains around his spirit.

All the villages of the land had their own stories and legends. Many were merely fabricated tales which had grown strong through the telling of them, while others were prophecies handed down from the ancients. Often fact and fiction had become mingled, the threads of truth interwoven with those of fanciful imaginations. The people of Athanan did not distinguish between this fearful speculation and the wisdom of the ancients. To them it was all one and to step outside of village tradition and customary beliefs was to invite suspicion, ridicule or, at worst, loathing and violence.

A young man of Athanan was free to choose a wife from another village but to choose one who was not of their land as Apheilio had done, aroused their primitive fears. Speculation on the threat posed by this interloper spread its own current of unease.

Shimmera kept her distance. Her only contribution to the village was to tend the gardens. No one deprived her of this for never had their gardens flourished so well – whether or not the rains came, food was in abundance.

From a new-born baby to the present day, Teilo accompanied his mother to the gardens. She taught him how everything travels a path and that all life, without exception, has a voice and every one of those voices has wisdom. She let him know this wisdom with his senses and speak his own. From Shimmera he learned that what you give to nature – to life – is always returned. Even the plants and the soil of the earth would offer back everything given to them. He learned the joy of true communion with the plants and creatures of his world.

Sometimes he would tend the plants with his mother but mostly he watched. From here he could see the life of the village that was denied him. He knew everyone. He observed them as they went about their daily lives – the women laying out their cloths in the sun to dry – their chatter drifting towards him. They talked of their children and the cloths they wove. They gossiped of other villages as well as their own. Never did they have the sort of conversations that he shared with Shimmera – those of the stories hidden beneath the visible world. When the women came to the gardens to gather their food, he noticed they often took without gratitude. Their hands did not honour the plants – their eyes did not see them. There were a few who were different. Lornaya was one. She stepped with care and her hands harvested with kindness. Often she would smile at Teilo or Shimmera. It was a smile that apologised – that sought to repair what was broken.

The men did not talk as the women did. Their words were practical – directive. They laboured over tasks – maintaining the stone walls around the village – building and repairing that which was old and worn. They never came to the gardens except to mend fences. Some would nod to Teilo and acknowledge him. He preferred they didn't. Athanan was like a dream he watched while wide awake and he enjoyed the dream – village children laughing and chasing each other – sounds and smells – the passage of people. It was a colourful story laid out before him – a book without pages. He knew the characters well – he read the language of their bodies and gestures. He saw the ever changing blends of patterns and colours. Each day created different scenes and none were ever the same. He knew more about these people's lives than they themselves did.

He accepted his separation. He was safe between Shimmera and Apheilio – that was his belonging.

The passing years had not dimmed the suspicious fears of the villagers. They had in fact intensified. Emanis, the father of Amis, was the chief antagonist in keeping Shimmera outcast. Quoting prophecies of old he foretold the destruction of their people by the one who was not their own – 'the one who came from the mist'.

Apheilio scoffed at his words. Shimmera would harm no one – her whole being was love – she could not, even if part of her wanted to – it simply was not possible. And yet, somewhere in his heart was the fear that one day he might lose that which he valued above all else.

♋

The three of them ate around the fire. Teilo happily recounted his adventures with Amis.

When the meal was complete, Apheilio spoke of his plan to become a warrior and asked for both Shimmera's and Teilo's blessings.

"I no longer have allegiance to the village of my birth nor to those within its walls," he told them. "To stay only for the security it offers would be to no longer flourish and soar. I know I must step aside completely."

Teilo was silent for a long time then he looked at his father.

"It is better for you to go where you feel freedom but why is it I cannot come with you? Why is it Shimmera cannot come with you?"

His father sighed. "This I would like more than I can say, Teilo, but I will have to stay at the warrior's compound while I am training – there is nowhere for you to live. Once I am a warrior, then I will receive payment, and we can live wherever we choose. Here you have a home, you have food – you will be safe."

"But we are not wanted here," Teilo argued.

Shimmera touched his hand. "We hold each other, Teilo – that is enough. Can you not let your father go that he may find his way?"

Teilo said nothing. For the first time in his seven years of life he noticed the shadows around their campfire could hold fear.

That night they walked together into the wood as they always did – listening to the sounds of the night – letting the stillness of the earth release the day's cares in them. The love between the three of them was not unlike magic itself. Teilo revelled in the feel of his father's arms around him – the strength and passion that made him soar. His mother's soft touch spoke within him like contented whispers that ignited his own joy and wonder. Let them be different, he thought, it mattered not – they were complete – like a circle appears in perfect peace with itself.

3

It took Romarrah several months to travel the length and breadth of the land. He witnessed no conflict along the way and his journey was one of pleasant encounters. He took interest in every village through which he passed, absorbing its flavour. Each was different and that difference he knew to respect.

In all matters, the villages were self-governing. All that was forbidden was for one village to take up arms against another or against the warriors. In turn, Romarrah would intervene only when such conflict arose, or the actions of one village threatened the peace of the land.

When he returned to Imoshtan, the old Romarrah, who was now called by his birth name O'Daewin, summoned him to his chambers. Though aged, O'Daewin was still strong and agile. Long had been his rule and he was honoured throughout the land. The two men greeted each other warmly but O'Daewin had no time for pleasantries.

"There is a dark force gathering beyond the land of Romarrah," he warned. "Word has come that the armies of Lemarron are being prepared for combat. You must be vigilant – Lemarron has never been a threat before – it may take years before they are ready to attack but attack they will – this I know. You will need to have warriors constantly moving through the land – preparation is your strongest foundation. You must always be ready – always prepared."

"Should we not send warriors to Lemarron to learn for ourselves what happens there? To perhaps end this before it begins?" Romarrah asked but O'Daewin shook his head. "We do not seek conflict. Never must we enter another land uninvited. That is how it has always been – how it must be. You will make your own choices as Romarrah but do not turn away from the law of the land – let it govern you."

Romarrah bowed to his old Master. O'Daewin smiled. "Each Romarrah should be wiser than the last. If that were not so, we would cease to be mighty – we would be like a stagnant pool where no freshness breathes.

Make your own way my friend but respect what has been put in place – what gave you your teachings." As he spoke O'Daewin poured them both a warm, spicy drink for the day was cool and the winter fast approaching.

"There is another matter," he said. "My daughter, Tharease, has spoken to me of her love for a young Fire Keeper, Vulone. Your face tells me you know this man. Learn to give nothing away, Romarrah – guard what you know – stay in your peace. What is he to you?"

"He means nothing to me," Romarrah responded truthfully, "I have only seen him briefly as I passed through his village."

O'Daewin considered these words carefully before he continued. "Each person is free to express their love – no law can bind that which exists between people. Yet, Tharease must rule beside you. Romarrah must have the woman's power to strengthen his own. For this Tharease has been prepared since childhood. Your wisdom and understanding must find a way that you may both be at peace."

There was silence for a time, both men addressing their own thoughts. Then O'Daewin continued.

"I will leave soon. I go back to the village of my birth to spend my last days in solitude. Fare you well, Romarrah – may your time be kind to you. Come – we will sit together."

They sat, eyes closed, each in the quiet of their being – freeing their minds and hearts.

♋

O'Daewin was right. There was a dark force gathering beyond the Land of Romarrah. Lemarron was a land of little light - an oppressive place filled with shadows and longing. Its ruler Myallon was a sadistic man. Cruelty and dominance were the creed of this heartless place.

The people were fearful and superstitious. Women and children were often neglected and mistreated.

Myallon detested the darkness of Lemarron and for many years had longed to rule a land of beauty and wealth and his lust for power was insatiable. He was a thick-set and grim looking man. What he lacked in intelligence and insight he countered with a brutality and animal cunning that made him a dangerous foe. Once determined he crushed whatever stood in his way and now he was intent on defeating the warriors of Romarrah.

♋

In due course O'Daewin left the compound and Romarrah assumed full control. Dutifully he summoned Tharease that they may find a way to be at peace with their lives together. The time was near for them to be wed – a symbolic union of man and woman – uniting their powers to govern the land. Romarrah had hoped to have a full life with Tharease but if her love was already given, their union was but one of necessity. This caused him pain even though he would not disclose such sadness.

Tharease bowed to him and smiled. There was an easy familiarity between them that came from years of friendship.

"Dear friend," she said, "I regret that my disclosure may have caused difficulty for you. My father has already told me that I am bound by law. If there was a way that I might relinquish this duty without compromising the protection of the land, I would surely follow that path. I have given myself completely to the Fire Keeper, Vulone, and long to stand by his side."

Romarrah watched her as she spoke – this strong, independent woman whom he admired and cared for more than he dare say. When she finished speaking he replied quietly.

"Tharease, I cannot, as you must know, release you from your duty. That we must wed is the custom and one of the reasons we have the power we do. We stay strong in our law – it gives us wisdom and understanding. Let us then be at peace with our fate. If Vulone be a man of strength, he too will know this and he will treasure what time you may spend together. For the rest, may he give of himself to his own duties and keep the land safe."

So it came to pass that they were wed and Romarrah pledged to rule with Tharease beside him. For several years all remained calm within the Land of Romarrah and when trouble did arise, it came from an unexpected quarter.

♋

When Apheilio left to commence his training, Shimmera was even more isolated and her presence barely tolerated. The thinly concealed hostility that began as a trickle, opened into a steady stream. Her home was watched – night and day. Whatever these people wanted to happen, they would make happen. She was aware of the pain that was to come. There was in her a deep grief, not for herself but for Apheilio and Teilo. Her purpose had been to give this land her son. It was a sacrifice that at times seemed too much to bear. She knew already what they would suffer – especially Teilo.

Each time Apheilio returned, in their quiet times together, she sensed the change in him. His training was opening him to his own wisdom – his power. He too experienced a presentiment of what was to come. Yet somehow they stayed at peace. The three of them laughed and played and walked in the forest at night, only now there was an intensity to their togetherness. They were savouring each moment, pressing it firmly into memory that it may stay alive within them.

The years passed and, for a time, it appeared all would be well. It was however Amis who broke the truce.

4

It was difficult to see the blood at first. The dove's feathers were of a russet colour, camouflaging the extent of its injuries. Caught in a tangle of thorns and vines, it was very agitated but lacking the strength to escape.

"It is a Wandering Dove," Amis said in a hushed voice. He had never seen one before. Theirs was a rich history woven into myths. They were the carriers of earth spirits and good fortune but, if harmed, the bearers of sorrow. "Be careful, Teilo – you may add to its injury."

Teilo had reached into the thicket, ignoring the thorns. His hands gently closed around the bird and brought it to safety.

"It has been attacked," he spoke, gently inspecting the quivering creature.

"Then what should we do with it?" Amis was wary of interfering. "Perhaps we should leave it in some place of comfort and let it be."

"I will take it to Shimmera." Teilo was adamant.

The bird had become still in his hands which were now stained with its blood and that from his own scratches.

Amis hesitated.

"Come, Amis – if anyone can save this bird it is Shimmera."

It did not take long for them to arrive at the cottage. Shimmera greeted them and took the bird from her son. It moved its head to look at her.

"It is this young dove's time, Teilo," she said, shaking her head. "Its spirit paces inside."

"It is fully awake," the boy argued. "See – it still holds to life." His words were hopeful – as if they would spur the dove to sudden recovery.

Shimmera smiled at him. "It is but the body that struggles to live – that is what it knows best, but the spirit is waiting to leave."

He nodded, disappointed as his mother placed the bird in a nest of leaves. Again it tried to seek flight – searching for the freedom of the skies but its movements were feeble and clumsy.

"I will calm its agitation that it may release its spirit." Shimmera spoke touching but the tip of one finger on the dove's breast before closing her eyes and whispering words that no one could hear or understand. Within seconds the small body went limp.

When Shimmera opened her eyes, Amis was staring at her. His look was unmistakeable. He had witnessed her love and wisdom but he had not seen it – his vision clouded by all he had heard of this woman. He saw only that Shimmera could summon death with the touch of her finger and a whispered command.

"Amis," she smiled at him reassuringly. "The dove no longer suffers – its spirit is grateful for your kindness."

But Amis was gone.

"What is it?" Teilo asked in alarm. He felt the disruption between them – like a quiver of pain somewhere deep inside him. When he tired to look for its source, a vision shattered his sight and innocent knowing. He was holding the red dove and the blood flowed from its body – his hands were covered in it. The dove was looking at him when suddenly, it became Shimmera – they were her eyes looking into his own – saying their farewell.

"No!" he screamed as in his heart he knew something, cold and hard, hidden behind the comfort of his life.

Shimmera grabbed him. She held him tightly. "My love," she murmured into his thick fair hair – smelling the warmth and sweetness of him. She too had felt the rupture beneath their most treasured existence and she could not deny it to him – she could only soothe it and fold it, for a time, into silence.

The men came the next day. Shimmera waited for them to speak but when their fear touched her, she tried to put them at ease. "What is it you want, good men?" she smiled. They looked away.

"We want you to leave now," one of the elders spoke. "You are not wanted here. Our council has met and this be our decree. You, woman, will only bring sorrow and destruction to our village – to our land. We know who you are – you have come to destroy us."

Shimmera did not have a chance to respond for Teilo stepped out from inside their home. In his hand was a sword his father had given him. He was now twelve years old and tall for his age. The gentleness of his mother was evident in his eyes and hands but there was also an unwavering strength that, when given his passion, emanated from him. At this moment his intent was clear.

The elder who had been speaking took a step back.

"Do not speak to my mother with your cowardice hiding behind your words." The boy spoke with authority. "It is you who have no place here. Our home does not need the disappointment that comes as the breath of your hatred."

He would have continued but Shimmera laid her hand upon his arm. "Teilo, I ask that you not raise your sword to these men. They come only to speak their concerns – we must honour them."

Once more she addressed her accusers. "What is it I have done to cause you harm? Pray tell me that I may ask your forgiveness."

The men were confused. There was nothing this woman had done to inflict injury. It was Emanis who came forward from the rear of the group. Emanis held his own grudge with the world and he bore it like a scar across his life.

"It is what you will do – what you have come to do – that is what we seek to prevent. Leave our land, woman, or face your own destruction."

Shaking his mother's hand away Teilo raised his sword and Emanis smirked. "As to yourself, boy – I have no fight with you even if you are of evil spawned."

The sword cut through the air. Emanis stumbled sideways to avoid injury. Regaining his composure, he spat at Teilo. "If I carried my own weapon, son, I would not hesitate to teach you the price of such stupidity."

To Shimmera he threatened, "If you do not leave we will drive you out. Already your influence has turned the boy. No child of this village would bear arms against an elder. You hold destruction in your heart – it is a silent weapon but it reaches far - of that there can be no dispute. Go before there is blood shed."

They left. Shimmera hugged Teilo but when she spoke, it was the only time his mother had rebuked him, however gently.

"To harm with intent, Teilo, is to deny your goodness. To raise your sword against another in anger will not bring calm to any situation – that is not where your power lies."

"Why do they treat you thus?" the boy was still outraged. "Tell me what it is they fear? From where has this tale of destruction arisen?"

Shimmera touched his arm – there could be no agitation once her hand rested its quiet upon him. She smiled. "You must go to your father," she said. "Tell him it is time to return. I will prepare food for your journey."

"I cannot leave you," Teilo fought back his tears – he feared so much for his mother's safety.

"I will come to no harm. In part they spoke the truth – I am not from this land and my power is far greater than their own. I will not allow them to harm me while you are away. Go without fear, my son. On your return we will talk of this – it is time."

Shimmera had no concern for her son travelling the distance to Imoshtan alone. Unlike the warriors' patrols which could meander a lengthy course from village to village, he would take a direct, much travelled path. Children were honoured in the Land. It was likely a passing dray would give her son the comfort of easy transport.

As he left the village Teilo saw Amis watching him but when he greeted his friend with a wave of his hand, Amis spat and walked away.

By the time Apheilio and Teilo returned to Athanan the men stood guard outside their home. The menace of their intentions visible on their faces and, although their resolve was strong they stood aside when Apheilio approached. He still wore his warrior's garments and the men were taken aback by his formidable presence.

Placing his hand on his son's shoulder, Apheilio spoke quietly. "Go inside to your mother, Teilo – I will come when I have dealt with this."

He then addressed the gathering. "What is it you want?" His voice was calm – inviting confidence. These men – some of whom were related to him, knew him well. This, and his lack of aggression, momentarily clouded their mission, erasing any justification to vent their anger.

Again Emanis acted as spokesman." We want her gone, Apheilio," he nodded in the direction of their home, "and the boy. He raised his sword against us – he tried to kill me. Do you not see her evil is in him also?"

"He was frightened, Emanis – he is but a child who thought you would attack his mother. What boy would not take up arms to protect his mother? Where is this evil of which you speak?"

"It has been prophesised. Already she has robbed your sight of clarity. Can you not see that which she is – the one who commands death – the one who will destroy our village?"

"Emanis, I live with this woman – she has no desire for this destruction of which you speak. What would be her purpose? Does your prophecy name Shimmera? Does it even suggest a woman? No – I think not. Here is my prophecy, Emanis – you are the ones who will destroy this village – all of you who feast off this superstition and fear. When I finish my training we will be gone – let us be in peace until that time."

"It is too late, Apheilio – there are rumours that this new Romarrah knows of her origins. Once he learns that she can command death he will tear our village apart if we harbour this curse. Give her up, I beg you, before we are all doomed."

Apheilio could have laughed – their fears were absurd, but in his own lifetime he had witnessed others who were accused of wrong doing being cast out by the elders. Often the accusations were baseless. They arose from the same ignorance of those before him now. He had seen the invisible walls of exclusion that would hold people in banishment as if they were dead and gone from the earth. It was why this village suffocated him.

"Romarrah will not destroy Athanan," he said in an effort to quell the seething tide of their misguided fervour. "Go to him now – tell him Shimmera is this one of whom you speak. Do you think Romarrah with all his warriors, of which I am one, would fear this woman?"

"If he knows her magic he would do well to be fearful – it is already in the earth." Emanis retorted.

Apheilio sighed. "And this magic – has it harmed the earth? Has it harmed our gardens? Do you not eat of its abundance?"

Emanis stepped closer. "Apheilio – we are kin – our blood unites us and therefore I have an allegiance to you. But I cannot let this pass. I am now an elder as was your father. It would be foolish of me to ignore our way of being. We must honour the wisdom of the ancients – we must acknowledge the prophecies."

Apheilio's patience became entangled in his rising frustration. "You can eat your prophecies for all I care," he snapped. "If it be a true prophecy you cannot prevent what will be. And, I say this for the last time – it is not Shimmera you need fear. I am finished with this – leave us be."

He turned his back on the group and walked away. Furious, Emanis raised his sword and two others followed his lead.

Not expecting to be attacked by his own people, Apheilio was caught unawares but his training had prepared him well. His movements were swift and measured and in no time he had rendered his assailants defenceless. Emanis was sent sprawling face down in the dirt. Blood flowed from a deep gash on Apheilio's shoulder where a sword had struck him. The other villagers stared at it. To spill the blood of a warrior of Romarrah meant to threaten the land. The punishment for such an action was to be sent to Manon – the place of desolation.

"It is of no consequence," the warrior said, seeing their fear. "Nor will news of this reach Romarrah – you have my word. Now leave us. I beg you desist in this persecution."

Brushing the dirt from his tunic, Emanis glared at Apheilio. "It is not finished," he snarled. "It will never be done while she still lives and breathes in this place. Give her up to the council, Apheilio."

Ignoring him, the warrior walked into his home.

While this exchange was taking place outside, Shimmera had taken Teilo into the room they all shared. It was his favourite place when he was indoors. The warmth of their love hovered here – it was a womb place – soft and nurturing, where he felt safe and protected. But it was here that his mother told him who she was and why it was she must now leave him. She talked of many lands through which she had passed. She told him of an ocean that would one day open before him and carry him to other places. She spoke to him of his own greatness and destiny, but it became blurred with the pain that was throbbing in his body – as if his blood had turned leaden and no longer flowed vibrant in his veins. He wanted to scream his denial but no sound came from his lips. He simply crumpled in her arms and let her hands take his pain away.

That night they sat together around the fire. The moon was full – a time they normally celebrated the goodness of the earth and the splendour of the heavens. They welcomed the moonlight and valued its healing. But this night, they sat mostly in silence – drinking their togetherness for the last time.

Earlier Apheilio had argued with Shimmera, then pleaded and finally wept as she held him. Death would be preferable, he thought, than knowing this beautiful relationship was nearly over.

Teilo had never seen his parents argue and even through his pain, he saw the difference between them. It was in fact only Apheilio who argued – his whole being bent on changing the course these events had taken. Shimmera remained steady. The tears flowed down her cheeks but her peace was constant. Even in his youth, Teilo knew his mother saw more than they – there was a distant horizon somewhere in their lives and she already knew its promise. He failed to understand why they could not simply leave Athanan together. Surely they would find refuge somewhere. Apheilio also posed this same argument.

"There must be no threat, Apheilio," Shimmera said sadly as she placed her hand upon his wounded shoulder – hastening its healing. "This wound tells me I am no longer silent upon this earth. You do not see the things I see. Never have you questioned my knowing before this day – you have honoured it. Trust me, my love – there is no other way. If I were old and tired in my living, would there be sadness? Know that I am with you – I am still the hand that touches your heart."

One last time they walked through the forest bathed in moonlight and softness. To Teilo every tree held a memory of their time here and now wept their sadness into the air around them.

'You will all live here forever,' the voice spoke inside him. He looked at Shimmera and she returned his look. 'I will live in you,' her eyes smiled.

One last time she lay beside him whispering the words that brought sleep to his eyes and eased the aching in his heart. And then she was gone.

Sometime in the night his father came to him and lay beside him, holding him so tightly he could hardly breathe and together they cried silent tears into the empty space beside them.

As the sun rose in the morning, father and son gathered their few simple belongings and left the village of Athanan. They walked side by side – neither looked back – Apheilio's hand on Teilo's shoulder – there was nothing more to be done.

5

News of what had occurred in Athanan did reach Romarrah. It was his business to know what was happening in the land – just as he had read the myths and legends of every village. He knew their prophecies, their folklore – he had an understanding of the customs and beliefs. Now he pondered what to do about these villagers who had stood against Apheilio. It was indeed forbidden to spill the blood of a warrior unless that warrior's actions were proven to be remiss. Apheilio had done nothing wrong – he had remained calm and had not sought conflict. He wished only to protect his family.

"It is best we wait and see what becomes of this,' he spoke to Tharease. She agreed.

"Apheilio will be a great warrior, Romarrah – you too must see this. I am certain he will become a chief warrior. Why not let him bring his family here now. Could not we find work for his wife within the compound?"

Romarrah appeared to consider her suggestion but did not respond.

"Is it the prophecy that troubles you?" Tharease asked. "Do you think that Apheilio's wife is the one?"

Romarrah shook his head. "She is not of their tribe that is for certain – or of this land. And she has something – an intangible quality – a sense of something magical – so indefinable. If you could but have seen the way her hands played with the earth, Tharease, you would understand. But what is prophecy and what is myth – do you know? If I lived by the legends I would live in constant turmoil."

"That is true." Tharease pursed her lips, a slight frown troubled her forehead. "I am not sure either, Romarrah, but you must also agree Athanan is the closest village to Avarinsa and no other has such a prediction. Whilst it is not definitive, it is indeed direct."

"That is why we have the Law of the Land and the Great Wisdom to guide us," Romarrah countered. "We cannot interfere – only when a threat comes alive do we seek action. Let us see what Apheilio has to say when he returns but these villagers will have to be punished in some way. They have shown aggression to the Land and that must not be permitted to pass without consequence."

Tharease agreed but something about this story troubled her. It was unlike Romarrah to be evasive yet he had not answered her question. Why had he not offered this family refuge from the beginning?

♋

As they spoke, the Land of Lemarron echoed with the sound of marching feet. Like a huge angry machine its army pumped a war message into the earth and now it had been set in motion, it gathered momentum – a huge beast, writhing – open mouthed – poised to savage, devour and lay waste what stood before it. The vibrations of its hostility spread like ripples in all directions.

Walking beside his father, Teilo felt those ripples beneath his feet and he shivered. He could not name this feeling. It arose in him like a panic. Was it simply all that had happened these past few days still coursing through him – much like a nightmare lingers even in the brightest day? Was it dread for an unknown life ahead and the huge hole that had opened up and swallowed the joy and beauty of his world? No – it was something else. Something darker that came to him and he sensed that darkness moving between himself and Apheilio. He cried out in fear and his father grabbed him. "What is it, Teilo?"

"Something is coming," his son whispered. "I am so cold, Apheilio." and he would have fallen to the ground had not his father held him.

He is his mother's son, Apheilio thought sadly.

♋

Romarrah watched from his balcony as the pair entered the compound. There was no sign of Apheilio's wife but the sadness that accompanied them as they made their way across the courtyard told its own story. The Great Master sent for them.

As Teilo ascended the stairs behind his father, he saw a young girl watching him from a doorway above. Although a few years younger than he, she stood with such confidence – observing him with an open, almost bold stare. Her long black hair framed her strong face and her eyes danced with curiosity. He returned her look briefly.

"Syrath," a woman's voice called and the girl was gone, closing the door behind her.

Romarrah motioned for them both to sit, then poured them a warm drink – a soothing decoction of herbs and grains. When he spoke it was with concern. "Apheilio, I was told of your absence and the necessity of your leaving. Am I to believe that this matter is now resolved?"

He wondered if his warrior would reveal all of that which had transpired between himself and those of his village. Instead Apheilio simply stated, "It is done, Master."

His tone was flat and it pained Romarrah to hear the emptiness in his words. This man's soul had been torn and it would take him time to replenish his essence.

Apheilio cleared his throat and continued. "My only concern is for my son, Teilo – he has no home and I seek a place for him close to my own."

Romarrah looked at the boy and to his surprise Teilo returned his gaze fully for a moment before he looked down at the floor. There was too much in that look for Romarrah to grasp it all. Extraordinary, he thought, I cannot read this young man – there is a part of him that is closed to me.

Aloud he said, "He is too young to commence his training. Do you read and write, Teilo?"

"I do, Master," the boy responded.

"Then perhaps time spent in study would benefit you – that is, if that be your wish also." When Teilo did not respond, Romarrah continued. "Is there something that claims a passion in you, son?"

He remembered the voice in the forest – 'I am the Great Romarrah Himself' – but the child before him was devoid of ambition.

"I wish only to be with my father," Teilo responded, his voice breaking beneath the weight of his sadness.

Romarrah knew the interview was over. "We will talk more when you are both rested. Take your son with you to your quarters, Apheilio – I will see you have everything you need."

Apheilio bowed his gratitude. As they made to leave, Romarrah touched the other man's arm and spoke softly. "May I inquire as to your wife?"

"She is no longer with us," the warrior replied and Romarrah asked no more questions.

No sooner had they left than Syrath entered the room. "Who was that boy Romarrah?" she almost commanded. He smiled at his daughter's forthright manner. "They did not touch their drinks," she observed. "He is different – don't you agree – and sad – very sad."

As she talked she walked around the room as if she was inspecting it. "What is his name? I have seen his father before – is the boy visiting him?"

Romarrah sighed, "Do you wish for me to answer your questions, Syrath, or is it that you simply desire to hear your own voice?"

The child ceased her inspection and sat down, looking at him expectantly.

He nodded his approval. "It is true – the boy is sad. His name is Teilo and he has come here to be with his father."

"Where is his mother – why is he not with her?"

"Perhaps she has died, Syrath."

"Is that why he is sad?"

"I think so. With your consent he might join you, if he wishes, in your instructions."

Syrath was overjoyed at this prospect but she pretended to consider the proposal. Her father watched for her reaction. What pleasure he derived from this relationship with his daughter. Though so young she conversed with him on many issues. He loved her spirit. She was both headstrong and considerate – a delightful combination and so easy to love. For Romarrah it was such a balm to receive her love amid the weariness of being the Great Master.

"I think I would like that," she stated at last.

Later when he sat alone, Romarrah pondered what to do about Athanan. He could not ignore what had taken place there. Not only had the villagers wounded a warrior, it would appear they had destroyed the life of this family. Of all the villages in the land, none had clung to the old ways and superstitions more than Athanan. His informer had told him this woman – Apheilio's wife – was said to have thrown herself off the edge of the land to save her son from persecution. Could this be true? Or had she come from Avarinsa and returned through the mist?

If so, it meant the prophecy, if it was a genuine prophecy, would not be fulfilled – at least not for the time being. He was not convinced of Shimmera's suspected origins. Still, he knew better than to waste time on supposition – he must deal with the matter at hand. The people of Athanan had turned against a Warrior of Romarrah and at the very least had driven away his wife. It appeared she had committed no crime – a discipline of some kind must be enforced. When he arrived at a solution, he sought out Tharease and told her of his plan.

"Would that be wise, Romarrah? I am not sure. Would it not be better to send those who attacked Apheilio to Manon for a time, to reflect on what they have done?"

"But would Manon only serve to strengthen their primitive ways," the Master countered. "It would not be enough to break this cycle, Tharease. I fear that we may have, in the past, overlooked what happens within some of our villages. Is it advantageous for the Land to allow villages such as Athanan to continue teachings that promote fear and distrust? Would it not be of greater benefit to insist that these practices cease? Yet whether we ignore or banish it, such behaviour only encourages further suppression and secrecy. By separating these people we have the chance to create change – to educate their children – to show them another path. Would that not be a more honourable way?"

Tharease was uncertain. "Are you proposing we separate families, Romarrah? Is that not similar to what those of Athanan did to Apheilio's family?"

The Great Master shook his head. "There is surely no comparison between what I am suggesting and that which has occurred in Athanan. I wish only to maintain peace in our land. Think how easily the order that has been the backbone of our peace for so long could fray if we allow the villages to harbour such blatant hostility."

Tharease suddenly felt her voice would not be heard above the clamour of the law of the land. To speak her truth would be to challenge the very foundation that had given them generations of contented abundance. Still, she was troubled. Romarrah had not reached out his hand to this family before and yet now he favoured this boy in a way that had never happened previously. There must have been many warriors who had experienced similar hardship to that of Apheilo. What was the Great Master's motive?

Tharease chided herself for holding such thoughts and also for her own selfishness – the longing in her heart that begged to be free. Smiling, she touched Romarrah's hand and looked into his eyes. She always saw in them an uncertainty that tainted their colours with sadness. "You are a good man, Romarrah – I bow to your wisdom."

Thus Tharease gave her consent. Within the passing of a few years, Athanan would cease to exist. All that remained would be the dwellings – the people scattered - the ghosts of their lives still evident in the overgrown gardens, the neglected tools and the crumbling stone paths.

Apheilio's prophecy became flesh.

♋

Romarrah made no attempt to move Teilo from his father's quarters, nor did he insist he do anything. Instead he sent his young daughter to show the boy his new surroundings that they may become familiar to him.

Although he did not desire Syrath's company, Teilo was fascinated by the size of the compound. Even his young guide was unsure where to begin her tour.

"Start with the place you like most," he prompted and immediately she set off through the orchard to the North West corner – the very edge of the compound where a swift stream flowed, separating Imoshtan from the forest. Teilo stared into the forest as if he could see in its depths a familiar story. Then he calmly wiped away the tears from his cheeks.

The stream bordered the compound on two sides and so Syrath led him back between the fruit trees to the eastern side where the gardens were laid out in neat rows. Never had he seen such gardens – many workers were tilling the soil, harvesting and sowing.

Along this eastern border were fields of grain that stretched a patchwork trail into the distance.

"What lies beyond the fields?" he asked.

"The compound is surrounded by villages where the warriors live with their families,"

Teilo blinked and turned away.

What could she do to cheer him, Syrath wondered. "Come – let me show you the kitchens."

He followed her simply because he could do little else and he had no wish to offend the child. The kitchens were like nothing he had ever seen before or, for that matter, imagined. They were alive with aromas, steam, clatter, orders being given and people carrying laden trays, large bowls and a great variety of foodstuff.

Syrath moved among the bustle with the complete confidence of one who is assured of their place. He watched her calmly take a basket from a hook and into it place bread, fruit and messa – a thick paste made from herbs, seeds and oil.

"Follow me" she commanded. "I know a lovely place where we can eat."

She led him past the rows of warriors' quarters, across the main courtyard and into the large building where he had come with his father on their arrival. He knew Romarrah's chambers were upstairs but Syrath walked instead across the main hall. Here Teilo could have lingered, such was the magnificence of this room with its tapestries and ornaments but his host continued on beyond the large doors at the end and into a walled courtyard. It was a place of great peace and beauty, but he felt as an intruder. He had no claim here – no part of it reached out to him.

"Should we be here?" he asked his guide.

"I can be anywhere I choose," she answered wilfully, with a toss of head. "Besides there is no one else here – Romarrah and Tharease will be training the warriors. It is beautiful is it not?"

Teilo nodded even though, to him, this beauty did not sing – it merely fell into the hollowness that had carved its own nest inside him.

♋

"He is very sad," Syrath told Romarrah later that day. "He does not smile but he is not afraid of his tears – he does not hide them. He is strong."

Romarrah looked at her almost quizzically. From where did this child draw her wisdom, he wondered. Aloud he counselled her.

"Leave him be Syrath, he must be his own healer now and he will have to find his life again – it will take time."

She smiled at her father. He was always steady – always calm. He was her tower and she loved him dearly. As a mother figure, Tharease was warm and loving but Syrath knew that her mother's heart was not fully with her daughter or her husband – there was a part of her that was a stranger to them. It did not matter, for between Romarrah and herself there was no distance.

Gradually Teilo became accustomed to his new life. He attended teachings with Syrath, aware of the honour that was being bestowed upon him. Frequently Romarrah would join them and exchange a few words with the boy. Although he found the Great Master to be most attentive, it puzzled Teilo why the man took such an interest in him. He always felt as if Romarrah was probing for something – as if he expected Teilo to divulge a secret.

"Does he want for me to be more familiar?" he asked his father.

Apheilio smiled. "Perhaps it is the Great Master who wishes to be more familiar with the one who spends so much time with his daughter."

"I do not desire his attention," Teilo replied. "It is not my need that pursues this relationship – therefore it must be his own."

Apheilio laughed and ruffled the boy's hair. "You are far too astute, Teilo, but also outspoken. Shimmera's sight is strong in you but I entreat you to guard your comments wisely."

Tharease also engaged Teilo in conversation. He warmed to this softly spoken woman who asked nothing of him. One day she took his hand in her own.

"You have such fine, strong hands Teilo – they speak their own language."

The boy raised his head and looked at her. She felt bare. "I am sorry, Master*," he said. "Your heart cries for the words it cannot speak. It is such a sadness when the flowers within us are not free to bloom."

How could this child have given voice to her own silent pain?

She did not speak of it to Romarrah. For reasons unknown even to herself, Tharease did not want to draw his attention to this boy. But his words remained in her like a bookmark on a much read passage.

Syrath both amused Teilo and annoyed him. She was precocious, outspoken and demanded his attention while he preferred either solitude or the company of his father.

Often Romarrah, from his balcony, would observe father and son at the end of the day either walking towards the forest or in the training arena where Apheilio would instruct his son in the art of combat. They played hard, they laughed and hugged each other – the affection between the pair was like a strong cable that could not be broken.

Romarrah, had he allowed himself to, may have felt envious of the ease with which they loved. Shimmera was still present in their togetherness – they carried so much of her love with them.

"The boy will be a warrior before his training begins," he told Tharease, "His skills flourish beneath his father's guidance. Already he displays what can only be described as a gracefulness."

"Then perhaps he should begin his training earlier," his wife commented, "although I fear Syrath would miss his company. She adores him and although he is kind to her, I think he prefers mostly to be within himself. What do you think of him Romarrah? Have you observed his eyes and hands? It is difficult not to be drawn to him."

---

* Master does not denote gender – only mastery

Romarrah considered her suggestion for a moment. "Let him commence his training when he is fifteen – a year earlier than usual but he will be more than ready." He looked at his wife. "I cannot say that I am drawn to him – there is too much uncertainty in him. I do not mean that he lacks confidence – far from it – no – it is something else that keeps him at a distance."

So it was settled and in the space between that time and when he began his apprenticeship, Teilo grew taller and stronger and gained a vast knowledge about the land. He read all the histories of each village but from the book of Athanan, he read only one prophecy and never touched it again.

His new life was so different to his childhood in Athanan and in one way, he was grateful for this privileged existence he owed to Romarrah's generosity. He still felt the blackness come upon him and lately it had been stronger – a consuming, suffocating evil that stole his breath and left him cold and shivering. Not wishing to concern his father, he kept it to himself but it filled him with dread.

6

The warriors of Lemarron were ready. Myallon had planned well. His army was enormous and certainly outnumbered the warriors of Romarrah. They would attack from different quarters so that the might of Romarrah's armies would be fractured.

For years Myallon had watched his enemy's patrols – he knew the pattens and methods of their planning and he laughed at the rumours that these warriors had special powers. Never had he seen evidence of such superiority. They were simply well trained and they stood their ground. That they used women as warriors, as far as Myallon was concerned, weakened their force rather than enhanced it. And he had found a great weakness which, given the chance, he intended to exploit to its fullest.

His time had come. The adrenalin pumped through his veins and he lusted for battle – he hungered for the kill and the taste of bloody victory.

Tharease and Romarrah stood in front of their assembled warriors. Romarrah set off to patrol the east while Tharease led her warriors towards the west.

Syrath watched them leave, a petulant expression on her face. Everyone had gone – even Teilo who, having reached his fifteenth year one month previously, had commenced his training. This was the first time he had been permitted to accompany the warriors. She missed his presence at her morning studies. Now there was only her tutor, chief warrior, Ortarian, to keep her company. She would tell Romarrah when he returned that she wished to commence her training also even though she had not yet reached her thirteenth year.

Teilo took an interest in every village through which they passed. Initially they walked north from Imoshtan to the mountain ranges that separated the Land of Romarrah from Yeshotruen. From this point the patrol followed a course from one village to the next along the western border. In his mind Teilo recounted all he had learned about each village. Of an evening he would spend time around the campfire with the other warriors and listen to their talk. It was as if he suddenly felt older sitting beside his father and being part of something that almost resembled a family. When he lay beneath his blankets and stared up at the stars, he experienced a sense of freedom and the excitement of possibilities he had not allowed himself to dream for a long time. He would have been more content than he had been in years were it not for the blackness which claimed him nearly every day.

On the second week they passed by the gates of Manon which towered above them against the horizon. Teilo wanted to satisfy his curiosity – go to the gates and look down upon this place of which no one spoke – the one place of which no history had been written. Although he had searched among the volumes, the book of Manon was the only one missing and he wanted to know why.

The warriors moved quickly on and Teilo had to be content with speculating on what the next village would hold.

♋

Vulone whistled as he worked for he knew Tharease was coming. It had been some time since they had last been together and although she had told him she could not leave her warriors while on patrol, he thought of a plan that might tempt her away. Long had he laboured and his body ached but at last it was finished in readiness for her visit.

He reached the warriors' camp and stood for a moment observing the scene before him. He could see his beloved, sitting separately from the others, as was the custom of the chief warrior. He made his way towards her, feeling as nervous as a young man when he loves for the first time.

Tharease knew he was there, long before he came into view, and her pleasure at seeing him was subdued by the fact that she was with the warriors – this was not the time for them to be together. She addressed her lover formally. "What is it you want, good man?" she asked, but her eyes smiled at him playfully.

"Tharease, I am here to beg you to come with me for only a small time that I may show you that which I have done and which I wish to give to you." His words came out in a rush and his voice pleaded with her not to refuse but she shook her head.

"You know, Vulone, that I cannot – this is my duty – to stay with my warriors."

"I have walked through this night to come to you and all around it is calm – there is no threat. Surely you have a warrior you can leave in your place – it is such a short time for which I ask." He smiled reassuringly.

Tharease hesitated, then summoned Apheilio. "I am called away for a moment Apheilio – I will return in haste – please stand my guard until that time."

Apheilio bowed. He felt immediately the bond between the two – the intense current that connected them to each other but he was troubled by her words. Never had he known a chief warrior to forsake their duty. He dismissed his concerns and took up his place of watch.

Romarrah instructed his warriors to set up their camp near the now deserted village of Athanan. So far their patrol had been uneventful yet he was apprehensive. He experienced a deep sense of foreboding although all around him appeared quiet and calm.

Such was his unease he took from beneath his tunic a small pouch from which he expertly poured a thin stream of golden sand into a circle on the ground. The warriors were immediately on guard knowing their Master had sensed danger.

Within the golden circle Romarrah placed different coloured sands and as he did so, he whispered words, as if in a trance. When he finished he bid the warriors to be restful but alert. Then he took up his place, on the edge of the camp. He waited, eyes closed, aware of every second and the sense of what lay around him. Suddenly he saw the woman – a vision – standing before him. He knew at once it was Shimmera.

"Save my son, Romarrah – do not let him die for your destinies be linked."

It was as if she held up a mirror and let him see within its depths the horrors that awaited him. As quickly as it appeared the vision was gone.

Immediately he commanded his warriors to hasten to the western border.

Myallon was pleased with himself. His years of preparation were finally bearing fruit. He had sent men into every village to befriend the villagers and learn of their ways and those of the warriors. All this information he had gathered, discarding what was of no use and keeping that which might be to his advantage. Thus he had learned of Vulone's relationship with Tharease and what might come about this very night. This was the weakness he had waited so long to glimpse. Even if Tharease had not left her warriors, he would still attack. But now, her departure was like a sign – an omen of his success. Nor had she made the golden circle. Not that he, Myallon, believed in the powers of the circle – that it offered an unnatural protection to the warriors. It was but a ploy to undermine the confidence of their opponents and nothing could undermine his confidence. Already he had told his men the land was theirs. They could have whatever they chose from any village – they could kill and plunder – satisfy their lust but the compound of Imoshtan and all within its walls belonged to him. That and the death of Romarrah would be his glory alone – to end the reign that had been dominant for so long. He could feel his heart pound its' desire.

♋

Teilo awoke shivering with cold – his whole body writhing. He vomited – retching violently. It was choking him again – worse than ever before. Instinctively, feeling weak and unsteady, he sought his father. Images flashed through his mind and he shut them out – he could not bear the horror of what he perceived.

Apheilio saw him coming and leapt to his feet. "What is it, Teilo – are you ill?"

The boy shook his head. He was shivering uncontrollably. "It has come, Apheilio – the blackness – it has come – we are not safe. It comes to us now and to Romarrah – it is everywhere – it surrounds Imoshtan – there is so much blood. I cannot look anymore – it hurts too much."

His father knew they were in grave danger – the land was in danger. He alone could not protect the warriors. Where was Tharease? He grabbed his son. "Listen to me Teilo – you must hide – go into the trees and no matter what happens stay safe."

Not wanting to leave his father, Teilo tried to speak but Apheilio stopped him.

"No, Teilo – do not! I have never commanded you to do anything but this I command you – do you understand? You must stay safe – your mother wishes it – I wish it. Hear me, Teilo – Shimmera told me you must be kept safe – you have a purpose. If I give my life this night I give it only that you might live – know this and know my love for you." Hugging the boy to him he again commanded him to leave. "The longer you stay my son, the more lives may be lost."

He wrapped his cloak around his son's shoulders – a final gesture of love and protection. Reluctantly Teilo did as he was bid and Apheilio turned his attention to preparing the warriors for battle.

He sent one to find Tharease, one to warn Romarrah and several others to alert those at the compound instructing all of them to give the alarm at every village they passed along the way that the Fire Keepers might spread the news throughout the land. He knew that if Romarrah's patrol had reached their expected destination that day, then they would be a full day's march from where he now stood but it was all he could do. What he didn't know was that Romarrah had already left, hours before, and he and his warriors travelled at a steady, fast pace.

Vulone had built a small dwelling beside the river. Long had he toiled to create a thing of beauty that reflected the love he had for Tharease. When she saw his gift, her eyes filled with tears. In that instant she knew the emptiness in his life and how he longed to have her with him.

"Vulone," she spoke at last, "know that my love for you remains unchanged and my heart soars when I see what you have created here but it is not good for you to be so alone. My life is full with being a chief warrior and I do you such an injustice in being absent so much in your own life. Should you not then seek another with whom you can share each day?"

Vulone put his arms around her. "I am content, Tharease. When you are not with me I live my life with the joy in my heart that you will return. I live my life with the hope that there will come a time when you are free. And still, I live my life to serve my village – that is enough."

They said no more but for the first time Tharease was disturbed by something she felt in him – an intensity that told her he would never let her go. She dismissed her fear – it was but trivial – and relaxed in his arms.

They listened to the sounds of the earth, letting the peace of the evening wrap itself around them when suddenly she startled. Her eyes were wide with the shock of what she knew.

"What have I done, Vulone – I must go – they are not safe – start the fires!"

She fled into the night.

♋

Myallon waited. It was a cloudy night and he had hoped to attack just before dawn when the light gave enough visibility and the warriors had not yet arisen to begin their day. It would be foolish to attack in the dark of night. His warriors would be closing in on Romarrah's camp – their orders to capture the Great Master unharmed. Even if his enemy eluded that first assault, Myallon had more men in the ready. The warriors of Romarrah were doomed. He issued the command for his men to be in position, then gathered others around him waiting to attack Apheilio and his patrol. The compound he knew was already surrounded and all forces would strike simultaneously. The time was drawing near.

♋

Apheilio watched – nothing stirred. Could Teilo be wrong? No – he knew that was not possible. But where was Tharease? The warrior he had sent to find her had not yet returned. He breathed deeply, releasing all fear, all anticipation – using his training to stay focused and calm. The warriors were in position – there was nothing more he could do. He only prayed that his son would stay hidden and free from harm.

♋

Romarrah stopped abruptly. There was something he had missed – he needed to feel his enemy. Already he had sensed the might of his opponent's army. Some were behind him – of that he was sure but now he realized that they were also before him. He split his warriors into three groups and gave them instructions – each party took a different path. They were no longer under his protection but at least this way they might stand a chance. They were all so well trained and they moved with great stealth – silent, and when they needed to be, deadly.

♋

The world was still in that pre-dawn hour. Not even the call of the birds anticipating the sunrise disturbed the stillness. Myallon stood like one who has already tasted the flesh of victory as he gave the signal to attack. His warriors flowed like a dark wave through the trees and into the clearing where their enemy still slept. Only they did not sleep – they stood as shadows around the camp, without movement. Once Myallon's men were inside their circle they closed in. The carnage had begun. The clash of swords and the cries of combat shattered the early morning stillness. The warriors of Romarrah, though outnumbered, danced their way through the conflict. They knew the art of evasion and the skill of attack. Still they fell, together with the warriors of Lemarron, each one's life blood draining into the earth and turning cold.

♋

Vulone found Tharease's body half way along the path that led back to her warriors. She had been killed with her own sword and her eyes stared lifelessly into the heavens. Not far from her side lay the warrior Apheilio had sent to find her – a young man whose body had been ripped apart by the savageness of the attack.

The Fire Keeper fell to his knees, unable to bear the weight of all he knew in that instant. He cradled Tharease in his arms. No sound came from his lips – no tears fell from his eyes. It was as if he too had died.

♋

Syrath had been awakened by Ortarian. His primary duty was to protect this child and so he led her into the underground passageway. He had told his charge nothing of what was happening but she knew they were under attack. She did what she had seen Romarrah do – she closed her eyes to sense what was, fearful for her father and mother. Suddenly her eyes opened wide and she looked at Ortarian – her face pale, her dark eyes afraid. "It is bad, Ortarian," she cried. "It is very bad."

He held the child. "We are safe here, Syrath," he soothed. "Romarrah will protect the warriors. Do not be afraid."

The warriors Apheilio had sent to alert those at the compound were still days away but each village they passed during that first night sent the warning smoke belching into the sky. Those on guard at the compound could see the red streaks against the dark night. They knew what to do – they were prepared. Not a light burned inside the compound. Warriors were awakened and moved through the darkness in readiness for the attack. Others crept through the night to surrounding villages summoning the warriors who lived beyond the compound. In some villages close to the compound the warriors of Lemarron had arrived before them, slaughtering those who slept in their beds.

Within the compound, two chief warriors placed the golden circles in the main courtyard – the compound would not fall into enemy hands.

♋

The battlefield seethed with the sheer force of the conflict. The sound was deafening – a constant discordant rhythm of steel against steel. The smell of sweat and blood filled the morning air. Myallon strode through the conflict like one who is invincible – killing with pleasure – revelling in satisfaction each time he drove his blade deep into flesh. And each time he killed, he made a point of staring into his opponents eyes so that his gloating face would be the last thing they saw as death claimed them.

Apheilio fought without emotion – completely focused – at one with each movement – like a machine except, for each life he took, he honoured them with the compassion in his eyes. Although it gave him no pleasure to kill, he allowed no feeling to disturb his rhythm. Face after face passed before him.

From where he stood, Myallon beheld this mighty warrior and began to make his way towards him, seeking the glory of this man's death.

Romarrah was almost there. His other warriors, having taken a different route, had circled and come to the rear of the warriors of Lemarron who were waiting to intercept them. They would hold them at bay to allow their Master access to the battlefield.

Romarrah felt the pain of what he was about to witness and paused in order to release it. All thought and feeling must be surrendered that nothing disturb the surface of his calm. When he came into the clearing there was no reaction in his mind or his body. Purposefully he moved into that battle and his presence brought with it an energy that affected every one of his warriors. It lifted their flagging strength and cleared their vision. Romarrah brought with him a sense of protection.

But at that very moment, as Apheilio withdrew his sword from the chest of a Lemarron warrior, Myallon came up behind him. The warrior spun around. He was staring into the gloating face of contempt as Myallon's blade entered his body with a force that brought him to his knees. Myallon drew back his sword, holding it aloft to the heavens, admiring the blood on its surface.

Even above the cacophony, Romarrah heard Teilo's scream. The boy had left the cover of the forest and ran across the battlefield, grabbing a sword from a fallen warrior as he went. Myallon too saw him coming and grinned. A boy, fair haired and innocent, not yet a man, would die like a lamb – bleating for its mother.

The Great Master knew he could not cover the distance between himself and Myallon before Teilo reached his father's assailant but, wielding his sword before him, he attempted to force his way through the warring bodies towards the boy. Shimmera's plea echoed in his mind,

'Save my son Romarrah – do not let him die'.

Myallon was not expecting the force that accompanied the first blow from the boy's sword. He staggered a little but quickly regained his balance as the two faced each other. Teilo became suddenly still. He held his weapon in front of him as his father had trained him. Myallon could not read his expression so he spat in the direction of Apheilio's fallen body, goading his young challenger to make the next move. Teilo remained motionless.

"Are you scared, boy?" Myallon sneered. "Can you feel in your bowels you are about to die?"

Still Teilo did not move. He could feel the sweat where his hands gripped the sword, the pounding in his ears but it didn't matter – nothing mattered. He was ready to die. There was only one overwhelming urge within him and that was to destroy. He did not feel himself a boy – or that he was anyone. He did not feel sadness or hate or even fear. He felt nothing except a compulsion to annihilate the suffocating blackness. He did not see the warrior in front of him – he saw only what this man gave to the world.

When Myallon lunged at him intending to drive his sword home, Teilo stepped to one side and his blade sang as it cut through the air, again hitting Myallon's with a force the man was not expecting. Time and time again the blades slammed against each other but Teilo always avoided the full force of his opponents swing. He was light and agile and he was not afraid.

Romarrah was not far from him when Teilo's sword drew the first blood, cutting through the flesh on Myallon's arm. The leader cursed. Two of his warriors moved towards him. But it was then Vulone, driven by grief and anger, suddenly entered the fray – his staff in his hands, his giant frame towering above the rest. Oblivious to the battle between the boy and the man, aware only of the two warriors moving in his direction, he delivered them a mighty blow as he strode past - cracking their necks and sending them crashing to the ground.

Teilo's sword seemed to twirl and flick so fast that Myallon could not keep up with it. Whereas he attacked with brute force, smashing into his opponent, this boy seemed to use his sword like a flicking tongue – a venomous snake that stung the flesh and tormented relentlessly. His body danced the combat as if some instinct moved him away from harm. He was unaware that he was covered in Myallon's blood – he was unaware that the man before him was dying.

The last vision Myallon saw, before the darkness took him, was the blood-splattered face of a boy with eyes that told him nothing.

Romarrah could not believe what he had witnessed and it was as if, for a moment, a hush settled over the battlefield. When he looked around him, he saw Vulone was not the only villager to have entered the war – more came with their swords, prepared to give their lives for the land. Red and grey smoke filled the skies above them.

Teilo knelt beside his father. He was no longer aware of the fighting or the need to defend himself. The blackness before him slowly melted and with the easing of that horror, came the pain of knowing who and where he was. Romarrah at last came to his side.

Apheilio could see the mist. He was walking through the forest towards the edge of the land – the white curtain parted. For a moment the light blinded him and then he saw her – Shimmera – waiting to hold him and he moved towards her. Someone tugged his hand and when he looked down a beautiful little boy was pleading with him not to go. Instantly, as he looked into that face, he experienced a sudden pulse of life.

Teilo watched as his father opened his eyes. "I have to go, son," he whispered and smiled – then he turned back to the mist. Something inside him seemed to open and spread – he became everything – the memory inside the forest trees – the joy that flowed like a stream through the land, the love of Shimmera's dance as it played between the earth and the heavens. Nothing could be greater than who he was as he rushed towards the mist.

"He has gone, Teilo," Romarrah spoke gently, his hand on the boy's shoulder. A number of warriors had formed a protective circle around them, keeping all others at bay.

Teilo had only one thought – to run to the edge of the land and let the mist take him also. He leapt to his feet but before he could flee, Romarrah grabbed his arm. When he tried to shake free, the man held him tighter. The boy was no longer the warrior who defeated Myallon – he was but a grieving child. He hit out at the Great Master, trying to break away, fighting like a wild animal but Romarrah only wrapped his arms around him in a vice-like hold. "Live, Teilo," he whispered in the boy's ear. "Live for Apheilio – honour him – bear witness to his life, his courage, his love. He died that you might live, son – do not let him die in vain."

The boy sobbed in his arms like a child.

Before nightfall, Romarrah knew this battle was all but over although others would continue for days to come. Never had such carnage occurred in the Land of Romarrah. He walked among the bloodied corpses of his warriors and his tears flowed openly. He knew them all – they were husbands and wives, brothers and sisters – they were sons and daughters and they died because of one man's hatred. He saw Vulone sitting wearily at the edge of the field. No, he thought, these warriors here died because they were not protected. Word had reached him that Tharease had forsaken her duty and gone with the Fire Keeper. He felt the pain of her last moments as she knew in her heart what she had done but at this moment he could not forgive her. That Apheilio had given all he could to protect and prepare the warriors showed the worth of this man. Romarrah was determined he should be given a hero's burial at the compound.

His attention turned again to Teilo, sitting where he had left him, guarded by two warriors. Romarrah did not yet trust that the boy would not do himself harm. What have I here in this young man, he wondered – the way he fought Myallon was almost not human – like he was fighting something else beyond the physical form. It was almost frightening to see that power – as if he was playing with his adversary yet not in a sadistic way. I must keep him close, the Great Master mused, for I do not yet know who he is.

It was the custom in the land that all bodies be returned to the village of their birth for burial – an almost impossible task now considering the extent of the carnage. Romarrah sighed. He walked towards Vulone – he did not wish to speak to the man. It was very difficult to stay within his training and not give rise to the anger he knew was within him. He paused for a moment to let it pass. When he stood before the Fire Keeper, he saw everything this man suffered – he was but an empty shell.

"You may keep Tharease's body – that be your right," he said, "but look on this waste before you and wish you too had died. I have not the care in me to even banish you to Manon. Go where you will but do not stay in this land for you can never repay that which you have dearly cost us all." There was a part of him that knew the injustice in his words but he walked away. This will never happen again, he vowed to himself.

Teilo refused to let the Great Master take Apheilio's body back to the compound.

"Where do you wish him to be buried?" he asked the boy wearily.

"In the forest – near our home." No longer tearful, Teilo spoke with quiet determination.

"But Teilo – there is no one there – Athanan is no longer a village."

Teilo frowned. He was unaware that Romarrah had scattered the inhabitants of his village far and wide. For the briefest moment he recalled the story book of his childhood but he had too little care to hold the memory.

"It matters not, Romarrah," he said flatly, "the forest is where he will be."

"As you wish."

Romarrah instructed his warriors to accompany the boy and take Apheilio's body home.

♋

In the months that followed, Teilo remained unreachable. He gave himself completely to his training.

Syrath watched him from her balcony knowing he was lost to her. She begged Romarrah to begin her training also. Eventually, despite her youth, he gave in to her demands. Ortarian went from instructing her in literature, art and history to instructing her in combat, stillness and the Great Wisdom.

When Amis arrived unexpectedly at the compound to commence his training, Teilo's deepest instinct was to ask his friend to hold him that he may feel something again of himself – who he used to be. Instead he saw the unmistakable hatred in Amis' eyes and he knew there was nothing left of who he used to be.

Romarrah wished so much to reach Teilo. The boy's skills for battle were second to none – so too did he grasp the Teachings, but he would not allow genuine love in his heart and he showed only a perfunctory compassion. If the young man's heart remained cold, Romarrah would be forced to reject him as a warrior and this he was loathe to do. No, he must find another way to reach Teilo for he held him dear and yet, he was still fearful of what he had seen on the battlefield.

The Great Master missed sharing his concerns with Tharease. He did not wish to burden Syrath with his duties and his aloneness weighed heavily on his heart. He did not see that, like Teilo, he was in danger of losing his own understanding.

In time the land and its people became settled again and as when one has suffered an illness, once health is regained, there is a new surge of life that flows through the veins. Thus it was with the Land of Romarrah. It was a time of healing and the only danger that could threaten was the part of the land that remained unhealed.

7

Syrath had become a most powerful young woman. Now in her eighteenth year, she was also a fully trained warrior. Only recently had she moved back into the main building with her father having insisted on completing the last two years of her training in the warrior's quarters. She wished to feel one with the others and not separate. It had been a happy time except for the distance between herself and Teilo. As always he was respectful of her and polite but there was no light in his eyes when he looked at her.

Now as she sat on her balcony combing her long dark hair, she thought back over the events of the day. She had been training the new warriors – mostly young men and women who had left their families and friends to come to Imoshtan. They were insecure but, for the most part, eager to learn and Syrath loved to instruct them, sensing in them their urgency to know and understand. These young proselytes were not yet aware of the need to be still and focused. Their minds were alert but they lacked the steady calm that would come with the understanding that all could be achieved without struggle. Too much effort would only harden them and keep them defensive.

Yet she loved their liveliness – the freshness of their thoughts, the glint of their ambition. She treated them all with the gentleness that was her way. Her instructions were clear and quiet and she was very much aware of, and interested in, each individual – watching their reactions to what she was saying and showing them and also to what happened around them. Her students loved her dearly and many spoke to her of their loneliness and fears for she counselled wisely.

However, on this very day, she had trained alongside Teilo. He was instructing a group of young warriors and she could see that they were in awe of him, as were most of his peers. Syrath could hear the emptiness in his voice as he spoke to these young men and women and it filled her with disappointment. It was when a chief warrior asked Teilo to demonstrate particular movements of combat to the young recruits, her disappointment turned to concern.

Amis was asked to partner Teilo and the minute they raised their swords, she could sense the bitterness between them. Amis had nearly completed his training. He was strong and ambitious and although he showed himself as an able combatant, she knew he cared little for the Great Wisdom. That he was also no match for Teilo's skill was apparent as the latter disarmed his opponent with such force she thought he would do him harm.

When the day's training was complete, Syrath observed Teilo and Orphaele, a young woman who worked in the kitchens, walking towards the forest and her sadness intensified. Perhaps this girl can open his heart, she thought, for he is lost to me.

Now as she sat in the fading daylight, she pondered whether or not she should inform Romarrah of her concerns. She was frightened Teilo would indeed do harm. And Amis – surely he could not continue as a warrior – it was impossible. She was at a loss to understand them. That Teilo had lost his father so tragically was a sadness she understood. Many people had lost their loved ones that day. Tharease had been the only mother Syrath had known and the tragedy of her death had grieved her deeply – especially the manner of her dying. But the grief had served to open her heart even more. She found deeper levels of love and tenderness in her being and readily would she have given this to Teilo but he no longer saw her. Instead she gave it to everything she did – there was a reverence about the way she lived and she honoured each day that opened before her.

Why does he not see me, she puzzled. It pained her so much to feel this separation. Abruptly she left the balcony to seek counsel from her father.

Romarrah had made many changes in the years following the Great Battle, as it had become known. In his heart he held himself responsible – that he had not been vigilant enough. That remorse, and the changes he had made, had etched lines on his face and a sorrow in his eyes. His daughter read in those eyes how much that black day had cost her father.

"You are troubled, Syrath," he smiled, rousing himself from contemplation as she entered the room. He welcomed her calm, soothing presence.

"Forgive me," she apologised, "I have disturbed you."

"It is nothing – it is delightful to have your company again. What is it you want?"

"I do not wish to trouble you, Romarrah, but I – "

Her father held up his hand and sighed. "I know what it is you wish to discuss Syrath – it is of course Teilo. I too have been pondering what to do. He does not respond to my attempts to reach him. I have puzzled why he holds me in such contempt as I have given him more than I have given any other. Gladly would I have taken him as my own son had he not turned his heart away from me."

Syrath was surprised by this response. Never had she known him to reveal his feelings so strongly but now he openly spoke his sadness – perhaps as he might have done with Tharease.

"Before the battle," Romarrah continued, "I had a vision – it was that alone which sent me to Apheilio. It was a vision of Teilo's mother and she begged me to save her son."

"You have never spoken of this before," Syrath interrupted.

"It is past – it holds nothing – at least it didn't, but these past months, I have seen the same vision in my dreams and I have heard the same words. Perhaps his mother was not asking me to save her son's life, rather to save him from a different death. I fear I do not know how. I am not sure what ails him. That love should be his remedy – this I do know – but he rejects my love – he rejects your love." Romarrah looked fondly at his daughter. "I know how much that costs you, Syrath, for you have loved him for a very long time."

Syrath had not wished her father to perceive the depth of her feelings – perhaps it would reflect for him his own pain and loss.

"He meets with a young woman from the kitchens," she said lightly. "There is the hope that she may soften his heart."

Romarrah shook his head. "I do not think Teilo's heart is open to anyone – he is merely acting out an existence. I must come to a decision on this, Syrath, for chief warrior, Ortarian, has already petitioned that I address this matter. There is also Amis. I know you are unaware of the history between the two. It is of no importance to you to know this – such knowledge may only colour what you see. But they must be summoned – I fear I have no choice."

♋

Teilo stretched fully in the water. It was icy cold but he did not seem to feel it. At last he was alone. He let his body sink beneath the surface.

Lately, more and more, he felt the urge to run away – to find another way of being. There was a tiredness to his living. He awakened to the same numbness day after day. Sometimes he could almost feel a flicker of warmth when he gazed into the forest, or lay with Orphaele or looked into the eager face of a young warrior but as soon as he reached out to that warmth, it turned cold again. He still felt everything around him – Syrath's sadness, Romarrah's frustration with him – Orphaele's longing for him to be more open with her. Yet he was powerless to give of himself. It was as if the blackness had never left him since the day of Apheilio's death.

Although he had become a hero in the land for his actions on that day, he could remember little of it except holding his father as he died. At times he would see flashes of scenes that he knew were of the contest between himself and Myallon. They were like pieces of a puzzle that didn't quite fit together and they brought with them a sickening deep in his core.

Gasping for air, his head broke the surface and he swam to the water's edge. The bank was steep and he had to pull himself up using the strength in his arms. His body had grown strong and powerful yet he had inherited the lightness and grace of his mother. Perhaps the most striking feature of this young man, the thing that made him different to the other warriors, was that, also like his mother, he had long fair hair and compelling grey-green eyes. Such fairness was not common in the land of Romarrah.

As he dressed, he sensed the presence of another and through the orchard he glimpsed Ortarian making his way purposefully towards him. I am to be summoned, he thought grimly and went to meet the chief warrior.

"Teilo – Romarrah requests your presence," the older man spoke looking directly into Teilo's eyes and holding his gaze.

"What do you want from me, Ortarian? Your eyes ask many questions."

Ortarian picked up a stone, holding it loosely in his hand, feeling its weight.

"I want nothing from you, Teilo, but what I would like for you, is that you feel your lightness again – otherwise," he threw the stone into the water, "like that stone you will slip below the surface."

"It is peaceful there," Teilo replied, walking towards Romarrah's quarters.

The chief warrior watched him thoughtfully and for an instant he saw a darkness surrounding him. He carries something – some fragment that is outside himself, the chief warrior thought – he has taken it into his own soul and like a parasite it takes the life from him. Romarrah must know this. And Ortarian hastened to tell him.

Amis and Teilo stood before the Great Master. There was no doubt in Teilo's mind why they had been summoned. He expected Romarrah to request they both leave the compound and it relieved him to see Syrath was not present. How often he had wanted to speak to her – to tell her what he was feeling, but he could not explain. He had no understanding of why the coldness never left him – why it lived inside him like a reptile, unable to warm itself in the sun.

On the other hand, Amis was unsure of why he had been asked to present himself before Romarrah, but it pained him to stand side by side with Teilo. Amis was of average stature but he carried himself with a confidence that only an astute observer could see was but a façade. This man's true confidence was blighted by an overriding sense of injustice. It was this that left a grudge hardened into his otherwise handsome features. He carried his father's legacy. He had trained hard as a warrior for he desired power more than anything else. To feel powerful and to be seen as powerful meant to stand alone, without fear. It guaranteed respect. Although he had studied the Great Teachings, he saw them through the haze of his own ignorance and their essence never came alive within him.

Romarrah looked fully at the two warriors but before he could address them, Ortarian appeared in the doorway. He bowed respectfully to the Master who excused himself and went to speak to his chief warrior.

Teilo frowned. He did not want Ortarian's intervention on his behalf for he longed to be free – he wished for Romarrah to dismiss him. The burden of others' expectations was too much and he ached for solitude.

When the Great Master returned and again stood before them, he appeared relieved and Teilo detected the change immediately. Do not relent Romarrah, he begged within himself, let me go.

When the Master spoke, he did so looking directly at Teilo and the latter knew he was being challenged.

"You are both good warriors, possessing certain attributes that would serve to make you great warriors, but you both harbour anger. You use this anger like a weapon and it makes you weak – it limits your compassion and understanding. I am loathe to dismiss you and so I propose a challenge – a pilgrimage for you both. I command you relinquish your weapons to me and make your way to the forest of Maurapin. Therein you will find the Pit of Maraka. On this journey you will take the vow of silence and you shall surrender your power to Syrath, my daughter, who will accompany you as your protector."

Here he paused watching for a reaction. At the mention of Syrath, there had been an almost imperceptible flicker of Teilo's eyes.

"Once at the Pit of Maraka," he continued, "you will adhere to the wisdom of the ancients and summon the spirit of the Great Serpent by dropping a stone into the pit. It is said that it takes one thousand breaths for the stone to reach the bottom and one thousand breaths for the Serpent Spirit to awaken. The seeker must then remain in stillness awaiting their fate – to be granted that which is your longing or to be devoured by it. I will give you but a few moments to consider this offer. If you should refuse you are at liberty to leave the warrior's compound and make you way in the world – but not as a warrior of Romarrah."

With that he left the room. It was an uncomfortable moment – the two of them alone together. Teilo ignored his companion and walked out onto the balcony – he needed to look out on the world, as if there he would find his answer.

Maurapin was an ancient forest at the very heart of the Land of Romarrah. Often had he walked on the outskirts of the forest as part of the warriors' patrols but never had he ventured into its mysterious depths – not many did. It was a place of shadow – not an evil place – more like a sacred temple of the land that was left in peace. Of the Pit of Maraka he had only heard stories – somewhat fanciful tales and yet it was spoken of with awe and reverence. Was there then some credit to this talk of Serpent Spirits? He had heard it said that to awaken the spirit was to relinquish life itself – to offer oneself as a sacrifice. His life meant little to him and he was drawn to accept this challenge.

Amis also knew little of Maurapin and the Pit of Maraka. He was angry that Romarrah had directed his words mostly at Teilo – as if he, Amis, mattered little. I will take this challenge, he thought, but I will do it my way – for my own purpose – not his.

When Romarrah returned, both warriors agreed to his proposal. "Syrath will inform me if either of you have broken your vows," the Master said. "Whosoever successfully completes this journey may commence training as a chief warrior if that be their wish. You will leave Imoshtan this very night. May you both find that which you seek."

It was settled. The warriors handed Romarrah their swords and left to prepare for their journey.

In the dark of night they departed the compound.

At first the silence between them was awkward and the fact the men carried no weapons gave them an initial feeling of discontent and vulnerability but they soon fell into the rhythm of their steady pace and the quiet of their own thoughts.

Syrath walked ahead. She, like her companions, was not attired as a warrior but in simple dress and she gathered her cloak about her against the cool of the night. She had not wished to be part of this journey and already she was aware that Amis resented her presence – that he perceived she had power over him.

Maurapin was a dense forest and often provided refuge for those who preyed on others and those who had escaped the harshness of Manon. Most could not stay in its shadows for any great length of time for the darkness and density led to confusion, even madness. Syrath knew she would need to be watchful once they entered the trees.

For the first time in years, Teilo felt lighter. At first he was a little bemused by Amis' seething anger towards him. He wondered how long it would take for this discontent to burst open but from the moment Teilo had surrendered his sword and turned away from being a warrior, he felt as if a huge burden had been taken from him. He was revelling in the first sense of freedom he had experienced in a long time and he was grateful for the silence – he could stay within himself.

The first days of their journey were uneventful until they entered the forest. Even of a daytime it was like night with just enough dim light to see the path ahead. It was this path that puzzled Teilo – who kept it clear of vegetation for it was more than a mere track made by animals. How did Syrath know the way, he wondered – had she been here before? He watched her – he knew her senses were alert – she was expecting trouble and no sooner had he thought this than she suddenly stopped and held up her hand. All was quiet and still but he had heard it too – they were being followed. He closed his eyes allowing his awareness to take in more of what was around him. Although this was a technique mastered only by chief warriors, Shimmera had taught him such skills from birth.

There were three presences – not powerful in themselves but menacing none the less. He opened his eyes. Syrath was looking at him. He held up three fingers and indicated with his eyes three different directions. She nodded slightly. "We shall camp here tonight," was her only comment.

Amis had seen the exchange between the two. Again he felt irritated. It was as if he didn't matter and his presence on this journey was unnecessary.

The three travellers silently went about their business – collecting wood, lighting a fire and preparing food – waiting for those watching them to make themselves known. They did not have to wait long before three men stepped out of the shadows. All carried thick staffs and wore swords.

Syrath acknowledged their presence. "What is it you want good men?'

One of them sneered. "We'll take what we want and it's no concern of yours."

"It is indeed," Syrath answered quietly, "for all we have is what we need for our journey. I forbid you to take what is not rightly yours. If you were to tell me what you need then we may be able to share some of what we have."

"Did you hear that?" the man shouted to his companions. "They might be able to share!" He turned to Amis and Teilo. "What poor fools are these that let a woman talk for them? What say you then?"

When the two warriors did not reply the man again turned to his companions. "They come unarmed – they are but mute simpletons," and saying this he hit Amis hard in the stomach forcing the air from his body. Another struck the warrior across the back and he would have fallen had not Teilo's hand steadied him. The third man hit Teilo sharply across his shoulders.

Syrath stepped forward and drew her sword. "I order you to stop. I have no wish to harm you but if you do not leave us I will have no choice."

Something in the way she spoke made the men cease their attack and look at her. In the light from the fire the sword in her hand almost glowed and the brightness of her stare was unnerving.

"And who are you?" one of them asked.

"I am Master Syrath, daughter of Romarrah," the young woman replied quietly. "This is Master Teilo and Master Amis. We are on pilgrimage at the Great Master's request – I command you to leave us in peace and there will be no retribution."

There was no need to say another word. The men were now aware of the identity of those they had chosen to attack. Teilo's reputation assured his safety. He was the living legend – the boy who had slain the giant. Syrath was the daughter of Romarrah. They did not even take the time to exchange glances with each other. Offering no further argument, they simply disappeared hastily into the surrounding darkness.

Teilo looked at Syrath and smiled and she felt a warmth flow through her. It was so long since she had felt that smile lighten her heart.

From his sack, he took a small pouch containing oiled herbs which he placed against his skin where he had been hit to reduce the swelling and bruising. He offered the same to his companion who only scowled and turned away. Amis was furious with Syrath for allowing him to be beaten. Had she intervened only when Teilo was set upon? Why had she waited? Were they playing a game with him? If so, he vowed he would repay them in kind.

Watching Syrath, Teilo became more aware of her calm and gentleness and how when she spoke, she easily commanded respect. What a powerful woman she had become. She did not seek to draw attention to herself – here was the perfect balance of will and reverence. When next their eyes met, he bowed his head in admiration.

And so their journey continued.

On the last night, before they reached the Pit of Maraka, they set up camp in a small clearing. Here in the deepest heart of the forest there was no menace – no unrest. Teilo lay beneath his blanket contemplating the journey so far. It had not taken him long to realize the sacredness of this place. It was this more than anything else that offered him respite from his colourless existence. For the first time since the day of the Battle, there was clarity – as if a veil had been lifted and he could see once more. Why had he not noticed Syrath before now? Had he been blind to whom she had become – so much more powerful than he because she was at peace with herself while he had floundered in some wasteland. He did not want for this journey to end for he dreaded stepping back into the sunlight and returning to the life he knew. It was as if, within this forest, the hardness in him melted and he could feel again. Tears slid down his cheeks – not sad but joyful – he was alive. Within him there was warmth and love – he had so much to give and he longed to do so. He was aware of Amis lying close by – the anger still rising like a fog around him. How had such venom found its way into his heart? They had once been carefree children – conquering mountains, riding waves of dreams and fantasies. He yearned for that friendship again – as men – to walk side by side – to be the keeper of each other's dreams – to have the freedom to hold each other and know each other's strengths and weaknesses. Let this journey take its course, he thought – who knows where it may lead us. A peace settled around him and he closed his eyes.

Syrath had been watching him from the edge of the clearing. She had seen his tears glistening in the glow from the fire and felt the peace at last come to him. Romarrah had been so right to send him here.

When Syrath was but a child, Tharease had brought her to Maurapin – bidding her not to be fearful of the shadows because if she understood them, she would have no fear.

"There is light in the shadows, Syrath," she had told her. *"There is joy. If you run from them, you will never know it, and you will always run from that which you fear."*

But Syrath had been fearful – there among the towering, ancient giants and she had clung to Tharease. It took many visits for her to feel what her mother understood and to let herself melt into the forest and simply become part of it. That was peace – that was when her heart felt light. Tharease had given her the greatest gift – she had taught her the completeness of all that is – the smallness of her own being and the great expanse that was also within her and around her.

It pained Syrath that her mother figure would be remembered for a sad mistake that cost her life.

The fire had burned down to a bed of hot coals casting very little light in the dark forest. It was quiet and still. Suddenly, Teilo was awake – aware of danger. A dark shape was moving across the clearing towards where Syrath lay. He knew it was Amis and he could sense his intent to harm. Bound by his vow of silence, he could not call out a warning – nor, as Romarrah had instructed, could he raise his hand against another. So instead, he quietly stood and blocked his companion's path.

Amis smirked. "You are a fool, Teilo,'" he hissed, "Did you really think I would be unarmed?" From beneath his coat he drew a knife.

"No I did not, Amis," replied Syrath from the edge of the clearing.

Both men turned. She was not lying beneath her blankets but standing a short distance away, watching all that had occurred.

"Do you wish to take my life," she spoke as she came closer. "Your hatred speaks for you." Calmly drawing her sword, she offered it to a surprised Amis. "Do your deed," she said.

Defiantly he took the sword and raised it. She did not flinch.

"Is this the power you want?" she asked.

He knew then that he was doomed. What he saw in her eyes reflected for him who he was at this moment – someone to be pitied. He threw the sword to the ground and turned to leave. Again her words stopped him.

"Do not walk away. Return to Romarrah and tell him what has happened here this night."

He felt not her pity, only her care. He wanted to weep – to reach out to her.

"Tell him what you feel in your heart," she urged, "take his counsel – whatever task he sets you – redeem yourself."

Without a word, he gathered his few belongings and walked away but not before he let Teilo see his loathing for him.

It is not Syrath he wishes to kill, Teilo thought – it is my life he detests – my life he holds accountable.

When Amis was gone the pair rekindled the fire and sat in silence awaiting the dawn.

The Pit of Maraka was simply a black hole in the centre of Maurapin. There was nothing to warn an unwary traveller of its location – it just appeared – a gaping mouth in the earth.

Syrath knew precisely where it was for instinctively she had come to this place once when she was troubled – after the death of Tharease. It was as if loving hands reached out of the earth and took all burdens from her. She had not seen another living soul. Although she had heard the rumours that Maraka was a place of demon voices – a place to be feared, she did not find it to be so.

In the early morning light, she led Teilo to the Pit and took her place of watch a respectful distance from the warrior.

He waited to gain a sense of his surroundings. There are indeed voices here, he thought – old, ancient voices from deep within the earth. He sensed lost and forgotten secrets of the land and its people. This is a burial place, his mind leapt to a conclusion but his heart said no – it does not hold the bones of corpses – it holds memories – wisdom – longings. He walked to the edge of the Pit.

Syrath expected him to sit in the position of stillness as was the custom of the warriors but instead, to her surprise, he unburdened himself of what he was carrying, unfastened the ties of his thick, cloth shoes and placed them to one side. Next he removed his coat – his fingers expertly untying the straps that held it firmly – then folded the garment and placed it beside the shoes. When he was finished, he lay on the ground. Now he could feel the earth against his skin. For a moment he gazed into the dark canopy above him then calmly closed his eyes as if he was going to sleep.

She watched his hand close over a stone by his side. He held it for a moment and then dropped it into the Pit.

The waiting had begun. She knew he was counting his breaths and that he was completely surrendered to his fate.

One thousand breaths, Romarrah had said until that stone would reach the bottom. One thousand breaths it would take to awaken the Serpent

Spirit and for all that time Syrath would remain alert – assuring nothing or no one disturbed the warrior. The breath of a warrior is slow and measured. Minutes passed into hours.

Teilo felt his awareness falling with the stone – going deeper and deeper. Nothing disturbed his inner watchfulness. He was no longer aware of his body or his surroundings – the sounds and smells of the forest – the ground beneath him. Time ceased. Then suddenly he knew the stone had reached its destination. He waited. Once more he became aware of his body. It was as if waves were washing over his feet, bringing with them a pulsing warmth alternating with tingling cold. He did not stir. Then came a sense that someone or something – a spirit form – was ministering to him. The waves spread into his legs. A strange force was moving slowly upward through his body. It washed over his pelvis. The spirit form was drawing something out of him and bandaging the wound.

A searing, lonely ache briefly shattered the soothing warmth and then melted away. The spirit voice whispered – *you will never again be abandoned*. The waves flowed across his abdomen and with them came fear - cold and gripping. He was powerless to avoid what was to come – he gave himself to the fear – he let it rise in his blood and consume him and just as the lonely ache had done, it melted into the warmth.

It was when this probing tide moved into his chest that the swirling blackness leapt from his heart. Many spirit forms gathered around him like thousands of stroking hands drawing the dark stain away. Still the waves would not stop. They reached his throat and something within felt as if it would snap. When at last they flowed to the top of his head, his entire body writhed as though in pain and a deep, groaning sob escaped from his lips.

He felt Shimmera's endless knowing uncurling within him. Again he knew Apheilio's loving strength and laughter like fire in his veins. The spirit forms continued to hold him and stroke him until he fell into deep healing sleep. It was then the warrior came to him – the golden warrior with the face of an eagle – a powerful radiance emanating from his form. Teilo heard the words *'I sit in peace'*. And in peace he stayed – long after his awareness of what lay around him returned. Even then he did not open his eyes – to do so would be to allow the world to flood back in and he was not ready. In this place where he rested, he knew himself fully. His wisdom rose like a swelling tide and filled all that was hollow in him. There were no barriers to check the immeasurable joy of who he was.

Syrath's presence came back – stronger than he had ever felt it. Her power was calling him and it too became a voice in his flesh that he could not deny.

She had not wavered in her duty. She had waited throughout the day – only stirring once when Teilo moaned. Two hours had passed since then. She had watched him curl his body into a foetal shape and there he had stayed. The love in and around him was palpable and she longed to be part of that love – to feel it soar inside her for she knew she had never experienced that which he now knew.

He stirred slowly, as if reluctant to move, and assumed a sitting position. Finally he stood and turned to her. Their eyes held each other.

"You may speak if you wish," she said softly.

But he did not speak. He simply went to her and held her and in that touch of their bodies, they surrendered to each other.

She longed to know him within her. To know that which she had seen in him from their first meeting – an unknown colour – a secret that held the answers of all time – something that echoed all of this world but was not part of it.

They lay together – allowing the colours of the earth and the heavens to flow through them. The waves that had moved through his body now engulfed both of them while the spirit forms held them and stroked them until they slept. And just before sleep claimed him, he again saw the vision of the golden warrior with the face of an eagle but this time it came to him, not in the form of a man, but as that of a woman.

In the morning when they awoke, they were still holding each other, their bodies curled together in childlike trust. They stayed in silence, not wishing to move, having no need to speak. What they now understood could not be given to words. Teilo stroked Syrath's arm. He had lain with Orphaele many times. Their being together was warm, affectionate – a physical knowing – a tender, earthly pleasure. Syrath had given him her essence – that which poured from the very core of her being – her gentle power – the reverence of her soul as it sang of greater truths. Her essence bled into his own, so that no part of him could be closed to her – he could not refuse her entry. It let him know his own love – in its deepest form – opening every pathway of the spirit and uniting it with that beyond.

Syrath looked into his eyes. Nothing was hidden. There was no part of him unknown to her. Never had she, nor would she again, experience such joy and tenderness and such aching desolation. Her heart had felt as if it was soaring to unreachable heights and yet, at the same time, a fire scorched through her soul – she knew the ecstasy and the despair of all earthly experience.

"Teilo," she spoke at last but he silenced her – holding her tighter.

"I know, Syrath," he whispered, "I know."

Still they stayed entwined – each nursing the realization that when they left this place they would also leave what had just occurred between them. She had so longed to be with this man and now she understood why that could never be possible. It would surely destroy her. That fire would scorch her again and again until she would no longer be able to breathe.

He smiled at her. "We hold each other, Syrath – always – and this forest now holds our memory of each other. It alone is the witness of our love, our knowing. This past day I have again found my father and my mother within me. I now understand what they sacrificed to know each other but I have no words with which to explain this knowing. This past night, I have known you also within my soul and you will stay there – I will carry you always. But we cannot make the same sacrifice Shimmera and Apheilio made. I do not understand how that happened but in my heart I know that is not our destiny."

She smiled back at him. He spoke the truth – of that she was certain and she was content. She could never feel closer to anyone than she did to him now. Nothing could change that. Gently she moved to cast aside the blanket covering them. It was then she saw the man.

Seeing the look on her face, Teilo turned.

Not far from where they lay, stood a man – grinning widely as if savouring some great amusement. He had the look of a wild man – thick dishevelled hair and beard and shining eyes that seemed to jump from one thing to another as if awaiting a sign. He was naked except for a tattered loincloth but it was not a smooth nakedness. His body was hairy and gave him the appearance of being half beast, half man.

Sensing the intruder was not dangerous but that his spirit was one of playful mischief, Teilo eased himself from under the blanket. The man looked him up and down. "The master looks very well this morning," he spoke in a voice that was surprisingly soft and clear.

Teilo smiled at the other's obvious glee in finding them thus. Nevertheless he was puzzled. He had not been aware of the intruder's presence. How could this be?

"What is it you want, good man?" he asked as he reached for his coat.

"Replace what you have taken," the wild man replied tilting his head to one side as if that angle was more pleasing to him. His look was comical and mocking but his words were earnest.

"I assure you I have taken nothing," Teilo responded.

"But you have, Teilo, and it must be given back."

"You know my name – you speak with familiar voice and yet I know you not – I have no sense of you – nor do I understand this riddle you speak."

Teilo calmly dressed as he spoke. Syrath was now sitting, wrapped in the blanket, listening to the strange conversation. The wild man turned his attention to her. He bowed, again almost mockingly. "And you – good lady warrior – many times I have followed your footsteps here – do you too think you can keep taking with no consequence?" He did not wait for her response but turned back to Teilo.

"Master, know what this forest has given you – do not take what you cannot give back or surely it will die."

Syrath shivered. Was this the raving of a madman? Had he followed her on her visits to Maurapin?

Then Teilo did the strangest thing. He walked towards the intruder and placed his hand on the rough, hairy arm. "Show me your pain, old man," he said gently.

The wild man's eyes glistened with tears. "There is a burden too great to bear and it spreads a poison in the earth, into the soul of my brothers and sisters – they weep at night when no one hears. Listen," he held up his hand as if he could hear something and his face distorted in pain. Teilo listened. He kept hold of the old man's hand that he might feel his voices. There was a deep grinding sorrow – like a crippling thirst – a timeless suffering.

"You asked them to hold your memory, Master Teilo, but you must take theirs – you must – if you hold this in you now – when the time comes you will know it and you will have their counsel – you will have their wisdom in you – their living and dying."

Teilo continued to feel the old man's words, the murmuring of the forest earth. His companion's eyes suddenly fired with intensity. "You have the warriors' stone." It was almost an accusation.

To Syrath, Teilo's reaction to these words was unexpected. His head, which had been bowed, listening, almost snapped into position as he stared at the wild man.

"Do not use it, Master, without listening to their counsel first," the old man spoke. Suddenly he laughed insanely. "So my children – continue your loving – my brothers and sisters thank you – they cherish your play." He was almost skipping as he spoke – his mood changing instantly from intense sadness to one of jubilation. "They tell me it was a good night in the forest."

Teilo could not help but laugh at this infectious joy and the teasing insinuations present in the words.

"Laugh out loud, children," the man whooped, "you have been blessed – the earth needs your laughter." Then he hugged Teilo. "I have missed you so much. Your spirit is strong again, Master." His eyes again became intense. "Do not forget my words."

Teilo answered him with his eyes and then the wild man was gone – his body simply blending into the shadows from whence he came.

Teilo said nothing. He began to make a small fire as Syrath clothed herself.

"Who was he?" she asked as she braided her hair. "What did you feel of him? Was he indeed demented from living too long in Maurapin? He appears to know you – have you met with him before?"

Teilo looked up from the fire and smiled. "Ever since I have known you, Syrath, you have never asked but a simple question."

She laughed, enjoying the lightness of their being together again.

"He may very well be suffering from madness," Teilo continued, "but he speaks well. He has lived here for so long, he has the language of the trees – his brothers and sisters – and he is one with them. He is a tree man – hence we did not feel his presence. I have not met him and yet he is familiar."

"Then is the forest dying?" Syrath looked around her. The forest, though ancient, looked very much alive. "It does not appear that is so."

He considered her question. "All is not well within this earth but it is not clear to me what ails it – perhaps such knowledge is not meant to be known to us yet."

They sat silently for a long time, sipping the tea he made, until Syrath, carefully confining her curiosity to one question, asked, "What is the warriors' stone?"

"I do not know," he replied but she saw his hand instinctively move to the pocket inside his coat. Sensing her doubt, he reached out to touch her. "I really do not know Syrath."

From her he would withhold nothing but nor would he talk of that which he did not fully understand.

The return journey through Maurapin was punctuated by their laughter. They were like children playing in the forest and it was as if the forest laughed with them. Not once were they troubled by thieves or the shadowy figures that hid beneath the dark canopy. As they neared the edge of the trees Teilo stopped. "Let us stay one more night."

"Do you fear returning to Imoshtan?" she asked, surprised at his reluctance.

"I am hesitant." He frowned. "It is as if here, in this forest, I belong to the earth as surely as the trees. I know my place – I have an anchor. In truth I have always felt as an impostor in Imoshtan – I came there you will remember, not by choice, but to seek refuge. In so many ways it remains foreign in me."

"I too, Teilo, have often experienced those same feelings and were it not for Romarrah, who I love dearly and upon whom I would never inflict grief or pain, I too would have questioned whether I truly belong. But can we not anchor each other? Do you wish to stay and become a chief warrior? Is there another life that takes your heart?"

He laughed. "Too many questions – let us make a fire and spend one more night close to the earth."

They talked quietly through the night. Together they set their path for the future – to become chief warriors and anchor each other with their friendship.

Here at the edge of the forest, the stars were again visible through the thinning canopy. The gentlest breeze fanned the flames. The forest was alive with scurrying creatures. The scene brought with it memories of Teilo's childhood within the forest of Athanan. He let the feeling spread its warmth in him.

"How is it you knew what to ask the tree man?" Syrath's question sent ripples through his reverie.

"Did you too not feel his pain?"

"I thought he was but rambling," she replied. "I did not know what to say to him."

"Shimmera taught me that everything has wisdom – even the humblest leaf or insect and that when we die, the memory of our wisdom is absorbed by all the earth, the air and the water for others to feel. And, to some extent, it is absorbed by those who truly see us. If you would know something, then you must make a space for that wisdom to be heard. Sometimes that space is in the stillness of your soul – at other times it is in asking someone the right question and hearing the answer within your heart."

Listening to him speak, Syrath knew it was Teilo's wisdom she had longed for from their very first meeting. But how was it that his understanding did not serve him when he needed it most?

The fire was but dying embers when she asked him that which had bothered her nearly every day for the past five years. "Teilo – tell me what happened to you on the day of the Great Battle." No sooner had she spoken than she regretted her words – her curiosity. Did her love for him give her the right to pry – to ask him to relive that which had cost him so dearly.

"I have no pain," he said sensing her regret. "Is that not why I came here – to heal? My father's death was indeed vibrant. He reached for it without fear and he took me with him for a short moment before he let me go. I felt his joy – his freedom. The pain I nursed of his death was but the grief of that physical separation." He hesitated – almost unwilling to say the name upon his lips. "It was what I did to Myallon, "he sighed, "that which I could not bear to look at – that was my deepest grief. I did not see him, Syrath," he shook his head sadly. "I saw only the blackness of his deeds and I destroyed him."

"But Teilo – did he not deserve to be punished? Had he not inflicted such cruelty – such misery – on our people?"

"No one deserves to die without being forgiven. No one deserves to die unloved and unseen. Each spirit should be released with great care that they may leave, not their fear and loathing, but the truth of their wisdom."

Syrath was indignant.

"Did he care when he killed our people? I am told he sneered and even spat at our warriors when he took their lives."

"Even his contempt would have served our warriors. If you faced death with Myallon's disdain staring you in the face, where would you go but into your own peace, just as Apheilio did. But you do not understand, Syrath – I left Myallon no peace – I tortured every part of his being. I did not just take his life – I destroyed every part of him – who he was – who he had been – what he held sacred – what he loved. When I had tortured his flesh I started on his spirit. I left him nothing – not even his own knowing and I took that blackness into my own heart. I want to weep for what I did to him. Even now as we speak, I do not understand from where that power in me came but I do not wish to know it again. Come," he sighed, "this fire has lost its spirit and these words do not keep peace in my heart or in the earth. It is done and does not need to be visited again. I am grateful to Romarrah, and Ortarian, for their wisdom in sending me here. And I am eternally grateful to you, dear Syrath – a gratitude that words cannot match." He smiled at her then added playfully, "Even if you do torment me with your endless questions. Come – let us sleep."

In the early morning they would step back into the bright sunlight and return to Imoshtan.

♋

The first Romarrah knew of their return was when he heard laughter in the courtyard below his chambers. Initially, he experienced a deep sense of joy upon hearing Teilo's mirth. It was obvious the pilgrimage had brought the desired outcome. Yet he felt a slight consternation at the sound of that laughter for it was accompanied by a sense of freedom – almost abandonment and bound to draw attention for that very reason. The compound at Imoshtan was a place of steadiness and calm. Each person knew their place, their way of being. That there was laughter – a small bubble of mirth among the daily activities was only natural and never appeared out of place. But this was a different sound – it brought with it different flavours that were in some way disconcerting. Nevertheless he prepared to greet the pair openly and when they entered his chambers, he welcomed Teilo warmly as if it were his own son returning.

As he appraised the young man before him, he beheld the Teilo of old – the softness and strength – the quiet knowing that was tinged with an effervescent joy and, of course, the mystery – that deep pool which was most beguiling and at the same time, unnerving.

Romarrah was not used to being unable to have a full sense of someone.

When he turned to greet Syrath, the Great Master saw immediately the difference in his daughter. She stood before him a full woman. When she saw his recognition, her face coloured slightly. Romarrah turned away, gesturing for the pair to sit while he poured them a tisane, but the real reason he had turned away was the pain he felt in his heart. His daughter had looked at him fully and in her eyes he saw that, like Teilo, a part of her was now hidden from him – as if some gentle walls had closed around a secret she nursed as one would a child within.

The three of them discussed aspects of the journey through Maurapin and it was evident to Romarrah that Teilo and Syrath now functioned as one – their knowing of each other complete and at ease with itself. Finally they spoke of their desire to become chief warriors and he was surprised by this decision. Since the death of Tharease, he had declared that those who chose to become chief warriors renounce the life of man and woman – that they instead devote their life to their calling, relinquishing the relationships of family. He had vowed that never again would a chief warrior be torn between their duty, according to the law of the Land, and the love of another.

It was evident that Teilo and Syrath had become known to each other and yet here they were before him choosing to forsake this knowing. He felt both disappointment and concern. He wished only that his daughter be spared the loneliness he suffered. If they became chief warriors the only way they could be together would be if Teilo became his successor.

"And are you sure this is what you both want?" he asked, watching for the slightest hesitation but both warriors showed no uncertainty.

"Very well," the Great Master responded, rising to his feet and thus indicating their discourse was at an end.

"Romarrah, what of Amis," Teilo asked, "did he return?"

The Great Master simply shook his head. "Amis was never going to make that journey," he replied adamantly.

Teilo frowned slightly – an expression which did not escape his Master's watchfulness.

After the young warrior had left for his quarters, Romarrah again questioned his daughter of her commitment to becoming a chief warrior, elucidating the vows and responsibilities of such a decision.

"Romarrah this is my choice – it is what I wish. Do I detect that you are not in accordance with it? Is it also not my duty in keeping with the law of the land? Would you rather I chose to enter into family life? At this time I have no yearning for man or child – I am content to be within myself."

"If that be your wish, Syrath, of course you have my blessing on this matter. I had merely thought that you and Teilo might have feelings for each other and that perhaps you would prefer..."

She interrupted him. "Teilo and I made this decision together, Romarrah. We remain as always the closest of friends." She could not speak of their intimacy in Maurapin for already it was like a cherished gift – wrapped in the softest cloth and stored in a sacred place. To speak of it would be to give away something of Teilo himself and this she would not do. Instead she led Romarrah gently away from the subject.

"You realize that there is little need for Teilo to do this training. Already he has both the knowledge and power of a chief warrior. It is obvious his mother taught him from the earliest age. Why is it, do you think, that Apheilio knew of Myallon's advance? Why was he able to prepare the warriors and avoid an even greater carnage? It is because Teilo forewarned him – he simply knows these things – he has a rare wisdom which is difficult to explain."

"There is more to being a chief warrior, Syrath, than being able to sense that which is around you. One must understand the needs of each warrior, have complete understanding of the rituals, especially protection, and be skilled in all manner of combat. Understanding and compassion must move before them. They have conquered desire and fear. Their body can face deprivation and hardship and stay strong. Their mind is at all times focused and alert. I could go on, for there is much more, but I can tell you, Syrath, that Teilo is still too young and inexperienced – he does not yet have all the attributes of a chief warrior, however great you may think him already."

You are wrong Romarrah, his daughter thought – you are, as far as this matter is concerned, so very wrong. But she stayed silent. She could not tell her father what she knew of Teilo and so she let the matter rest.

After leaving the Great Master's chambers, Teilo did not immediately return to his quarters. Instead he made his way across the courtyard to the kitchens. His intention was to seek out Orphaele and tell her of his decision to become a chief warrior. He also wished to offer her his love, gratitude and loyalty for she had given him comfort and tenderness and, at times, had been the only thread that connected him to life. When he had no longer been able to see his reflection in those who cared for him – especially Romarrah and Syrath – Orphaele had suddenly appeared. Quiet and sincere, she spoke little – only what was necessary – but her eyes said all that she did not give to words. He knew she had let him be with her because she felt his pain and it was in her nature to comfort. The touch of her body was often the only true goodness in his day. How she had found her way through his unfeeling reserve, he did not know. She had simply been there one afternoon as he walked towards the forest. She was picking fruit in the orchard and he had watched her for a few moments. Her movements were unhurried and gently methodical. When she saw him observing her, she spoke without hesitation.

"Master Teilo – do you wish to speak with me?"

He was surprised by her forthright manner for he had observed in her a shyness – as if it would be too painful to suffer the intrusion of a stranger into her privacy. And so began their relationship. Orphaele asked nothing of him, nor did she treat him as someone different. She, like everyone else had heard the stories of Teilo. Most likely she, like so many others, had lost someone she loved in the Great Battle but she did not speak of it.

Their meetings were of the most part, silent. Occasionally a conversation would surprise them both but Teilo could not give of himself, even though Orphaele's eyes told him she would hold her knowing of him in that same private world she held everything. It would be safe.

Outside the kitchens, he hesitated. Now that he was free and his world had opened up before him once again, he felt the warmest love for this young woman who had held him through the darkness. They had made each other no promises – had pledged no vows, yet he wanted her to be sure of his loyalty. Although they could no longer be together as man and woman, he would hold their friendship for as long as Orphaele wished him to stand by her. He knew little of her, except that her bond with her parents was strong although he sensed they lived far away. He did not know where. Nor did he know how she came to be in Imoshtan. Here was a life he had shared intimately without taking the time to know it. A sense of sadness filled him as he suddenly knew Orphaele's aloneness in this world.

We nursed each other, he thought, through our own sorrows without ever knowing them. For an instant he contemplated forsaking his life in Imoshtan and taking Orphaele back to his home near the forest of Athanan where they could live as simple villagers – without a village, he thought wryly. The temptation was strong – he held it – feeling the weight of its comfort – but in his heart he knew that this was not his path. He stepped into the kitchen.

Riata, a large, strong woman with arms like a man's, smiled at him as she kneaded mounds of dough. "Master Teilo – you have returned then. What is it I can do for you?"

He returned her smile. "I wish to speak with Orphaele," he replied watching her hands begin to fashion the dough into long, plaited braids with a speed that was fascinating.

"That you cannot do, Master Teilo. Orphaele is no longer here – she left in haste some days past. Perhaps her parents were in need of her."

"Where may I find her parents, Riata – do you know?"

"I cannot say, Master Teilo. Orphaele was never one to talk. She just came and said goodbye to me. She looked very unhappy so I suspect there had been a tragedy." Riata placed the doughs neatly, side by side, as Teilo thanked her and left the kitchen, walking slowly towards the orchard.

Evening was closing in and the sadness he felt intensified, but part of it belonged to Orphaele and was accompanied by a feeling of panic and despair. What could have happened to take her away and cause her this distress?

The words Shimmera sometimes sang to him as a child suddenly became clear in his mind.

I have flown over valleys old and guarded
lost between mountains of mist
and silent passion
I have bathed in oceans like crystal glass
stretched between lands of shy mystery
and hope.
Do you know where my soul hides
little bird, little bird
Do you know who I am?

I have skipped through forests
laughter blessing my feet
I have spread like a rainbow
colours dancing behind me
I have like the rain flowed into the earth
and there in soft dark flesh
stayed hidden and warm
Do you know where my soul hides
little bird, little bird
Do you know who I am?

I have stroked your beautiful soft face
and played as music in your dreams
I have listened to your beating heart
and floated on your quiet breath
I have kissed your sleeping eyelids
scattered leaves of joy
upon your path
but do you know where my soul hides
little bird, little bird
Do you know who I am?

Fly with me to the valleys old and guarded
Bless the mountains' mist
with your rising sun
Let the oceans hold your body
Let the earth your spirit contain
Give the wind your breath to carry

> *Let your voice be the music of time*
> *Do you know where your soul hides*
> *little bird, little bird*
> *Do you know who you are*
> *little bird, little bird?*

How those words had soothed him to sleep. How he longed to hold Orphaele now and whisper those same words to ease her suffering – to bring her peace. He vowed to find her – to reassure himself that she was safe and had come to no harm. That was all he could do. He released his feelings and lay beneath the gathering stars, breathing the earth and the heavens.

I am home again in myself, he thought and smiled.

8

The training of a chief warrior differs greatly from that of a warrior. There are no instructors and all study and preparation is done alone. The aspirants know what disciplines, techniques and skills must be acquired and their entire life is devoted to practice. At the same time, they are expected to continue their work with the young trainee warriors, offering instruction, guidance and understanding.

Nor are the ways of combat a major part of this training as the chief warrior's path is one of stillness and intense study. The time taken to complete this study varies for each person. Every week an aspirant meets with the chief warrior chosen to be a mentor to discuss teachings and receive counsel. Romarrah was to be Teilo's mentor while Syrath remained under the guidance of Ortarian.

There were in all, at any time, between three to four hundred warriors in training at the compound. At least a further hundred accomplished warriors lived within those walls along with eight to twelve chief warriors. Imoshtan itself was, for the most part, a city of warriors. These men and women lived normal lives but regularly went on patrols and attended special instructions and rituals at the compound. They were, at all times, prepared to be summoned to duty and they numbered in their thousands.

Very few warriors chose to become chief warriors such was the intensity of this undertaking and now, since the Great Master's decree that they must forsake the relationships of man and woman to do so, their numbers were even fewer.

Romarrah knew to be Teilo's guide and counsel would be a challenge. This young warrior would always do things differently and perhaps not wish to hold with certain traditions. Therefore he would require careful handling – his influence was, however subtle, already noticeable. He was like a magnet – even when he had been so dark and distant, others still looked up to him. To his credit, he did not use or abuse this adulation – he simply let it be.

During their very first session together, Teilo had many questions – none of which specifically pertained to his recommended studies and endeavours.

"Why is it Romarrah," he spoke openly with not a hint of self-consciousness, "that the warriors are not shown more of the land – is this not where their instruction should begin – close to that which holds them?"

"They are taught to love and respect the land, Teilo, as you would be aware, but what has this to do with your own study?"

"Is that not what I am to study – that which is before me? I am aware of what we have been taught – to love and respect all is our first duty, but what does it mean if we do not fully feel in us what it is we love and respect?"

Romarrah was silent for a moment studying the face before him. Where was this young man heading now? If it was with arrogance he spoke, the Master would have cautioned him, but there was no arrogance in these words – it was more a calm, confident inquiry.

"What is it you see, Teilo?' he asked patiently.

"The warriors need to experience more of the world inside themselves. A leaf is but a shadow of something greater? And at the same time, what is something greater if not the shadow of a leaf? Why is it they are not encouraged to know more of what lies beyond these walls? If they cannot feel the journey of that leaf, they will never know of greater things – not fully. They are given instructions but these are merely principles. They must know themselves – in every part of life. They must be able to touch any part of life and feel the enormity of what it is. Then they will know joy. They need to play with life, Romarrah – to dance without weapons – to love the dance."

Romarrah smiled. "Teilo, as teachers we open the space wherein these men and women may expand. It is for each person to spread where they will with the teaching we give to them."

"That is true," the warrior replied, "but that space you open is too narrow."

The Great Master swiftly ended the debate. "Your feelings have been noted, Teilo. Now tell me of your own practice."

He must keep this young man steady – in his place – he was too powerful and Romarrah was unsure Teilo had the wisdom to wield that power safely.

♋

Jemai scowled at the thick, congealed wax around the base of the candelabra. For the past two days he had been scraping it into a large pot and his fingers ached. At first he had enjoyed the task, for his surroundings were beautiful and peaceful. He was in the sanctuary – the building where the warriors came to be in stillness. It was lit by hundreds of candles which stood in giant candelabras of intricately carved figures. It was said that the figures represented different aspects of the Great Wisdom and that meditating upon these forms would give one a deeper understanding of that Wisdom. As the candles burned, the wax dripped onto the figures. It had to be removed regularly – a task usually given to the young apprentice warriors.

Jemai had done more than his fair share of wax scraping in the six months since coming to the compound. No matter how he tried, when practicing the moves of combat, he was clumsy and awkward and he sensed his superiors watching him – most likely expecting him to fail. They never showed anger or displeasure at his ineptness – they were patient and kind, but he was often sent to perform some menial task elsewhere.

Suddenly the small tool with which he worked slipped and chipped a large splinter off the statue. Jemai cursed under his breath. He knew chief warrior Prisheed would see it immediately. Searching the hard clay floor for the missing piece in the hope he might be able to stick it back, he became aware he was no longer alone. Master Teilo was standing quietly to one side – just watching. The boy felt himself blushing. For how long had he been observed? He hoped the Master might go away again, but instead he came closer and to Jemai's discomfort, sat opposite him.

"I used to chip them on purpose," the warrior said with a smile, then laughed at the boy's incredulous expression.

"You do not believe me do you?"

Jemai shook his head.

"I speak the truth," Teilo continued, as if oblivious to the young man's discomfort. "I was angry then and there were many things I did not understand – including the value of ritual. These statues meant nothing to me."

As he spoke, he had taken the tool and was gently prising the wax away from the uneven clay surface.

Jemai glanced around him to make sure no one else had entered the room. Although he knew of no rule stating that silence be observed in the sanctuary, he had never known anyone to speak within these walls. Yet here was Master Teilo talking to him and laughing, as if they were seated in their own home.

"You know, Jemai," Teilo chatted as he worked, "people make rituals to which they attach so many conditions. For some those rituals have meaning, but for others they are like a hollow shell – they contain no flesh – no sustenance – they are but a mechanical knowing."

He paused for a moment and unlike Jemai, was aware that chief warrior Prisheed had entered the room and was observing them. Still, he chose to continue, for what he now sensed in Jemai made it imperative for him to do so. Neatly he brushed the wax shavings into the pot and returned to the scraping. "But do not forget that ritual is beautiful – especially when released from its purpose – when you give yourself wholly to the doing of it – the sound, movement and sense of it. I made a ritual of wax scraping and I would come to this place when I knew it would be empty – when I had not been asked to do so and remove the wax – feeling the form beneath the wax – letting the movement become part of me – not merely an extension – letting myself absorb the ritual and it absorb me. In this way ritual is for its own sake and it softens and crumbles the hardness and rigidity within us."

Prisheed quietly left the room and Teilo stopped his task, placing the tool to one side.

"Give me your hand, Jemai."

The boy was surprised, but obediently reached his hand across towards the warrior, his eyes downcast. Teilo's strong, fine hand folded around the boy's which was hardened by labour – a farmer's hand – used to bigger tasks than scraping wax. Beneath the surface was much sadness – aching for a voice and folding in on itself again and again.

"Jemai, hold my eyes with your own," Teilo spoke gently.

When he raised his eyes to meet those of the warrior, Jemai felt a shock move through him but he did not look away.

"What do you feel?" the warrior asked.

Jemai was flustered – his skin began to prickle with sweat and he attempted to stammer an answer.

"No, no – do not answer," Teilo soothed. "Listen – in your heart – what do you feel? There is no right or wrong to what you feel – it is but what it is. Your fear is blocking you, Jemai – let go of your fear – give it to me."

Feeling the warmth of Teilo's hand spreading into his own, almost involuntarily, Jemai allowed his body to relax.

"What is it that lies beneath your fear?" Teilo's voice was soft but very insistent and the boy's eyes filled with tears. The sadness spilled down his cheeks and he bowed his head.

"Let it come," the warrior counselled. They sat in silence as Jemai shed his tears. Then Teilo spoke again.

"Now what lies beneath your sadness – close your eyes – let yourself sink into your deepest place, Jemai – your most deepest place – tell me what you feel there."

Jemai followed the instructions intently – he even felt himself sinking as if a deep hole had appeared beneath him and he could not stop falling into it. Suddenly some place within him opened into the softest yellow sun and the most beautiful quiet white. As if from a distance he heard himself speak.

"I feel calm, Master Teilo – and love."

He did not know when Teilo took his hand away, or how long he remained still in that peace but when Jemai opened his eyes, the warrior was once more quietly absorbed in his task.

The boy watched how effortlessly the young Master worked – each movement was smooth, almost caressing. Without looking at him, Teilo stated, "Your parents were both killed on the day of the great battle."

"How did you know, Master Teilo?"

The warrior turned to face him. "It is in your eyes – your face speaks it – your body holds it. They were not warriors but humble farmers protecting their land and their family – protecting you. Honour them, Jemai – believe me, they are with you still."

The sadness returned to the boy's eyes but this time it was not as heavy.

"That is why I chose to become a warrior, Master Teilo." he said.

"Do you think a warrior is more honourable than a farmer?"

The boy thought for a moment. "No, Master, I do not, but I wish to learn things about myself. My intention was to return to the land when my training was complete."

"And, your intention now? What has changed?"

"I have no talent for combat," the boy replied miserably. "My Masters are patient but I fear they despair of me."

"Come," said Teilo brushing the last of the wax into the pot. "Your work here is done – let us play, Jemai."

The courtyard was still filled with warriors training – each one intent on their movements. Jemai followed obediently behind Teilo but inside himself, he shrivelled. He had no desire to be singled out by this man and, in front of all the others, instructed in the art of combat. To his surprise and relief, Teilo walked straight through the courtyard, pausing only briefly to say something to Syrath. Then they continued on in silence until they had reached the far corner of the orchard. The warrior laid his sword on the ground and bid Jemai to do the same. He then rested his hands on the boy's shoulders and stood facing him.

"Watch my eyes, Jemai – do not waver in your gaze – do not look at what I am doing but dance with me – be my mirror – feel which way I move and be there also."

Having given these instructions, Teilo, holding Jemai's gaze, began to move – slowly extending his left arm and letting it dance as if it had a life of its own.

Feeling very self-conscious, Jemai tried to do the same.

"You are trying, Jemai – too much effort – feel and trust yourself – do not think – do not yet try to anticipate – be with me."

As he spoke Teilo continued to move – only one arm – letting it flow – stretching and circling as if to music. When he knew Jemai was now at ease with the play, he began to move the other arm also. Gradually he let his body find its own rhythm – slowly bending and twisting – folding and opening.

At first the boy struggled but his gaze did not falter – he watched Teilo's eyes and somewhere in their grey-green depths, he saw the dance and he followed it. Never had he experienced such freedom in his body and before he could stop himself, he had closed his eyes and moved to his own silent music – almost as if he were no longer in control – something else was moving through him.

Realizing what he had done, his eyes opened with a start. Teilo was standing still, watching him. When Jemai looked at him, the warrior laughed and hugged the boy. The feel of those strong arms around him made Jemai want to weep with joy.

"Now you understand a little of what it feels like to trust yourself." Teilo spoke. Releasing him, he added with a smile, "but it will not serve you to close your eyes during combat."

Jemai returned the smile. "Master Teilo," he said shyly, "would you dance for me?"

"For what purpose?" Teilo responded.

"It felt so open," the boy appeared uncomfortable as he spoke. "I wanted to see what it looked like."

Teilo stared at him for a moment and then, without another word, he let his body dance. To Jemai it was as if everything else became still – but no, he thought, everything moves in him – it is beautiful and powerful – it is without fear.

When the warrior finished Jemai said quietly, "It is freedom."

"That it is, young Master," his teacher replied. "You have a deep understanding, Jemai. Now come – we are late. Meet me here at this time tomorrow and we will continue."

Jemai's world had suddenly been filled with a new colour. He felt his parents' smiles upon him and he knew all was well.

For many weeks they met in the orchard each afternoon and danced until one day Teilo said, "Pick up your sword, Jemai. You have played long enough – combat is no different – stay with my eyes – move with me only now, without trying to anticipate, be there just before me. You must trust yourself. If the mind gets in the way you are lost – you will listen to the wrong voice – do you understand?"

"I think so, Master Teilo." The boy was hesitant.

"No, do not think so." The warrior was suddenly very serious. "Thinking so will see you slain. Feel it – be it – this is ritual also. It all comes from one place only – not your thoughts, but your stillness. Come – raise your sword."

Nervously Jemai picked up his sword and immediately he became aware of his clumsiness. He saw himself as he had always seen himself – a plodder – someone who was not gifted with grace and ease of movement. He looked at Teilo who was watching him, eyebrows raised in quizzical amusement. Jemai laughed - that look said a thousand words. He raised his sword and faced the warrior.

"Eyes," Teilo reminded and they began. The sparring continued long past their usual time and was punctuated with laughter and exclamations of surprise and appreciation until finally Teilo called a halt to the play.

"You are tiring, Jemai – it is time to stop. A quick plunge in the stream will refresh you."

"Master that water is like ice – it is too cold to bathe in."

"I know." Teilo discarded the last of his clothing and leapt into the water. Jemai too then rose to his feet, quickly undressed, and followed his Master into the stream. The cold pierced his flesh like thousands of spikes and he couldn't help but scream out. But more than the cold, he felt joy – the joy of being. He was alive and each moment was vivid.

"Out," Teilo commanded appearing from beneath the water, "or I will be responsible for your demise."

The spread of warmth rushing back into his body as he pulled himself out of the stream only increased Jemai's joy and contentment. As he dressed, tears came to his eyes and with them an overwhelming sense of love and gratitude towards the man beside him. He wanted to reach out and hug him, but he feared it would not seem appropriate – that it would in fact, appear improper. Although Teilo was different, the warriors were always restrained.

"Jemai follow your heart," Teilo spoke, fastening his coat. "We were born to live fully, joyously – we were born to love. Do not restrain yourself in showing love." The young apprentice turned to the warrior and hugged him.

Several weeks later as they walked back through the courtyard after practice Teilo spoke seriously to his young student.

"Romarrah will most likely request that you continue your training with chief warrior Prisheed only." Here he held up his hand to brook any argument from Jemai. "He will have his reasons – it does not mean that we cannot practice sometimes together although," he paused as if thinking of the right words to say, "I feel I may have to leave Imoshtan for a time. Take your instructions from Master Prisheed with gratitude – he is a fine warrior – but remember to enjoy your dance. Remember also that freedom is an internal world. When I return, I will want you to tell me the difference between restraint and containment and what happens when you truly surrender to your dance. Remember this, Jemai, for it will be the first thing I will ask you when we meet in the future. Take heart, my young friend – you will not be forgotten."

Jemai felt the joy within him begin to crumple at Teilo's words. Just when he had found his footing in this foreign world, the one person who had held him steady now talked of separation.

"I am not your source of happiness, Jemai," the warrior said quietly. "Now you have found it in you, know its true source. Let this parting bring you strength." He took the boy's face in his hands and kissed his forehead. "I will tell you what is to be." And with that he left to keep his appointment with Romarrah.

If Teilo had been sparring with Jemai, so too had he been sparring verbally with Romarrah and the latter had, in part, enjoyed their debates. He had been correct in assuming Teilo would break with tradition and when, on hearing from Prisheed of the meeting with Jemai in the warriors' sanctuary, he had been mildly rankled by such disregard. When next he addressed the warrior it was to chastise him for his failure to respect the silence of that place. He expected Teilo to be defensive but the young man stayed silent, sipping his tea until asked for an explanation.

"I was freeing the boy's heart, Romarrah," came the response. "Had I waited for another time, another place, the moment would have been lost. I do not think silence is bruised by love."

His words are as lethal as his sword, the Great Master thought.

On yet another occasion he inquired as to how much time Teilo himself gave to stillness, for he knew many evenings were spent talking to Syrath in her chambers. Their laughter often reached him as he sat in contemplation and gave rise to irritation in him. To his mind their togetherness did not augur well for their future as chief warriors. Teilo's days he noticed were spent in varied activities but rarely did he see him enter the warriors' sanctuary.

Teilo responded to his Master's question with a smile. "What part of me should be in stillness, Romarrah? How can one measure the stillness of one's soul? If you are asking of me when do I sit in stillness and contemplation, my answer to you would be, in the forest, before the warriors awaken or after they have retired. I do not neglect my times of solitude Romarrah."

Now as the Great Master awaited the young warrior's arrival he again reviewed the decision he had made – being especially careful to re-examine his own motives as honestly as was possible.

To the far north of Imoshtan lay the city of Yeshotruen. Here was another compound where warriors lived and trained, but unlike Imoshtan, it was not a place of quiet harmony or great beauty. The terrain was open and stark. The water courses were mostly dry and all water had to be drawn from wells. The people of this area were coarser, often uneducated, and there was a desperate violence that permeated their lives.

O'Daewin, in his wisdom, had ordered the construction of a compound at Yeshotruen in an effort to bring education and peace to the region. He also hoped such an undertaking would provide a stable governance and ward off resentment towards Imoshtan. Initially it had been moderately successful but for many years this initiative had floundered and was now in need of new life – new direction. Teilo himself needed to lead – of this Romarrah was certain – the time had come to give the warrior this freedom.

When told of Romarrah's decision, Teilo bowed. "You read me well, Master. I feel it is time for me to leave Imoshtan."

He was aware that to leave this place where he was most comfortable – to leave the forest where he prayed and the orchard where he played and walked in contemplation would carry with it a fleeting sorrow. To leave this place where he was known and loved and take up residence at the compound in Yeshotruen, would not be an easy task and yet he knew it was right – not only for himself, but for Romarrah as well. The Master's next words came as a surprise.

"You will take young Jemai with you," he instructed. "He may continue his training at Yeshotruen."

Teilo objected. "I have no wish to take the boy away from here – it is too soon – there is comfort here, Romarrah, and his soul needs comfort."

"If given a choice, Teilo, we both know which Jemai himself would choose. What is your objection to this action? You have given him too much of yourself and now you must take the consequences. You have created attachment – you are like a father to him – this carries responsibilities."

For a brief moment Teilo felt angry and he waited before he spoke – watching the anger dissolve.

"Attachment is not unhealthy, when it carries no dependence – no claim. It is but another feeling. I am attached in some way to my walks in the orchard, but my stillness remains without them. Are you not attached to your unspoken rules? Is that a healthy attachment?"

No one spoke to the Great Master in such a forthright manner. Not even Tharease would have challenged him thus. He looked at Teilo quietly for a few seconds before he spoke.

"There are upwards of four hundred men and women in training, Teilo. They each have a story – a past – some have suffered tragedies. We have not the time to give each one the attention you have bestowed upon the young Jemai. Is it not better that they be treated equally – that we give to them an example of living within the Great Wisdom – that we offer a foundation which holds them and allows them to find their own way?"

"And did Amis find his way?" Teilo's voice was quiet, but strong, and Romarrah's response was almost sharp. "Amis made a choice – he was given the same training as any other."

"He was taught principles – he was not shown how to feel his pain. What is it you see when you look at the faces of the new, young warriors? You know how to read them – you too must have seen the poverty on some of those faces – when the soul in them is starving – shrivelling within. They are the ones who need your love – not your teachings. Address the pain first and the teaching will open inside them without you ever having to say another word. Perhaps you would not feel your own aloneness so acutely, if you addressed the pain of its source in you – if you allowed yourself to be loved."

Teilo had not raised his voice. There was no superiority in his tone or frustration. He simply stated what he saw. Now it was Romarrah's turn to release his anger.

"I did not think this discourse was about myself," he finally responded, equally as calm. "It was of the young Jemai we spoke and what is to be done in his best interest. I am not in doubt of your love, Teilo – or your qualities – many of which are quite remarkable, but let us be very clear in this – I do question your judgement on some matters. You are young and you lack experience in many ways, which is why I have chosen to send you to Yeshotruen. My perception is also that your relationship with Jemai has extended too far – you have created in him a dependence. This now becomes your sole responsibility and why he should accompany you. I perceive him as too vulnerable to be abandoned by you at this time."

If you knew my love, Teilo thought, you would not use the word abandoned. He realized that if Romarrah questioned his judgement on this matter, words were now useless. "Then let Jemai come to us and make his own decision," he said.

Romarrah rang for Ortarian to send for the boy.

Unsure of the purpose of his being summoned, Jemai expected the worst but was relieved on seeing Teilo was also present. The Great Master presented him with the news of Teilo's imminent departure, but this came as no surprise.

When Romarrah asked if Jemai would like to accompany Teilo, the boy's face openly showed his delight. He turned to the young Master. The expression on Teilo's face said nothing, but when he looked into Teilo's eyes, Jemai had his answer. Teilo smiled at him.

"I will stay here at Imoshtan if I may, Master," Jemai bowed to Romarrah. "Master Teilo has set my lessons to learn here and, though I would like nothing more than to be with him, my strength is where I am."

Romarrah was astounded at this response. He had seen the unspoken exchange between the two – he also had been watching Teilo's eyes but frustratingly, he had seen nothing. Courteously he dismissed Jemai and turned to Teilo. "I bow to your wisdom, young Master," he said graciously.

"And I to yours, Master. You are correct – I have little experience of the world and I am in need of this pilgrimage and I long for solitude."

"You do not wish to be accompanied on your journey?" Romarrah frowned. The road to Yeshotruen was long and not without danger.

"No," Teilo replied without further explanation. "With your blessing I will leave after training tomorrow – there is one thing I must do to assure

Jemai's confidence in himself – then," he added, again smiling, "I leave without obligation."

Romarrah was unsure if he had misunderstood Teilo's relationship with Jemai – had he made a decision based on wrong knowledge and not taken the time to seek the truth?

The young warrior bowed. "You have my gratitude," he said. The two men embraced. Between them was a genuine love and affection but Teilo's words had opened an ache in Romarrah that he did not know he held.

9

There was a festive air about the compound. Flags, delineating the areas of combat, fluttered in the breeze. Long benches were set out against the walls, awaiting the feast that would come at the end of the day's competitions. The young warriors assembled, taking their places in readiness. They were in three different groups depending on the length of time they had been in training and they stood mostly in silence, mentally preparing for combat.

Each new season these young apprentices would undergo an intense day of combat. They would pit their fledgling skills against each other and finally against an experienced warrior – perhaps even Romarrah himself. By day's end, their bodies would ache and their minds would be filled with moving pictures – the clashing of swords – their opponents determined expressions – the blur of watching faces. Inside their heads would echo with the sounds of combat and the commands of their instructors.

This was the day Jemai dreaded more than any other. No one taunted him. No one paraded his ineptitude with their eyes or their words but in him it quaked – a silent terror. The practice with Teilo had not erased his fear among his peers – his overwhelming sense of incompetence. Now, without his mentor, this day loomed heavy and dull and broken.

Syrath and Teilo, like the other experienced warriors, worked tirelessly with the older students and Romarrah watched their progress, his face an impassive mask. It still perturbed him that Teilo appeared to make a game of something that required intensity of focus – humour only served to disturb the stillness of the surface. Syrath also had adopted Teilo's way of ease which, if the Great Master was to describe it, was akin to flippancy. He caught himself feeling pleased that Teilo was leaving and with that event, the work at Imoshtan would return to its usual steadiness. He allowed this feeling to pass, having no desire to hold it as resentment.

The morning's preliminary activities over, time came for the students to test their mettle against those more experienced. They drew lots to determine whom they would oppose. Chief Warrior Prisheed took their names and matched them with a warrior. Romarrah observed Teilo approach and speak with Prisheed. The chief warrior frowned momentarily, then smiled and nodded. The Great Master sighed. He was in no doubt that Teilo had changed the draw and it annoyed him. Again he heard the warrior's words – *'is your attachment a healthy one?'* Yet he also knew that without those rules, there would be no order – their discipline would fray as surely as an unhemmed cloth. Yeshotruen would teach this young man the value of such strict adherence to the law.

Throughout the day, student versed instructor – there was no exception – male against male – female against male – female against female – it mattered not. When it was Jemai's turn, he was surprised to see Teilo step out to confront him. The warrior smiled at his expression. "It is no different, Jemai – here or in the orchard – the game remains the same – shall we play?"

The young boy knew in that instant that Teilo had orchestrated their match – he was giving him the chance to step away from all that crippled him. As he moved into position, Jemai became acutely aware of those watching.

"Remember," Teilo said as he bowed in acknowledgement of his opponent, "they are not part of the play. It is between you and your opposer and that, my friend, is me." His eyes laughed at his opponent. "Challenge me – I swear I shall rise to it."

Jemai laughed out loud at Teilo's humour and with that laughter came freedom. Their swords clashed. For those who predicted the competition would be over in seconds, their indifference soon became disbelief. Jemai moved with expert precision and ease. It soon became apparent the two combatants were locked into a serious play of their own. Twice Teilo moved to disarm his opponent and twice the young Jemai slipped away with an effortless cunning. For the first time he fought as if his life depended on it.

Standing beside Romarrah, Prisheed shook his head. "He has taken a boy – ill at ease with the world – a seemingly clumsy, untalented young man and given him the grace of a fargaleen (earth spirit).

Romarrah said nothing – he simply looked on as Teilo finally disarmed Jemai and then embraced him heartily.

Aware of the silence around them, the young apprentice spoke. "Master – you are an inspiration to us all."

The young Master shook his head. "Jemai – it is you who is the inspiration. Twice you have out stepped me – do you know what that means? I gave you no consideration – no leniency – it was your play alone that saved you – twice Jemai. You are equal to any other apprentice here today and now you will stand alone."

With that he bowed to the boy and walked away. Jemai would not see him again – not for many years and by then he, himself, would be an accomplished warrior.

"Are you sure you will not wait until after the feasting is over?" Syrath asked as she walked her friend a short distance from the compound. Teilo shook his head.

"How can it be that I keep finding you and losing you again?" she spoke quietly. It had been a gruelling day – her body was tired and her head ached – partly with the sadness of his leaving. "What is it that takes you away, Teilo – I know it is not that Romarrah sends you – you wish this for yourself. Why can you not be content here? What has changed in you that you must leave?"

Teilo smiled to himself at the tumble of questions but he did not make light of her words. He felt the sad weariness beneath them. For a moment he wondered if he was doing the right thing. Did he place a greater burden on his dear friend? Stopping he dropped his sack of belongings on the roadside and sat, bidding her to do the same. She settled herself beside him, laying her head wearily in his lap. He gently loosened her braids, releasing the thick mane, and rubbed her scalp – drawing the tension of the day away from her body.

"This is what I will miss," she murmured. "No one has your healing hands."

She closed her eyes and felt the warmth of him reaching into her tiredness.

"I go, Syrath," his voice was soothing, "because my heart tells me to. It is not a question of being content – that is but a practiced way of being – but discontent serves to show us we need to be aware that something is not as it should be. I have felt that discontent for many weeks now and it leads me to Yeshotruen."

She could not argue with that – she knew he must follow what was in his heart. Often had they discussed this very matter – the knowing that could not be discarded. It was like a heart song waiting for its colours to be sung. But had they not promised to anchor each other through this time? Did not Teilo bring joy to everything he did and affect all around him, including herself, with his warmth? Alone she did not know if she could stand against Romarrah's will as he did. The Great Master was after all her father. And then there was the smallest doubt – did these two men struggle merely to assert themselves over each other? She almost felt guilty to so much as whisper this thought within her and yet, she could see the rightness of them both.

Suddenly he laughed. "You are teetering, Syrath – I can feel it in my hands – your mind wavers."

She opened her eyes and stared up at him. They were soft, dark, and cloudy.

"Ah," he murmured, "so that is it – I see uncertainty and it creates its own spiral – if you go too deep you will be left clinging to the sides of your unrest."

"Tell me my answers," her eyes begged him, "you are hiding from me."

The warrior sighed. "Syrath, I do not do battle with Romarrah. Is that what you think? That my spirit is rebellious against one man – that like a beast my instinct leads me to usurp the leader – to claim my supremacy? For how long have you held this? It is not about one man. Old ways must die – old ways of thinking and being. Not just for survival alone – more than that – for the purging of that unified soul. And I know my heart is not clouded by vows and rules. It beats to its own knowing – that which comes from inside life itself. It is that which tells me now that something is wrong with this land – something hovers, out of sight yet, but it moves closer."

Syrath had closed her eyes again letting his voice soak through her skin but now they opened in alarm and she sat up to face him.

"Do you mean like the Great Battle – another war?"

"No – this is different – I think it is what the old tree man in Maurapin spoke of – the poison that spreads in the earth – I can feel it. But do not dwell on these words for they belong to another time – it is not now."

For a short time they were silent. She took his hand, tracing a lonely finger over its story. She longed sometimes to have his absolute knowing – her heart beat a fragile, human rhythm.

"There is no need for you to stand against Romarrah." He took her hand in both of his. "This you do know, Syrath. Imoshtan lacks joy – it always has – joy has been tucked into little corners – it is not permitted to be vibrant within those walls. The warriors' training brings a reverence and respect, but true joyful being is lost among the forest of teachings. Often have I sat with you into the night and we have laughed and given our spirits freedom. Keep your laughter alive in Imoshtan and perhaps give back to Romarrah the time with his daughter that I have stolen from him."

Still holding her hand, he stood and gently pulled her with him. Then drawing her closer he whispered. "Nothing has changed – we hold each other – I am still your anchor and I will come to you – I have already found a way."

He felt the slight stiffening of her body as she made to speak.

"No," he said laughing, "do not pester me – let it be my surprise."

She let him go then, watching him as he walked away. She loved him in a way that he could never love her. His love spread from his eyes and hands like a blessing to all who stood before him.

As soon as he was out of sight, Teilo again stopped and sat waiting. He needed to be free of what he was leaving behind – to make sure that when he did step forward on his path, he carried nothing but an open heart. He closed his eyes and became still. The sounds from Imoshtan were barely audible. The day was leaning towards its end. Syrath was foremost in his mind and he took time to feel her sadness. It was like a birdsong without an answer. His stillness became disturbed by his own conflicting emotions. He opened his eyes. "Oh Syrath," he groaned to the space around him. "I too am flesh and blood – do not think I am without this passion but it is a thirst I would rather leave unquenched than rewrite our destinies. Give me your blessing that I may go in peace."

He did not have long to wait. She arrived like a hastily painted picture – out of breath – hair streaming and in a flurry of soft tears and tangled feelings. In her flight she strove to give her thoughts to solid words that would bring strength to their farewell, but when she stood before him, they fell away no longer necessary. Instead she handed him a small green pouch and silently he emptied the contents onto the palm of his hand – seven stones – a mystery of colours and patterns – smoothed and oiled – begging inquiry.

"I am told they were my birth mother's," she explained simply. "An ancient art – reading the stones. May they speak only goodness for you, dearest Teilo." She touched his cheek and walked away. He watched her serenity fall back into step by her side then, placing her blessing safely inside his coat, he continued on his way.

10

It is a private thing, pilgrimage; a communion between a soul and a greater story. Each footstep is known. Time and identity are trod surely into dust. The body finds a rhythm that gives no bother to its keeper. Every moment strokes eternity as a wave does the shore, before its flavours slip and spread into the unknown; like scattered letters upon a page; a meaningless scramble until they find a verse.

Thus Teilo walked. Each day was a quiet picture that moved past his eyes without disturbing the steady rhythm of his journey. Each night he sat alone, beside the fire, in contemplation, or writing his thoughts into a memory.

Before my eyes the horizon is a mystery of mountains, as if here the earth ends at its highest point glorifying the sky. This ribbon of earth and stone begins to the north east of Imoshtan and flows its ancient path through the land. It has allowed the rains to carry its life blood into the valleys; to feed the earth its stories of other times. The earth here takes pleasure in its secrets.
Imoshtan has faded; set free. I have no claim upon it. I offer it no disturbance. The earth takes my steps and asks 'what is your purpose?' I make myself small, becoming blind to distraction; waiting; watching.

The answer came in a prayer some kind soul had left beside the road.
I have no purpose
and that is my release
I am no one
and that is my freedom
I neither suffer nor rejoice
and that is my peace.

This fertile land opens before me, step by step. Rain comes and hangs like crystals long after the clouds have passed. Sometimes a face; a recognition; a nod or a smile. Or perhaps a wariness; a suspicion; sometimes a solid greeting. I hold my words still within me; they have no meaning. There are those who understand. They have taken this path before me; a newborn who wails with the weight of its body, not yet familiar; a woman who holds her dignity close, tucked beneath her shawl; a child whose light still glows with the knowing of each secret moment; a man who tends a garden, sifting earth through hands that have memorized a spectrum of flavours and colours in each turned clod. I take the garden with me for it means something that is not yet clear.

The figures which pass have become like ghosts; shadows of life that fade and disappear. The path darkens and becomes a thread between known and unknown and the voice becomes insistent. "Give up your comfort and seek a different path. Be truly blind."

And that is what he did – Teilo left the road that would see him safely to Yeshotruen. He gave up the comfort of the known and placed himself at the mercy of the unknown. A forest closed around him and he, like the ghosts, disappeared.

♋

Chief Warrior Pauroseng roused herself from contemplation. The room had grown cold and dark and she slowly eased her body into movement – lighting candles and drawing the shutters closed. A tall, quietly spoken man entered the room with a tray of food. Together they sat in silence until their simple meal was finished.

"The young warrior we have heard so much about has begun his journey, Osarien," she spoke. The youthfulness and strength of her voice denied her age. "He has come to me in my dreams. I fear it is a troublesome path he walks – he may arrive at Yeshotruen a far different man to the one of which we have heard so much."

Osarien frowned. "Should we not then send a warrior to guide him?"

"He has chosen his way," Pauroseng smiled, "it is his purpose."

She had trained so many warriors. She had been Romarrah's mentor when he too studied the way of a chief warrior. She had fought alongside O'Daewin and her name was known throughout the land. Then she too had done what Teilo now did and come to Yeshotruen – forsaking her comfort.

Pauroseng was the mother of Ortarian. Osarien was his father. They had lived for a time as man and wife but now shared their lives separately with an ease that comes from knowing each other's place in the world.

Pauroseng was Master of Yeshotruen – a world that had challenged her to her very core – at times filling her with despair and at other times, indescribable joy. Its people cursed her and loved her, mistrusted her and gave their lives to her care. This harsh land had buried itself beneath her skin and she could not leave. But now there was a faint sense of anticipation as she awaited the young warrior who was to be the new Master - partly for practical reasons – her body had grown weary and she longed to relinquish her duty to someone with youth and vitality. She knew in her heart that she was destined to know this young man – that their lives were in some way linked by what they held for each other. At the same time, she feared for his safety, as though she had a presentiment of what may befall him. Knowing this was not her concern, she put aside these fears and went about her life although often, during the coming weeks, she would let her gaze rest upon the road to Yeshotruen and wonder what the young warrior was facing on his travels.

♋

Ortarian sat opposite Syrath. "What is it that troubles you?" he asked. He had known her for many years – he could see her story so clearly on her face.

"Do you remember, Ortarian, of the night when you took me to the underground chambers when the compound was under siege?" Her tutor nodded and she continued. "And do you remember, I told you it was bad – very bad?" Again he nodded. "Ortarian I saw it – I saw everything – Tharease's body and the bodies of the other warriors. I saw Teilo and the darkness around him – I knew what was happening. Now, I see nothing. It is part of our study to develop this knowing but it is lost to me. I have no visions – I sense what is around me but I have not the clarity."

Ortarian studied her thoughtfully before replying. "Perhaps it is because you give your power away. You give it to Teilo. No," he shook his head, "do not argue with me – be still for a moment." He smiled at her haste to come, not to her own defence, but to Teilo's. "I did not say Teilo takes your power – I said you give it away. Because his gift of sight is – I suppose a birthright – it comes to him without effort and you have relied on him for your wisdom. You think he is wiser than yourself. Syrath, Teilo knows this – it is one of the reasons for his leaving. Now is your time to find your own power. I watched the same thing with Apheilio."

"Apheilio?" Syrath looked puzzled.

"He was my dear friend," Ortarian explained. "After he lost Shimmera, we became closer for he needed love and comfort. But Apheilio had looked to Shimmera for his wisdom also. When she was no longer with him, he was forced to find his own. He became so powerful Syrath – he was a man unlike others. I wept openly that he should die so young without having fully experienced that which he had found within himself. Teilo has since told me that his father's death was glorious and that it was his time. Be that as it may, I am pleased he lived to touch his power. There is another point here also. What Shimmera gave to Apheilio opened his world for him – it lay the foundations for him. Has Teilo not given you the same?'

Syrath sighed. "I still feel him, Ortarian. I fear for him – I know he is in danger."

Ortarian took her hand. "Teilo has chosen his path – it is not your destiny – it is his. Be very clear on this, Syrath – understand it fully and it will give you peace."

♋

I am not alone; this world speaks in me, swells in me, recedes in me. Should I stay here and adopt madness as my companion; the madness that comes from too many visions, too many voices. It is all too large for this world. I have seen my life come and go. I have lain in the firelight and watched Shimmera's dancing hands through childlike eyes. Her words have fallen all around me like leaves from an autumn sky; a soft blanket only a child understands.

And Apheilio; every day now I see him. There too is a sword; it glistens before me in this wilderness that knows no time. His love holds me close as I die, as I once held him.

Syrath, you have released me from your destiny; every part of me is now returned, except what is yours to hold. You stand so peacefully alone amid the colours we wove for each other.

Orphaele weeps in my dreams. Why is she hidden from me? Why do not the trees hold a memory of her?

I could just lie upon the ground and let these visions take me, piece by piece, until nothing of me remains. And now this mountain before me asks for my prayer, that we might know something of each other. Day and night have passed again and yet again and still I take no step towards its summit. In my mind's eyes I see the sword gleaming against its side; so climb then I must.

He began his ascent – his delusions becoming his reality. This was the Lonely Mountain – thus named because it stood alone – separated – as if at some point the chain of peaks had broken and cast this one aside.

The forest soon thinned and was replaced by rock and boulders. Rambling shrubs tore at clothes and raked the skin beneath. He paid them no heed – his flesh no longer belonged to him. The warrior was sure footed and his mission impelled him upward like a helping hand. Oblivious to the soft rain and gathering mist, his feet searched for safety among the slippery, moving rocks and stones.

It did not take him long – perhaps an hour – to reach the place of the sword. It was nestled among rocks – a quiet burial site above the earth – but when he reached out to grasp it, a coiled serpent, treacherously camouflaged, sprang to attack the intruder. The warrior's reaction was fast – perhaps too fast. The suddenness of his movement loosened the stones beneath his feet and he fell. There was no pain – only an abrupt, sharp moment when movement and light ceased. Then the drumming of the rain upon the earth - then nothing.

♋

There came the sound of sobbing – like a child – far away – coming closer – fading again. He opened his eyes. Light and shadow flickered – as if competing for space. Slowly the shadow receded. High above him, dangling by a thread, was a golden-white flower. Never had he seen a flower so large and he watched, mesmerised by its swaying. Then the pain came – it left him no breath – just fire – burning everything – even his thoughts – except for one. Who was sobbing? The shadow closed over the light.

♋

"Why do you sit here in the dark, Syrath?"

Romarrah had come upon his daughter sitting alone in their private courtyard. Normally she would put aside her feelings and rise to greet her father but, this time, she remained seated looking into the night.

"I have such sadness, Romarrah – as though my heart is being torn apart," she turned her face – turned away from him.

The Great Master felt uncomfortable – he was not one to discuss private feelings. "Would you like to speak with Ortarian?" he asked but she shook her head.

"His life essence is weakening. I can do nothing. This I can accept, but I entreat you to allow me my sadness. Perhaps you could sit with me and let our love speak itself to his spirit for although he vexes you, I know your love for him is strong. At least he may feel our comfort."

He knew she spoke of Teilo and he did not question her knowing. Instead he sat in the dark with his daughter and kept vigil through the night.

♋

The rain had stopped its drumming. The sobbing had ceased. But now a voice – mumbling – stricken.

"I did not desire your death – forgive me – oh forgive me. I should never have been given that choice – you understand – forgive me."

Sobbing again. The sound of rock against rock. More words.

"The warrior has to live – keep him safe – oh what have I done."

Then the rough hand – stroking his face. "You are so beautiful, but oh so pale – heal yourself warrior – you must."

He knew that voice – the touch of that hand – the intensity. He opened his eyes and stared into the wild madness of the tree man. Sparkling eyes crinkled in a smile, then dimmed with tears. "You should not have made me do that, Master Teilo, but not now – I will not reproach you now."

The tree man watched Teilo's eyes roll away from his gaze. "No – heal yourself warrior – I cannot do it – you know I cannot do it - you must not go that way. You bleed inside – like the earth bleeds and no one can tell. No one hears the bleeding. I hear your bleeding – like a weeping, somewhere beneath the cage of your heart."

The voice was fading – he could not hold onto it. There were hands – removing his clothing – fumbling – searching – the voice came back.

"Here it is, warrior – I do not want to touch it – it is not mine – there is no other way - take it – it is yours."

Something small and hard pressed into his hand. The voice was close beside him – whispering in his ear. "Go into the stone warrior – open it – you know how to do it – heal yourself."

There was heat in the palm of his hand. "Go on," urged the tree man, "become the stone – what are you waiting for?"

"What are you waiting for?" Apheilio spoke to the boy as they stood at the crossroad. "Are you coming son? Shimmera is waiting."

He looked at his father – he could feel the warmth of him. "Hold me, Apheilio – I am so cold."

"Take your time." Apheilio gently folded his arms around the boy. "I will take you only if that be your wish. And if you choose to stay, I will let you go. It matters not – it is but a different path."

The boy relaxed. He stayed by the roadside. I can take my time, he thought and drifted into sleep.

Pauroseng awoke suddenly. Where have I been, she wondered, as if surprised to find herself in her own room. "Oh I see," she murmured aloud. "Perhaps I may not meet this young man after all."

Wrapping a cloak around her shoulders she went into her private sanctuary, lit a lamp and settled herself on a small cushion. "There you are, dear boy," she whispered softly. "I will wait with you."

Something was shaking him. He groaned.

"Go away," his voice was but a whisper.

"You are not trying, warrior – try. You are cold – I will warm you – use the wretched thing." Sobbing again. "I have killed for you – to keep you safe."

He could feel himself being buried.

Apheilio released him. He was still at the crossroads but he was no longer shivering. He looked back. In the distance he could see Imoshtan. Syrath and Romarrah were with him in the orchard – watching over him as he lay sleeping in the grass. When he looked to the left, he saw the sword – the black serpent coiled around the blade – its beady eyes watching him, waiting. He felt drawn to that sword – its power. He longed to hold it, but then he heard Apheilio's voice. "I am still here, son." The words were reassuring. His father had moved further away but he was still waiting. There was something else – begging his attention – far away in front of him – an old woman with a light. He frowned – who was she? Then came the song. Someone was singing and they sang as Shimmera had danced. He was crying.

Aphelio knelt beside him. "I can see you have made your choice, Teilo," he soothed, "and you have chosen well. The sword and the serpent are but illusion and they will cross your path again – be prepared for them. Go son – find your song."

No sooner had he spoken than Apheilio was gone. The image of Imoshtan and all that went with it was washed away by a sudden mist of rain. He turned to the sword as it crumbled into the earth and he stared at the serpent until it too melted away. But the old woman stayed, and so did the song. When he looked again, the light became Shimmera. She smiled at him. The song became stronger, purer. It was in him – he saw it in his flesh and his bones – it rippled in his blood. He saw the brokenness of his body – the rupture of its life force. He found the weeping of which the tree man spoke and the lament of broken bones. His spirit soared into the ether.

There was a dance around him – like that of Shimmera's – sunlight sparkling on water except this light stretched into many strands. They pulsed with a deep continuous hum. Again he saw his body. Within it were the same strands – the same sound – but there were threads in him that no longer held certainty. He commanded their restoration. Then he went back to his form. He witnessed the pulse move into bones and flesh.

For a time the warrior watched the painstaking mending – the knitting and weaving of fibres – the colours and shapes decorated with memories, mind impressions – a complete history – a lineage that contained every thought and action of the human form. When he could no longer hold the vision, he let himself drift in the quiet humming that was slowly replacing the body's lament.

"Now you have found it, warrior, "said the fervent voice beside him. "You took your time. I beg forgiveness – I touched it – they told me – it was the only way."

Teilo smiled behind the mask and fell asleep beneath a blanket of leaves and earth, aware of the mutterings of the gentle tree man curled beside him like a faithful forest creature.

Syrath had not left her room. For three days she had stayed alone in silence and prayer. On the fourth day she opened the shutters to a watery sun quietly drying its eyes. The rain had left the earth sodden but on this morning, with the purge complete, there was a lightness to life – as if a window had been opened just long enough to glimpse a new vista. She smiled at the tray of food that had been left for her. She knew it was

Romarrah who had brought it – not Ortarian. Dear Romarrah, she thought, I will give him no more vexation – he only gives of his best, at all times – no one can do more than that.

For three nights she had forgone sleep until, on this past night as she watched the large waning moon rise against a distant sky, she knew he was safe. Only then did she weep her tears and it was Romarrah who came to hold her. Never had she felt the warmth of his love for her although she had sensed it many times. It was always unspoken – never did it reach out and touch her as a physical thing.

"Is it finished?" he asked.

"It is done," she replied. "He is safe."

She knew his question asked more than a concern for Teilo's welfare and she had answered truthfully – it was indeed done. She had felt her dear friend reach out to life and at the same time untie the strings that bound them – they floated gently apart.

And now, she had overslept. Already the warriors were moving about in the courtyard below. Syrath readied herself for the day, humming a song she had never heard before.

♋

"It has been a long wait, Osarien," Pauroseng smiled at her companion. "I could not sense for some time which way our young warrior would choose. How strange that he should come to Yeshotruen so purposefully since we are yet to meet."

Osarien spoke little but he was a thoughtful man. A sadness hesitated around his eyes and Pauroseng saw him fold it carefully out of sight. They both knew why the young warrior came.

♋

There was a weight on his chest – he tried to reach out and push it away only he couldn't move. Matted hair brushed his face as the tree man raised his head. "I am listening to your blood, warrior – it is quiet now and more content."

Still the weight remained.

He knew he had to speak and give himself sight but it seemed too great an effort to move eyes and lips. Instead he watched the images coming back to him – neatly fitting together to tell their story. There were still spaces –

dark and disconnected – as if their colours had drained away.

"I cannot move, tree man," he said at last, his voice foreign and unattached.

"Ha," – a gleeful response – "I have buried you, Master Teilo – but not your beautiful face."

Teilo smiled weakly. "Then unbury me, friend – I am not dead."

"You must lay still – your body mends itself."

Teilo opened his eyes. "I will be still but release me, good man," he was insistent.

His companion was peering at him as if he had something hidden beneath his skin. "You will bleed again, warrior – I cannot release you. Become a tree – let the earth hold you – you will be safe. Patience comes when you are a tree – can you not feel that? It does not imprison you, the earth – it only holds your body until your roots find their home."

"Enough, tree man – let me out of this tomb."

Suddenly the tree man's voice took a different tone – no longer rambling but fluent and strong. "Master, you have let yourself believe you are something other than this. You have listened to what others have said of you. Most of your kind fear death because they do not know who they are. You know who you are, warrior, but you fail to see how truly human you are. Let me tell you – you are human. Have you not suffered delusion like any other mortal – did you not scale a mountain to hold some form – some symbol that has no truth of its own? I have killed for your folly – one of my own. When I found you bleeding and broken, a she-dog had come to you first. You were her food and she forced me to fight for that claim. What did your illusion cost me? Bear no mistake here, warrior – had she been with young, I may have let her have you."

This was no longer the rantings of a wild man. The truth of his words was savage. The pain they gave rise to worse than the pain of a broken body.

"Ah, warrior – your tears tell me you have heard my words. It is sad, is it not, when we find our true wretchedness?" The rough hands stroked his face. "Be still and humble, my friend – you are nearly there."

When at last Teilo left the earth womb, his body felt weak and wasted. He saw the rock piled on the grave of the beast. He saw his clothes, washed clean and dried over branches. He saw his few possessions neatly placed in the hollow of a tree. The old man tended to him as if nursing a child and the warrior submitted to his ministerings without objection. Through most of this strange time of convalescence he said little and nor did his companion.

They watched each other and spoke a wordless conversation. The tree man brewed strange decoctions of leaves, bark and roots. Some tasted exceedingly vile while others were warming and soothing. He pounded leaves to a pulp and mixed them with water and earth then rubbed the warrior's body with the sticky paste. He told Teilo to stay without clothes, for only a naked body truly feels its healing.

Of an evening he made a fire and often placed leaves on the flames to fill the air with fragrance, insisting the warrior breathe the smoke until his eyes watered and he could not help coughing.

"I will leave you soon," he spoke one night as they sat, each within their own peace, watching the flames. "It is time you were alone – to be with yourself. You will go back to your new world and I will stay in mine."

He sat beside Teilo and stroked his arm. He did not like to leave this child he had nurtured. The child he had seen born in the forest. He had watched as the mother gave her infant first to the earth, then to the water, then to the heavens. She knew he was there and she called him to her. Handing him the child, she said, "Watch over him, kind soul – he is yours when he is alone in the forest – keep him safe."

And he had. He watched him as a boy give his memories to the trees. He watched him as a man do the same.

It was so long ago that the tree man had forsaken his birth kind. People were not part of his life – he mistrusted them, for they did not know their place on the earth. They sought dominance and not inclusion. But this one – this one was different. This one he loved. This one he had studied – every part of his body – the way he moved – the song in him. He knew his secrets. This one he had lashed out at as a mother reprimands her young, then held him close and breathed his love into him.

Teilo too did not look forward to their parting. This ancient, gentle soul had returned him to life. What had he cost this sweet creature who loved so purely? It was his turn to lie beside the little man and stroke him as he slept.

The tree man left but he bequeathed a legacy of instructions and four baskets made of twigs and vine – filled with herbs, fruits, seeds and roots. He had lectured the warrior in their preparation and application.

"You are safe here," he said as he took his leave. "I have protected the earth. Stay until your body tells you it is time to clothe yourself again, but before you do that, warrior," intense madness again, "you must stand up to your mouth in the stream. The water must cover all your spine – every pathway is to be cleansed. You will feel that – I need not tell you of that feeling. Then immerse yourself completely – offer yourself to the water – complete your birth."

He farewelled his patient with the same intensity - if he kissed him once, he kissed him at least a dozen times and Teilo watched him slowly becoming more creature like and less man like. The tree man's words again became erratic and, finally, he slipped out of sight among the trees.

At last the warrior was alone. How long had he been here – an invalid – lost in the gap between the reality he had known, the world of the tree man and the maze of his own dreaming. For a long time, his protector would permit him no activity. "Do not undo the healing with your impatience," he would growl if Teilo so much as thought of physical activity. Now the young warrior's body was in need of movement. He gave his time to dancing and training but it was a different man who moved in the forest to the warrior from Imoshtan. It was as if each movement had a carefully considered origin outside of himself. No more a deep sensual pleasure, it was an emptiness that was at once more peaceful and more holy and within it, he knew the abundance of nothingness.

When it was time, he went to the stream and walked into its depths until he stood as the tree man had directed – in water up to his mouth. He looked across the surface and into the forest at the trees that had been his companions for all this time. He had become like them – without need or expectation – without desire or avoidance. The cold of the water reached through his skin. I cannot stay much longer, tree man, he thought but within him he heard his friend's answer, *'be still and humble warrior – you are nearly there"*.

He gave his body to the water. It became the blood in his veins – it replaced the nerves – it spread swiftly – a liquid fire – until it possessed all of him. He became the water – no longer separate – he let himself sink into its depths.

That night, for the last time, he slept in his forest home. At daybreak he would continue his journey.

Sometime towards morning, he was awakened by drops of moisture falling on his face and when he opened his eyes he again saw, dangling in space, the golden-white flower. A giant vine hung from the tree above him – its flower opening in the light of the full moon – dripping its nectar onto his face. It was the purest white – tipped with gold. He stared into its splendour for a long time. He knew then that he had lain in this forest from one full moon to the next. The flower had been there to welcome him and also to bid him farewell. It is birth and death, he thought, beginnings and endings – all are one and the same.

Gathering his few possessions and leaving his love and gratitude in the earth, he walked quietly through the night towards Yeshotruen.

PART TWO

YESHOTRUEN

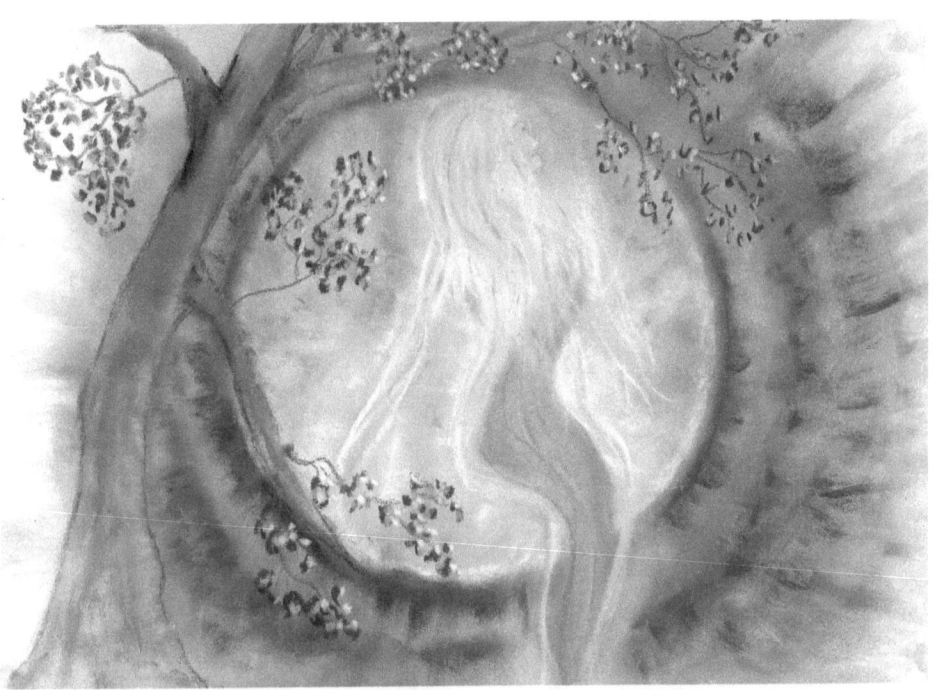

1

Broken lives – that is all that met his gaze as he approached the city. That and dry earth – barren poverty – the strangled sob of resignation.

The woman was the first to stop him. There were sores on her skin – a blindness in her eyes. Clutching him with a bony hand, she did not have to speak her need. He touched her face. "I have nothing to give you, good woman."

Next he came upon some youths throwing stones at a young, limping dog. He did not acknowledge them but simply walked to the animal and scooped it up with one hand. A stone hit him on the shoulder and he turned to face his assailant.

"Why did you do that?" he asked quietly.

"I didn't," was the insolent reply.

The warrior smiled. "Your face tells me you did although your friends share equally in your action."

By the way he spoke and the sword he wore, the group were in no doubt they had made a mistake but, as there were eight of them and only one man, their defiance remained unchecked. Teilo chose not to continue the exchange – their aggression begged to be provoked. Still holding the dog, he walked away. They would meet again – of that he was sure.

He made his way through the pathways of this disorganized city until he found the entrance to the compound. Lounging beside the front gates were two men, presumably warriors, although their demeanour cast doubt upon that assumption. In Imoshtan, these warriors would greet all who passed, escort any traveller who desired entry or deliver messages. Yet these two men did not greet him nor did they offer assistance. One spoke in a surly voice. "You can't take the dog in there."

"It is in need of care," Teilo replied.

The man smirked. "It is an animal."

"Of that I am aware. Perhaps, good man, you could take me to Master Pauroseng."

The second man looked at the newcomer warily. "What do you want with her?" he asked.

"It is she who summons me," the warrior replied.

Pointing to the first building inside the gate and across the courtyard, the man dismissed Teilo with a wave of his hand.

The compound, though smaller, was an exact replica of the one at Imoshtan but that was where the similarities ceased. In some ways it appeared like a tired, crooked painting that no one had taken the time to straighten.

Teilo had no trouble finding the chambers of Pauroseng as they were exactly where Romarrah's would have been. When he knocked on the door it was opened by an older man – grey and gnarled like an aged forest giant – clothed, not as a warrior, but in simple attire. He looked at the young warrior and smiled. Immediately his face softened like a new beginning.

"Welcome, Master Teilo," he said. "We have been expecting you. I am Osarien." He glanced quizzically at the dog which all this time had nestled happily in Teilo's arms aware of its reprieve.

"I will tell Master Pauroseng of your arrival," Osarien bowed. "Be at ease here." Indicating to Teilo to wait within the chambers, he left to summon the Master. It was clear Pauroseng did not inhabit these rooms – they were all but empty. Her presence here is strong, Teilo mused as he walked onto the balcony. He looked down at the courtyard. It too was almost empty except for a few children playing in the dirt – building miniature walls of sticks and stones. He watched them, fascinated by their play. He had little knowledge of children.

"I must confess," he said to the dog, ruffling its ears, "I am curious. What is this place?"

He turned when he sensed Pauroseng's presence and greeted her, bowing respectfully, as she came into the room. She was a small framed woman yet her bearing was one of strength and determination. Instead of warrior's clothes, she too wore the cloth of the village women – wrapped around her body and partially covering her head. Her eyes were exceedingly youthful and bright but her face was soft and wrinkled, holding many years of stories. She too glanced at the dog but, like Osarien, said nothing and Teilo offered no explanation.

"I believe your journey has been long, Master Teilo – you must be in need of food and rest." She noted the leanness of his body. His face held the shadows of what he had suffered. "Osarien will see that food is delivered to you here in your chambers."

"But surely these are your chambers, Master," the young warrior interjected.

"You are now the Master of Yeshotruen, Teilo," her voice was firm.

"That may be so, but I have no need of these rooms."

"And I assure you, I am content where I am – in fact, I prefer it. Now come – let us sit – there are things we both need to know."

As she spoke Teilo studied her eyes. What life played in their colours. He was immediately drawn to this woman – he knew something of her – something old and unknown – something perhaps she would in time reveal to him.

"I am sure Yeshotruen is not what you were expecting," she spoke, watching him as he settled himself on a cushion, laying the dog across his lap.

"I came without expectation, Master," he replied turning his attention to the dog – running his hands over the creature's body – exploring its bones – probing its flesh.

"We do not have animals in the compound," Pauroseng stated. Again he heard the firmness in her voice. "This is a harsh place and there are sicknesses that spread from animal to people."

Teilo raised his eyes to look at her. "It carries no sickness, Master – only injury and hunger. It would appear it is the victim of a human sickness."

"And," Pauroseng continued unperturbed, "we have barely enough food for those who live here without feeding the animals as well."

"Pauroseng – do not concern yourself with the dog – it is in need of healing and I will see to it. I have accepted the responsibility for its care – it will carry no imposition."

Osarien entered and placed a tray before them. He looked from one to the other then seated himself off to one side as if to witness their conversation but offer no contribution himself. Teilo felt the solidness of this man who carried no agitation only a sense patient service.

"There are no warriors in training?" Teilo's question to Pauroseng was more of a statement.

"Is that not why Romarrah has sent you?" she countered.

"There were many reasons why Romarrah sent me to Yeshotruen," Teilo smiled at the chief warrior.

"But it was what you wanted?"

"It was."

Pauroseng smiled too. "I think you are accustomed to people doing what you want, Master Teilo."

An image of the tree man came into his thoughts. "Not all," he replied softly.

They were silent.

"It is not easy here," the old Master began again, pouring their tea as she spoke. "Perhaps it would be best if you became familiar with the people and the ways of Yeshotruen. Take your time Teilo – there is no urgency. I know Romarrah wishes you to bring this compound to a standard closer to that of Imoshtan. That will pose many difficulties for you as this is a far different place – something you will already have noted."

Teilo reached out and placed his hand on hers. Something in that touch made him frown but for the moment he dismissed it. "What do you want for Yeshotruen, Master?" he asked, his eyes not leaving her face.

"Let us have that discussion after you have seen for yourself."

Withdrawing her hand, Pauroseng quietly closed the door on his question.

♋

During the days that followed Teilo spent his time learning about his new home.

"Are you sure this warrior is the right one?" Osarien asked Pauroseng. "He has spent his first weeks sitting in the dirt, playing with the children."

"He knows precisely what he is doing, Osarien," she murmured, "have no doubt of that. We will be informed soon enough of his intent."

♋

"What are you doing?" the child asked, looking at him as only a child could – bare, open inquiry – the purist expression.

"I'm making water channels," he replied. "Look."

Taking a small earthenware pot, he slowly poured water into a miniature stone and mud canal and then observed it flow into a network of others he had been building.

The child laughed. "Do it again," she squealed when all the water had disappeared into the earth. Obligingly the warrior released more water. The children watched its progress delightedly while he watched their faces – fascinated by what he saw. They know how to look, he thought – their vision is not yet impaired by desire – they are so very open to what is before them and their knowing of it is immediate – they see endless possibility and all is of equal value. Sadly he also noted that they were undernourished, in their bodies and in spirit. He knew these children fared better than those outside the compound.

Teilo had quickly discovered that what would have been the warrior's quarters housed mainly women and children, the elderly and the sick. The women spent much of their time making cloth to be traded for food and working in the meagre gardens which surrounded the kitchen. He watched them labouring to carry buckets of water from the well to the gardens.

The history of what had happened in Yeshotruen was evident in the buildings – the faces – the behaviour of the people. He could imagine the excitement when the compound had first been erected – a sudden possibility like an oasis rising out of the barren ground – new industry – new dreams. Anticipation would have lightened steps and voices – even the dullness of the earth.

He imagined that, for a short time, life in Yeshotruen may have seemed blessed. Young people no doubt commenced training and in time became warriors. Where were they now?

He sat with the children picking up handfuls of dirt – feeling the desolation slip through his fingers. Of course the warriors had left. Imoshtan would have hovered in their dreams - a golden city. We elevated their minds, he thought, and with that, this dry wasteland no longer resonated in their hearts.

Pauroseng surely would have seen the mistake – especially as it was not the women who had become warriors – it was the men. This land would not allow women to stand in their own right. The men had left and never returned – they had missed the essence of what they were being taught.

That was another difference, he pondered – the behaviour of men and women. They were separate here – as they had been in Athanan but much more so. He had noticed it the first time he stepped into the market place. Never before had he felt himself looked at as if he were an object – something that could be claimed. Yet this was how men and women in Yeshotruen beheld each other. In Imoshtan, male and female warriors shared quarters – shared communal baths – they were accustomed to being together. They saw each others naked bodies but never did they experience the covetous attitude he saw here. Relationships between the warriors were mutual, private and respectful. Respect in Yeshotruen was as withered as the stale breath of the earth.

♋

Wherever Teilo went the dog, bearing a splinted, bandaged leg, was never far from his side. It had found refuge and it would not be parted from it.

Of an evening the warrior would close the door on the world and sit in his chambers contemplating his day and planning for the next. He would write in his journal and draw pictures of the city, his plans and what he felt. Osarien would always bring food, bowing to the young Master but offering little conversation for which Teilo was grateful. He had instructed Pauroseng not to announce his arrival as the new Master - he was not yet ready to assume that title – not until he had found clarity and a definitive course of action.

The old Master and Osarien intrigued him. He knew they were the parents of Ortarian, that they lived together but apart, and that Osarien honoured Pauroseng with a quiet reverence – content to follow her footsteps. They live a life of devotion, he thought – she to her knowing of something greater and he to her. We are yet to meet – the Master and I, he mused.

For the first time, he was given the flesh of animals to eat. He was puzzled at first to think that Pauroseng and Osarien ate this flesh. At the compound in Imoshtan animals were not kept for food, pleasure or work. There were those of the city who ate the flesh of animals or kept beasts of burden, but at the compound the meat of animals was never part of the warrior's diet.

He understood the unity of all – that the flesh of animals would be absorbed like everything else and he did not take offence, but nor did he eat of it. Instead he gave it to the dog, consuming only the grain and dried food which he knew came from Imoshtan – though not often enough, he thought wryly.

"I will surely starve, my friend," he stroked the dog's coat, "if I do not remedy this situation."

Looking back over the day, he would make mental notes of all he had learned including the names of people, stories, legends, hopes and dreams. He knew from his own research that those who had first settled in Yeshotruen had been a nomadic tribe driven out of their own lands until finally they claimed this place of hardship and bitterness. Legend revealed it had not always been such a desolate land. The earth had withheld its waters – a punishment visited upon the tribal elders by the earth spirits whom they had offended. Teilo understood legend enough to see the truth of it. "We must find the place of injury," he muttered as he lay wearily on his bed. The dog licked his face then curled up on the floor not far from his side.

Each night the young warrior dreamed of the forest. The tree man would speak to him in these dreams but Teilo could no longer understand his words. So often he would awaken to a lonely ache – like a dry taste somewhere inside him. In the dim light of morning he would seek the quiet of the courtyard where he could train, as the buildings slowly stepped forward from the shadows.

Sometimes, as he walked through the city, he would recognize the youths he had encountered on his first day – he had memorized their faces. They knew he was watching them and it made them uncomfortable. "Discomfort will not harm them," he said to the dog, "but we must reach them before they are lost to us."

That chance came as most do – unexpectedly.

Standing in the market place as he was now accustomed to doing – watching people go about their day – observing customs and rituals, he witnessed two of the youths being accosted by an older man – perhaps their father, he thought.

"Animal filth!" the man shouted as he hit one of the boys with a solid tree branch. The boy cried out in pain. Another man appeared, drawing his sword and both youths cringed in fear. This man raised his sword as though he intended to inflict injury.

"Leave them," Teilo commanded quietly. Moving a little closer he asked, "What has this boy done?"

"You would do well to keep to yourself here, stranger." The man holding the sword looked behind him for the support of others in the crowd. Several moved forward through the gathering crowd.

"I will gladly keep to myself good man, but these boys are unarmed – what have they done to cause you harm?"

"They are thieves," replied the man with the branch. Again he savagely hit the boy. Blood spurted from a gash above the victim's eye.

"Enough!" Teilo drew his sword and sliced the branch in two. The speed of his attack left the man speechless, but it was all the provocation the small band of onlookers needed. Swords were drawn and held at the ready.

"I have no wish to cause harm," again the warrior spoke quietly, in vain hoping to diffuse the situation. Four men came towards him like a pack, about to feast on fallen prey. Try as he would, he could not avoid wounding two of them although he intended only to disarm and deter further conflict.

The affray ended swiftly and Teilo immediately offered to assist the wounded. They spat their disgust and walked away. Their injuries were not serious – they would heal but perhaps not their pride. He had no doubt they would desire retribution.

The boy, whose companion had fled during the conflict, was still standing to one side, his wound bleeding profusely. He flinched when the warrior touched his head and moved away.

"Now you know how the dog felt," Teilo said softly. "If you are in need of refuge son – come to the compound. My name is Teilo – ask for me – I promise I will see you safe."

Ignoring him, the boy disappeared into a nearby alley.

♋

Pauroseng was not pleased. She came to his chambers to confront him. "We cannot interfere with the lives of these people – beatings are common – you cannot prevent them, Teilo, but interfering will itself prevent us from doing what we do here."

"And what is it that you do here, Pauroseng?" Teilo asked. The steel in her eyes glinted at him.

"We endeavour, as you would have observed, to give these people a way to stand alone. They have not the skills – the continuity of their people is a broken line. They no longer possess the strength of their ancestry. You must see how flawed was this concept of building a compound in Yeshotruen."

"To the contrary, Pauroseng – I think it is a very sound one."

She was rankled by his answer. She had thought that this one, who had come to her in her dreams and her times of stillness, would be the one to take this burden from her.

"You have already been here some time, Master Teilo, yet you have not assumed the duties of Master – may I ask what it is that you are doing here?"

"I am gathering people and knowledge. Forgive me that I have not yet spoken with you." He took both her hands in his. "You have a sickness in you, Pauroseng – I can feel it – your body cries to be released from this place. You want me to take your burden but you do not want to give it to me. Your hands tell me of the work you do. I watch you each day – tending the sick – working in gardens that produce so little – counselling women – helping them with their work. And all the while, your heart longs for nothing but to sit in prayer – your heart weeps for the peace of Imoshtan. Why have you not yet left this place to appease your weary body?"

"You may be gifted by your birth with wisdom, Teilo, but you do not understand quiet sacrifice – men so often do not. Has not your own suffering been a selfish act?" She observed him blink for just a second too long. "Forgive me, I have spoken hastily without awareness."

"There is truth in your words," he looked away. "I have cost others dearly but," here he faced her again, "I cannot, nor will I, walk away and let children be beaten regardless of their misdemeanour."

"Nor would I once but you cannot be there to save everyone. The boy may have taken that man's food – this is how these people deal with such transgressions. Who are you to interfere with their law?" Seeing he was unmoved by her words, she guided the conversation down a different path. "So, Master Teilo, what do you intend to do here?"

"I will do as Romarrah wishes, I will train warriors."

Pauroseng did not show her disappointment at his words, but she felt an instant, almost overwhelming weariness. She imagined the women and children, the aged and the ailing, being turned out of the compound and sent back to lifeless homes to fend for themselves – beggars outside the gates.

Teilo was watching her. He shook his head. "You have little trust in me, Pauroseng and it puzzles me greatly for I know it was you who called me here. Do you think I would betray you? It appears Romarrah has little idea of what you do in Yeshotruen. I will train warriors as he wishes and I will find a way to nourish these people. They cannot embrace their wisdom when their bodies are so depleted. This land must support them."

The old warrior's eyes filled with tears. She knew then that he had recognised the plight of these forgotten people and wished to give them hope, but more than that, he had acknowledged their wisdom. He did not come to bestow upon them the Great Wisdom – he already saw them as having their own and therefore as equal to himself.

"You and I have a journey ahead of us," he continued. "Let there be trust between us, Pauroseng. I would not alter even the least significant part of your service here without first seeking your blessing. In all things I will be guided by my own knowing, yet, even then, I will place it before you first. But be assured – I will never stand back in the face of cruelty. There must be a point where actions are challenged."

As he spoke, Teilo had been slowly unbinding the dog's leg. "There," he said when it was done, "you see – it is healed."

"For how long, Master Teilo, do you intend to keep feeding this animal your own food? See how big it grows? If you do not wish to eat what is given to you, there are many people here who would gladly have your share."

"Fear not, Pauroseng – the dog has a purpose – all will be well. It is a beautiful creature is it not?"

She sighed and turned to leave then, changing her mind, posed one last question. "Teilo – how do you know you have not made matters worse for that young man by coming to his assistance? Those men you injured will vent their loss upon someone."

"Most likely I have created more strife for him, although I pray I have not. He is not a child and he has intelligence and now, he has a choice he did not have before."

"And what is that?"

"I told him to come here."

Pauroseng rolled her eyes. Teilo laughed. "You see," he said smiling at her, "I am gathering people."

"And who else have you gathered, Master Teilo?" She could not help but return his smile.

"You," he replied seriously.

In the quiet of early morning, Teilo commenced his training. The dog lay in the dirt, head resting on its paws, its eyes following every move the Master made. Teilo was aware of the sleeping form huddled in a recess in the earthen wall but he gave himself completely to his dance. When he finished, the boy was awake. "Come," the warrior said as he walked into the building. The boy hesitated for a moment then shuffled after him.

Once in the Master's chambers, he stood awkwardly as Teilo removed his sword, placing it on a stone bench. The boy watched him take an earthenware pot, fill it with water, and place it over a small flame. Into the pot Teilo placed leaves and seeds which he first crushed with a stone. Only then did he turn to face the boy. "What is your name son?" he asked.

"I am Deshan." It was a sullen reply.

"Then Deshan – tell me your part in the scene yesterday. What had you done to warrant such aggression?"

Deshan's story unfolded disjointedly with much prompting from Teilo. He had stolen precious oils from the man with the sword – Mercenta was his name – a trader who travelled far from Yeshotruen and one of the few people in the city with any wealth.

The man with the stick was Deshan's own father, furious his son had been caught and intent on being seen to punish the boy, even though it was he who had encouraged him to steal from the trader. Deshan's friend had helped him by keeping watch – obviously not very well. Beatings it seemed were a part of the boy's life.

When he had heard the story, Teilo said nothing but went back to the food he was preparing. From another pot, Deshan saw him take finely ground grain and mix it into the water, stirring the brew slowly and letting it thicken. The boy did not know from where the feeling in him arose, but he wanted so much to be close to this man.

Pouring the gruel into three bowls, Teilo put them aside to cool. "Well Deshan," he spoke, "what is to become of you?"

No answer was forthcoming.

"How do you feel about leaving your family?" the warrior persisted. This is going to be harder than I imagined, he thought.

He tried again. "What do you think would happen in your family if you were not there?"

"I don't know."

"Deshan – do you want to live at the compound with me, or do you want to go back to your family?"

"I want to stay with you," the boy mumbled. Teilo could see he was compromised. He has obligations elsewhere, he thought – not to his father but perhaps to his sister and mother.

"Then eat, son – we have a lot to do today." He handed the boy a bowl of gruel and placed another before the dog. By the time he sat down to eat his own, Deshan's bowl was nearly empty.

"Are you a warrior?" the boy asked.

"I am," Teilo smiled at him.

"Are you the new Master?"

Teilo nodded.

"Are you going to train me to be a warrior?"

"So it is food that loosens your tongue is it? I make no promises, Deshan – first we must seek your family's blessing."

The boy looked stunned. "My father will not give it – he is angry with me but more so with you. He said he would rejoice to see you dead."

"Do not be concerned for me, son – there will be no more fighting. This morning we will speak with your family – then we must find a way to appease this trader so that when you come here, you bring no debt. You must promise me, Deshan that you will not steal again."

The boy nodded. Teilo laughed. "That was the least sincere promise I have ever seen. There is a long way to go to earn your trust I see. So come," he took up his sword and placed it in its sheath, "take me to your home that this matter may be resolved."

"When do I get my sword?" the boy asked with a touch of boldness.

"Do not be eager for the sword, Deshan – it carries with it no glory."

Pauroseng watched them leave the compound – the man, the boy and the dog.

"Magnificence can come from the most humble beginnings," she murmured.

2

Romarrah looked at the letter before him. The demands contained therein were long and detailed.

"I cannot supply all these needs," he said to Syrath, "nor do I understand why he wants many of these materials."

"You set Teilo a seemingly impossible challenge, Romarrah – for what reason?" Syrath sighed. "Did you wish for him to fail? Did you not think he would need our assistance? The compound at Yeshotruen has not borne fruit – it has failed to become what it was intended to become and you send one man to cure its ailing."

Since Teilo's departure Syrath had spent more time with her father – taking the role that was once filled by Tharease – easing the burden of loneliness from his duties.

"Syrath, I sent only one man because Pauroseng would have it no other way. I should have relieved her of her office long ago – this has been my compromise, but I cannot send all that he demands. It would deplete our own stocks."

"We are always in surplus," she argued. "Our land is abundant – of that there can be no dispute. Perhaps Yeshotruen is worse than you have been led to believe. Teilo does not ask that these requests become commonplace. I urge you to honour his demands. If you do not, I must question your motive for sending him. Would it be harmful to the warriors of Romarrah to practice prudence? They have never wanted for anything – theirs is a privileged life."

"Do not forget, Syrath, we also deliver grains to Manon. Prudence is one thing but we also have responsibilities to others."

"And they need not suffer, Romarrah – we have the ability to do as Teilo asks. It may place us at a disadvantage if the following seasons are not as plentiful as is usual, but I fear to not comply with his wishes would be to ignore the plight of these people."

"They have their own governance with which we do not interfere.

Teilo's duty was to the compound at Yeshotruen – not to the entire city. I instructed him to begin by training a small group of warriors – to develop change from within the compound itself and let it spread as waves into the homes of the people. Pauroseng and Osarien achieved this in the beginning and they produced some fine warriors. I do believe it became too much for them – they failed to keep those warriors close. That they have had many seasons of hardship is unfortunate but.."

"Then let us extend a gesture of goodwill to these people and honour Teilo's requests," Syrath interrupted. "If it all be in vain, we lose little and yet, if it proves a success, we gain one hundred fold."

"You have a will cast in iron, Syrath," her father smiled. "Did Teilo also write to you and request you intercede on his behalf?"

"He made no such a request," she replied. But he had written. The letter was delivered in the same manner as Romarrah's. Slatoro, who carted the grain from Imoshtan to Yeshotruen and also to Manon, had as well become Teilo's trusted courier. It was Jemai who knocked on the door of her chambers to deliver a small parcel. He too had received a letter from the Master.

When Syrath opened the package, it contained a drawing of the most exquisite flower. Underneath he had written; *This in part belongs to you – my gratitude to you for holding me.*

There was also a smaller object, wrapped in a mat of sweet smelling leaves and bound with delicate vine. It was one of her reading stones and a page of verse.

> *How long can I sit in this place*
> *of forgiveness and calm;*
> *all else has expired,*
> *a quivering forgotten sigh.*
> *I have seen this vast world within me*
> *enveloped by fear*
> *and the torment of being unloved*
> *My hands, by the very nature*
> *of their belonging,*
> *have added to the sorrow*
> *of anguish inflicted.*
> *I too have given pain,*
> *wrapped within my words and deeds,*
> *disguised by the illusion*

of wisdom.
So falsely noble
to lay myself down
surrender this life
and ask forgiveness;
far far more
to know the origin
of this unlove
and there at its source
prise out the roots
of its clinging.
If I seek forgiveness
but not understanding
again and again
will I add to this misery;
a world of ungentle thought
and discontented action.

Underneath were the words;

This is the stone of origin, intent and purpose. It asks us to reflect on these; to gain an understanding of what it is that we do. It signifies the beginnings of journeys both internal and external. It offers a promise of renewal or warns of difficulties ahead due to mistaken views, depending on the stones which fall around it. Your mother's touch upon these stones was gentle, seeking without wanting. She gave them to you that you might know her in your own searching. This is your mystery, Syrath; trust yourself to read these stones; become acquainted with the feel of each one for they have secrets for you alone.

She held the stone, feeling the warmth beneath its surface.

"Is that not bribery or even worse?" Pauroseng asked. She sat with Teilo in his chambers as he told her of his plans. "You are now paying parents for their children."

"It is only fair that I offer them recompense," he frowned slightly at her objection. "Their children are after all needed to help fend for the family."

"You mean steal," the chief warrior corrected. "And how many children have you purchased now?"

Teilo laughed. "Is this how you were with Romarrah? His journey to chief warrior must have been long and arduous. Did you also try to rattle him thus? I do not purchase people, Pauroseng. I am simply making it possible for them to come to the compound. And they are not children – some are young men with wives and children of their own. Deshan, and his sister Edora, are the youngest but they are still of an age to be trained as warriors. I was nigh on my fifteenth year when I commenced training. Syrath was but thirteen years of age."

"And if Romarrah does not agree with your requests?"

"He will – of that I am confident."

But Pauroseng was still not satisfied. "Where will these warriors stay? What is their number?"

"For the moment they will remain in their homes and come here each day for training. This arrangement will only be temporary until I know how we will proceed. They will number only twenty." The young Master paused then added, "Pauroseng, with your blessing I must go away for a short time. I will take Deshan with me – there is something I must know. All being well, I will meet the supplies from Imoshtan along the way and return with them."

"Are you always such a mystery, Master Teilo?"

"I do not think for one moment that anything is hidden from you."

She smiled. "You do not need my blessing, Teilo – you are Master here remember."

♋

Teilo awakened early to prepare for his journey. Normally he would make his way to the courtyard and his morning ritual of training but instead he lay quietly absorbing the peace. His hand reached out and touched the dog's head. It reciprocated with a gentle thump of its tail.

Outside it was still dark and he let himself drift – perhaps he even fell into sleep again because suddenly he was back at the crossroads. It was dark and still – nothing moved. Then the old woman appeared with her lamp – it cast a strong light – probing the darkness which quivered in surrender and receded in a rush.

At first the song was barely audible, as if it was hiding among the shadows, but gradually it came closer. He watched it move into his body like a liquid prayer. Then as quickly as it had appeared, the vision dropped out of sight.

He was awake. The first light of day reached through his windows but he could still hear the song.

Arising from his bed and motioning for the dog to stay, he quietly left his chambers. A soft light from Pauroseng's room illuminated the hall.

The song wove its way towards him. Through the open door he saw her sitting as if in a trance, softly singing. Her voice must have been little more than a whisper and yet it penetrated and hovered and bled itself into the surroundings. The expression on her face was one of perfect, joyful devotion.

Noiselessly the warrior sat in the passageway, closed his eyes and let that voice wrap itself around him. He breathed it deeply into his lungs and watched it travel with his breath.

He did not notice when it was finished – he did not move. Images fell around him like scattered pages. Her hand rested upon his shoulder.

"Come, Master Teilo," she said. "It is late – your young friend will be waiting."

He rose slowly but effortlessly. Pauroseng smiled at his youth – his grace and agility. There was no steel in her eyes now. "What is it?" she asked seeing the way he looked at her.

"Teach me." It was not a command but a humble request.

"I do not know that I have anything left in me to teach, Teilo," the old warrior sighed but he shook his head. "You could have healed the whole of Yeshotruen with your song."

"Ah but it has taken me a lifetime to find it, my son. I am too old in this world, and you are young enough, to use it well. When you return, we shall sing together."

He took both her hands in his. At once he knew something of himself that he had not truly believed before. "Let me heal you, Pauroseng," he said softly.

Again she smiled at him – an old woman with her whole life gathered behind her. "Dear Teilo – it is not my time of healing, but when death comes, you may use your hands to calm my restless spirit. Then I may leave in peace."

There was no more to be said. He bowed to his Master and walked away.

♋

Deshan was waiting outside the compound, despondently throwing stones at his own impatience. He brightened when he saw Teilo and the dog. "I thought you were not coming." His relief was obvious as he leapt to his feet. "Where are we going?"

"For a very long walk, my young friend," Teilo replied, hoisting his sack over his shoulder and handing Deshan a smaller one to carry.

"Will we get there before nightfall?" the boy persisted.

"Deshan, it will take us days to get there – you would do well to conserve your energy. Your first lesson as a warrior is to watch – as you walk see what is around you – take in everything, without placing your thoughts upon it – let it be as it is. At the end of the day, recall all you have seen in as much detail as you can. Train your mind to truly see." And leave me in peace, the warrior thought.

Their journey was slow. Deshan was not used to such exertion and he tired quickly. Teilo adjusted his own pace to be more compatible with his young companion. The dog ran happily ahead of them, returning promptly if Teilo clicked his fingers.

Deshan thought there was little to see – just hour after hour of dust and rock. An occasional lone tree, bramble, or tuft of coarse grass struggled to break the monotony.

That evening he took great delight in sitting at their fire, questioning his mentor almost incessantly. Teilo gently corrected the boy's unintentional rudeness.

"Have you ever killed someone?" Deshan asked abruptly.

His feet were sore and blistered. Never had he walked so far in one day. Teilo was rubbing them with pungent oil. The boy was fascinated and embarrassed. He was not used to such intimacy and, although Teilo's hands were so soothing, he suddenly realized they were the hands of a warrior – in essence they had been trained to kill.

Teilo paused and looked at him. "Deshan, it is courteous to acknowledge someone by using their name on occasion when you speak to them – it implies that you have seen them – they have your honour. And I beg you to think carefully about what it is you intend to ask of them and why."

There was silence for only a short time before the boy spoke again.

"Should I call you Master, or Teilo?"

"It does not matter – at Imoshtan you would call me Master or Master Teilo. If we were better acquainted you would call me Teilo. I have no preference."

Silence reigned again but only briefly.

"Master Teilo, have you ever killed someone?"

Placing the wooden stopper into the neck of the oil pot, Teilo took a candle from his sack, held it above the flames of the fire until it danced into life, then dripped the wax around the wooden stopper. When he was satisfied the pot was sealed, he once more gave his attention to the boy.

Sometimes when their eyes met Deshan recoiled. There was never a hint of anger or irritation in the warrior's gaze, but it was as if he looked at a part of him that the boy himself did not know – it almost hurt.

"What is your purpose in asking that question, Deshan? What do you really want to know?"

Deshan was not good at having to account for himself – he did not have the language or insight to be clear about his purpose.

"You are very good," he attempted at last, stumbling over his words. "You touch my feet as if you really care and – I just thought – how do you feel when you kill someone?"

Teilo kept looking at him. Deshan worried his words may have caused offence.

"A warrior is not trained to kill," his mentor spoke at last. "That is a misconception. A true warrior is trained to avoid killing – that requires the greater skill. To kill at all does not rest lightly on any heart. The warriors of Romarrah are trained to never be the aggressor – only the protector and if, inevitably, they do take a life then they must do so with compassion rather than disdain or hatred. Your sight is astute, Deshan. I have taken a life – no matter how much we justify killing, it still leaves its mark. I would much rather give my hands to healing."

The instructions continued each night. Deshan delighted in the attention he received. So too, of a day, the changing landscape intrigued him – never had he been so far from Yeshotruen. His dreams became more vivid and colourful. His imagination reached into the shifting scenes before him and made stories that had lain dormant within him.

When at last the pair reached the mountain range, he was eager to arrive at the summit and discover what lay beyond. Teilo took pleasure in watching the expression on the boy's face as he stood on high and beheld the forests below opening into fertile valleys which stretched forever into the distance. He pointed out different landmarks, such as the dark green stain of Maurapin.

Deshan had endless questions about the land. That night was the first he had ever spent in a forest. He felt fearful of the sounds and shadows and he huddled close to the fire, seeking its protective warmth. But he could not help noticing the difference in his companion, for Teilo seemed completely, if not joyfully, at ease – as if he had just returned home to a loving family. The boy often observed him gazing into the trees having an unspoken conversation with whatever stayed hidden in the shadows. The dog too appeared to see and hear invisible things that hovered outside the circle of firelight.

Deshan watched the warrior gather leaves and shape them into a mound. He is so caring, he thought – so soft and yet so strong.

"You shall sleep in comfort tonight," Teilo said, taking a blanket from his sack. "I am going for a short walk, Deshan – have no concern – I am close by – you only have to call if you need me." He could feel the boy's fear. "Do not be frightened, son – believe me you are safer here than you have ever been in Yeshotruen."

He tucked the blanket around the huddled form and smiled reassuringly. "You will come to no harm but I must ask that you do not follow me – it is important for me to be alone. Do you understand?"

Deshan nodded.

Before he left, Teilo placed more wood on the fire making it burn warm and bright. Then, motioning to the dog to follow him, he slipped between the trees and was out of sight.

♋

The mound of rocks was still there. A creeping vine had begun to knit a blanket over the grave. Though the moon was not yet full, it cast enough light to silhouette the Lonely Mountain against the sky. The sight of it made Teilo shudder and he smiled at this reaction. There are ghosts in me yet, he thought. The smell of this place was still familiar – the smell of birth and renewal. He felt a sudden urge to be closer to the earth that held him – to shed the weight of the world he had chosen and be at one with his forest home. He made a small fire, removed his clothing and lay on the ground – letting the coolness of it seep into his skin. Through the canopy above him he saw the heavens – he felt the play of the unseen spirits that flitted between the earth and sky. The dog, patiently waiting, alert and protective, growled softly. Soundlessly Teilo rose to his feet and looked into the night.

"How is it you know where I am?" he asked.

The tree man came forth from the shadows, wrapping his hairy arms around the warrior and sniffing the skin of his neck and shoulders as if there he would detect all he needed to know.

"You are still clean, warrior," he said. He studied Teilo's face and body. "And you have healed well."

Impulsively he laughed and hugged and kissed the warrior – stroking his hair and face. Teilo hugged him back with genuine love – almost as a child for a parent.

"I have brought you a gift," he said and summoned the dog to his side. "You took a life for me, now I give you a life that needs to be guided towards her freedom."

The tree man approached the dog warily. Without warning the dog sprang. The tree man caught her in his sinewy arms. They wrestled playfully, the dog whimpering and licking the face of her new protector.

"You have not yet answered my question, tree man," Teilo said as they sat beside the fire. "How is it you always know where I am?"

"You were given to me."

Teilo frowned. "I do not understand – how was I given to you."

"I watched her, warrior – she birthed you on the forest floor – she knew from where you came – she gave you to me – keep him safe tree man – that is what she said. When you are in the forest, you are my child. They tell me when you are coming – they feel your feet upon the earth."

So Shimmera had given him to the tree man. As a child he roamed freely in the forest as no other child would be permitted to do and he never felt alone – he always felt safe. Now he knew why.

"My gratitude," he said simply, then added quietly, "I need your help again, my friend."

The tree man suddenly became erratic and appeared distressed. "Then why did you bring him here?" he whispered. "He has seen me. I should not be seen."

Teilo put his arm around his guardian. "Have no fear – he is but a boy who has not learnt to keep faith with his word. He will not breathe of this to another living soul. If he does, I will cast him aside for he could inflict no greater injury or betrayal."

Hiding among the trees, Deshan cringed. Teilo had spoken loudly enough for him to hear every word and he was in no doubt that they spoke of him. Ashamed he went back to his dying fire, rekindled the flames and wrapped himself in his blanket, but he could not sleep. His mind was filled with images of all he had witnessed. So foreign this place – it revolted him and excited him.

But how could Teilo permit that creature to touch him? How could there be such intimacy between them. Their nakedness disgusted him and yet he saw the joy of their being together – joy such as he had never known.

There was something else that he struggled to define. To Deshan it seemed that Teilo and the tree man were part of the forest, the earth, and he was the one who didn't belong. Almost as if here, he did not exist – he was nothing. He thought of his family in Yeshotruen. Their existence was dry and empty. There were brief times of affection and laughter. There were also many times of bitterness and tears – even cruelty – but never the love he had just witnessed between the man who was his hero, and the ugly beast-like man who looked at once fiercesome and tender. Deshan quietly wept until sleep came.

He was awakened by Teilo gently shaking him. The sun was well up but it was still cool and dark among the trees. The warrior had already prepared their morning meal of thick gruel only now, it contained more ingredients. There was also a bowl of fresh berries. The dog was nowhere to be seen and the morning seemed subdued without its presence.

Teilo was silent. Deshan mistook this silence for anger towards him but, in truth, the warrior had much to think about. He had stayed with the tree man until the pre-dawn hour – neither had slept. They had talked or sat in silence and his wild friend had left him much on which to ponder.

"How is it you knew of the warrior's stone?" he had asked the tree man. "Pray tell me about it – I need to know."

At first his guardian was evasive but when at last he did answer it was with quiet eloquence.

"The warrior's stone is the stone of life and death. It gives and takes – it creates and destroys. It is a gift or a curse bestowed upon few. At your birth she blessed it also in the earth, the water, the heavens and lastly the fire. Then she wrapped it in cloth against your heart that it may bleed into you without causing you pain. See warrior – you still have the mark," he pointed to a small birthmark on Teilo's chest. "Thus she gave you to the elements. All this I saw. It knows you this stone – thus it is for you alone to use. Only a child of your heart may touch it without stealing its heat. All others will rob its power like leeches take blood. I touched it because I could not let you die – fear not – I did not take of its life force. You have used it but once."

"I have used it twice, tree man. I know now it was how I destroyed Myallon."

The old man heard the sadness in Teilo's voice. He reached out to take his hand.

"Myallon had to go back to nothing, warrior – do not fear that nothing – you know it remains everything."

"Help me bring life to Yeshotruen, dear friend," Teilo asked after a long silence. "I am unsure of where to begin."

He spoke of his plans and for a time they were like boys plotting an adventure. Before they parted, the tree man offered the advice for which Teilo had hoped.

"Use the stone, young Master – bury it – in the earth – let the prayer come to open its power – the earth must feel of it. All else will follow."

♋

At last Teilo looked at the boy whose misery and self-pity were crying out in his untouched food and the redness of his eyes.

"Deshan," he began, carefully choosing his words. "I grew up knowing only the love of my parents. Neither of them ordered me to do anything, except once, before my father died, he commanded me to hide – to save myself. They chose not to order my behaviour because they wanted me to always know freedom. I will never command you to do something, Deshan – I will only ask and I will have my reasons for doing so. If I had to order you, it would mean I did not trust you – just as my father on that day did not trust me to stay hidden – and rightly so. I need to know there is respect and trust between us and I meant what I said last night. If you did so much as breathe your knowing of the tree man's existence, I would sever the hand of friendship I have extended to you. Do you understand?"

The boy nodded, but Teilo could see that his grasp on this understanding was not firm at all – it wavered – a fickle flame which would lean the way of the wind. This boy did not know of trust. He did not yet trust Teilo and the warrior said no more on the subject. Instead he spent time with him – teaching him the lore of fruits and herbs and collecting seeds to take back to Yeshotruen. He let him explore this new world fully. He laughed at Deshan's mixture of trepidation and excitement as he bathed tentatively in the mountain stream – warmed by summer heat – more water than the boy had ever seen in his life.

When it came time to return to the city, Deshan was becoming accustomed to his strange surroundings. Teilo had collected hundreds of seeds of many varieties and each species went into a different pouch.

"We are going to bring the forest to Yeshotruen, Deshan." His confidence was that of one who has complete faith in their own capabilities. On the other hand, the boy could not even conceive that such a grand plan would ever reach fruition nor was that of any consequence to him. His thoughts were dominated by this man himself – the warrior who showed not the slightest sign of violence or aggression and who seemed free of fear – never did he hide within himself. Deshan was used to secretive behaviour that courted suspicion at every opportunity.

Slowly he became more open – laughing and allowing himself be seen.

♋

They caught up with the drays from Imoshtan bearing the food and materials Teilo had requested when they were still several days from Yeshotruen. Three warriors accompanied the supplies. Deshan looked on as Teilo embraced one of them. The friendship between the two, and their delight at seeing each other, was obvious.

"I did not expect this pleasure, Ortarian," Teilo said to the older man, "or have you been sent to ascertain what it is I do in Yeshotruen? I imagine some of my requests were puzzling to Romarrah."

"I am sure they were, Teilo," Ortarian smiled, "though my feeling is that Syrath persuaded the Master to honour them."

Teilo said nothing but Ortarian responded to his look.

"She is well, Teilo." He nodded, handing the young warrior a small bundle of letters. "I came to visit Pauroseng and Osarien – it is many years since we have been together. I feel the urgency to be with them for a time."

Teilo remained silent – something that did not escape Ortarian's attention. His young friend had changed greatly in such a short time.

"You have an apprentice I see," Ortarian bowed slightly to Deshan.

Teilo raised his eyebrows at the boy who then returned the chief warrior's courtesy, but he was resentful of this intrusion. He wanted Teilo to himself for just a little longer.

That night the four warriors talked quietly around the fire. Afterwards Ortarian and Teilo sat together in contemplation.

Deshan felt lost in his own wilderness of mixed feelings. The day had begun so joyfully – striding beside the Master – full of his new place in the world. Now it was as if a barrier had suddenly come between them. He was no longer part of this man's world.

As he was finally drifting into sleep, Teilo came and sat beside him. He ran his hand through the boy's hair.

"Deshan," he spoke in a whisper, "I am still with you but you cannot hold on so tight – see how you seethe inside? You create this separation – it is your own doing. Learn to be by yourself, son – it is a much fairer place to be."

Those words and the touch of the Master's hand were enough to let sleep come peacefully.

The boy awoke to the clashing of swords and would have leapt from the ground in panic were it not for the accompanying laughter.

"You seem to have lost your lightning edge, Master Teilo," Ortarian mocked.

"I fear it is lack of practice," Teilo laughed, neatly side dancing away from his partner's attack.

Deshan watched in awe of the two men. That Teilo's skill was superior was discernable but Ortarian himself was a master with the sword and they were tireless. They had long since discarded their coats and the sweat glistened on their bodies, spraying into the air as they twisted and turned.

"Enough, my friend," Ortarian said at last, sheathing his sword and extending his arm to place around Teilo's shoulders. "It will not take you long to find the swiftness of old. Do my parents not partner you?"

He had noted that Teilo had avoided talking of Pauroseng and Osarien – he could not help but wonder why.

"Osarien no longer wears his sword," Teilo's response was short. "And Pauroseng's body is ailing, Ortarian." He looked at his friend. "Your visit is timely."

They said no more.

♋

3

Their arrival in Yeshotruen caused a small commotion. People were curious as to what was happening at the compound to warrant such activity. Deshan helped the warriors unload and store the supplies. When the task was complete, Ortarian was surprised to see Teilo bolt the doors.

"Do you expect these goods to be stolen Teilo?"

"This is not Imoshtan, my friend. My gratitude for your work, Ortarian – perhaps you would like to visit your parents now. Deshan and I must attend to some duties before I can join you."

Ortarian bowed. The young Master is in control, he thought as he walked across the courtyard.

As soon as Ortarian had left Teilo turned to the boy.

"So, Deshan – let us pay our debts shall we?"

"I do not see why we must give Mercenta more oils, Master Teilo. I did not steal them – I only tried to."

"The intent is the same, Deshan. Mercenta still harbours resentment. Do not forget that, however slightly, I did wound him – we must offer just recompense to the man and others who were with him. Come – let us be finished with this – it must be done."

Mercenta accepted the gifts readily, with grudging courtesy, but his animosity was ever present in his eyes and the curtness of his speech.

We are not finished yet, Teilo thought on the way back to the compound. He read Mercenta well. This swarthy, angry man would come for him, of that he was certain, but he did not expect the manner in which the trader would take his revenge.

Teilo escorted Deshan to his home. He offered the boy's parents food and supplies – the agreed upon payment for their son's absence. It saddened him to see the way the boy's mother could not look at him – at least not in the presence of her husband. Edora smiled shyly and asked when she too would be summoned to the compound.

"We will begin training in several days," he returned her smile.

Their father said not a word. He turned his back on the warrior and left the room. Yeshotruen would guard its resistance for some time to come.

♋

"It defies belief, Teilo," Ortarian had sought him out in his chambers. "I confess to being stunned by what I see. It is no more than a hospice for the sick and needy."

"Show me, Ortarian – where is the wrong in that?"

"But it changes nothing – it holds a burden that is never-ending. It breaks Pauroseng's body and gives Osarien a weariness that makes him older than his years."

"That is their choice, my friend. You of all people must see the rightness of it."

"Are there any warriors here?" Ortarian sighed.

"There are two men with little training who offer their service to protect the compound – fortunately they have never been put to the test. Until now there has been little here to steal. Ortarian," Teilo fixed his gaze on the chief warrior.

I know that look, the older man thought, what does he want of me?

"Stay with me," Teilo urged. "To have you here would give strength to my own resolve. Pauroseng is right – it was a mistake to teach but a handful and let others suffer. There is another way – we must give life back to this earth – it can be done – this I know for certain."

Ortarian looked at the young warrior – he could read his passion and conviction but this was one man. Together they would be two men against a city of people who barely survived among the stench of their own poverty and decay. The lawlessness and disrespect for life was proof that these inhabitants of Yeshotruen would not seek betterment. He shook his head.

"You are judging them, Ortarian. I can feel it. You are measuring their behaviour against that which comes from decades of privilege – knowing the warmth of good food in your body – the peace of safety and the love that comes from gentle kinship. Their history is not one of peace, my friend – it is one of violence and struggle."

"You are correct, Teilo," the chief warrior acknowledged his own prejudice. "I beg forgiveness for my lack of understanding but I do not believe that my work is here. Allow me the time to see perhaps what it is that you feel for this place. I will give you my answer in the days to come.

Now – show me these plans of yours."

Teilo laid out his plans for Yeshotruen – an ambitious network of water canals, orchards, gardens and forests. Ortarian was impressed by the detailed drawings and calculations but it would surely take an army of hundreds to bring these ambitions to fruition. He voiced his misgivings to which Teilo responded adamantly.

"I have twenty young men and women who are ready to commence training at the compound. They will be warriors, Ortarian – have no fear of that – but they will be warriors who bring life and healing and their numbers will grow."

"Teilo – this is a small land on its own – it is not of the Land of Romarrah. Is this really our concern? Should we not let these people make their own decisions?"

"Did we not make it our concern when we built this compound here? Did we not say to them – we have something better to offer you? Do we give a people dreams and hopes only to let them rot because we can not make them fit our ideal? Pauroseng has given what should have been her years of solitude to hold a cup to dying lips – to deliver yet another child into this life that robs their dignity with their very first breath. She will not leave them and I," he hesitated and looked for a moment out the window at the scene beyond, then back to the chief warrior. "I will not leave her, Ortarian."

They talked no further and in the days that followed, Ortarian assisted Teilo in preparing the eighteen men and two women who came to the compound each morning in the pre-dawn hour to become warriors. Their day began with stillness. The new Master had cleaned the warrior's sanctuary and filled it with candles. He placed small pots of perfumed oils above some of the flames so the air was always fragrant.

Osarien, in his own quiet way, willingly gave his time, as always, to lighting the fires in the kitchens and preparing food only now, there were more to feed.

Before the day became brittle with heat, Teilo would lead the warriors in dance just as he had done with Jemai. At first they were embarrassed – some were openly critical and a few were hostile to the concept, but the warrior took no notice.

"When you understand movement in this way," he told them, "then you shall be given your sword. To attain this knowing you must first let the self die until it is no longer you who dances."

Often some of the children who were housed at the compound would join in the dance – something that delighted the young Master.

By afternoon he would have all his students digging canals and once again, the children joined in – carting dirt and stone.

Ortarian was fascinated by Teilo's manner of teaching. He was even more intrigued by the realization that his mother and the young Master sang together in the early hours of each morning.

The chief warrior acquainted himself with Yeshotruen as Teilo had done – walking the pathways that led through the huddled maze of the city but he did not feel drawn to the place or its people. His life had been one of books and study and teachings – it was how he offered the best he could – it was his vocation. He made his decision to return to Imoshtan. He needed only to inform Teilo of his decision but, as it so often does, fate took his intention and cast it aside.

♋

Leaving Pauroseng's sanctuary, their daily devotion finished, Teilo suddenly felt ill – a churning, cramping fear that came from outside himself. Closing his eyes and steadying his breath, he waited for clarity. Deshan was screaming – he could not hear it, but he could feel it. Edora's spirit was retreating, as if into a corner where it shivered – cut off from any sense of itself.

The warrior ran, grabbing his sword as he went. He did not wait to summon help. He was aware of nothing but the distress that awaited him – he had no time for hesitation. Edora and Deshan would be on their way to the compound and in his heart, he already knew what had befallen them.

As he made his way towards the kitchen, Osarien witnessed Teilo's flight. Without further thought, he followed the Master.

The city was not yet awake – it nestled quietly in the dim light of morning but now, as he ran swiftly through the semi-darkness, Teilo really could hear Deshan screaming. He let his mind become clear and focused.

It was Edora he saw first – the torn clothing exposing her crumpled body told its own story. Unfastening the cloak he wore against the cool morning air, he placed it over her and touched his hand to the top of her head.

"Do not move, child – you will soon be safe," he whispered.

People came out of their homes, still clutching their blankets around them. They formed a stoic wall of silence although none stepped forward to offer help.

Deshan lay a little further along the path – his face bloodied and already swelling. A stake had been driven through his right hand and into the earth. No longer screaming he was whimpering in pain.

When he bent over the boy, Teilo knew these children had been used as bait. He had walked into a trap. He stayed calm, giving no thought to what he was seeing – letting his mind be steady. Placing his sword on the ground beside Deshan, he put his hand on the boy's chest.

"Be still, Deshan," he said.

"My sister," the boy mumbled through swollen lips.

"I will look after her," Teilo soothed.

He took a deep breath. For a moment he hesitated and waited. When he knew Mercenta stood ready to take his life, he moved.

Osarien too walked into the trap. He carried no sword – he came only to offer care to those who needed it.

Mercenta had ordered his men to make sure no one prevented him from exacting his revenge. When he saw the warrior place his sword to one side and kneel beside the boy, he stalked his prey, assured of vengeance.

Osarien had reached the girl. He was aware of the men, their swords drawn coming towards him.

"I carry no weapons," he said calmly, "I wish only to care for the injured."

He knew death would come anyway.

♋

Pauroseng let her tears fall – it was over – this time of friendship and sharing – of being known. She held Osarien in her heart as she felt him take his last breaths. "Come," she whispered, "take my hand."

They walked together through a lifetime that had passed so quickly – a dream that now closed its eyes and became lost to the world.

♋

Deshan saw Teilo spring like an animal from his side. Every movement seemed to slow down. The warrior's sword split the air with its lethal whine then the sound shuddered and thickened as it severed the trader's head from his body.

To Deshan it was as though the warrior became motionless – caught in full flight, but to Mercenta's men watching in horror, it was not so.

Still clasping his sword with both hands, Teilo let his body steady itself as his feet touched the earth. He then raised only his eyes to meet their stares.

"Do not walk away from this," he spoke as they turned to flee.

But it was Ortarian who suddenly blocked their path to freedom – stealing himself for what he already knew he would find.

"Put down your weapons," he commanded. "If you choose to fight now, your death is all but assured."

Perhaps they would have complied with his command had it not been for Andeysen, Deshan's father. Like a crazed beast he came from nowhere swinging his sword wildly. Ortarian tried to stop the man but the latter's rage propelled them both forward. Andeysen would not stand a chance against the five assailants. Both warriors were forced into combat.

"Leave this!" Teilo almost hissed at Andeysen as he came to the man's side, fending off the attack.

"I have a right to vengeance," the other replied. It fell from his lips – a worn out platitude.

"Go to your children." Teilo's response was sharp. "They are in pain – what is your vengeance compared to their suffering?"

Andeysen stepped back as if he too was wounded. In that instant, the fire in him was lost. He stood dazed, looking at the hopelessness of his life reflected in the violated bodies of his son and daughter. He did not know how to comfort them.

It was Freyora, his wife, who came to him.

"See to your son, Andeysen. I will tend to Edora."

He was frightened to look at Deshan – that he might see there too much of his own fear and incompetence. He sat numbly beside the boy in the dirt, a short distance from Mercenta's body, staring at the thick red stain slowly soaking into the earth. He had no sense of the battle being fought before him. His son no longer appeared conscious and Andeysen fumbled in his mind to find the things he wished to say to him. Nothing came – not even the tears he was crying inside.

"Hold him while I release his hand."

It was the warrior again – kneeling by his side. "It is better he is not conscious."

He watched this man touch his son. Even when he drew the stake from the boy's hand, it was with tenderness. Like his son had done, he found himself wondering how those hands could kill.

"Andeysen," the warrior was talking to him. "I would like to take Deshan and Edora to the compound to see to their wounds. If you would rather they stay with you, with your permission, I will come each day to ease their healing."

Teilo glanced at Ortarian holding the body of his father. For a second Apheilio was there, dying in his arms. He let the image go. Andeysen had given him no answer.

"Come," he said softly, "we will all go together – carry your son."

♋

By the time the dawn broke over Yeshotruen the pathway was empty – only the stains remained waiting to be erased by the movement of life passing over them. Just like the stains in people's minds and hearts that would take time to heal and dissipate into the past.

♋

The sun was setting and he was watching the colours spread – a visual analogy of the day – awash with violence – smeared with the numb quiet that follows in its wake. The air had lost its heat – already the cool of night flirted with the creeping shadows. The heat of Yeshotruen during the day could be stifling, but of a night a cold would descend from the heavens and seep into the earth.

Teilo sat atop a small rocky outcrop. He had needed to distance himself from the compound and those within its walls – to find a space among the shock and grief of the day's events.

Deshan and his family were safe within the walls. He had tended to them all, depending on their needs – bathing Deshan's wounds, binding them with herbs and tinctures to guard against infection and all the time talking to the boy, reassuring him of his recovery.

He had sat beside Edora, feeling her pain – so different to her brother's because it sprang from a different violence – one that was intended to debase – to strip the dignity from her soul. The process of Deshan's healing would be open and visible, but Edora's pain was secretive – invasive – an indelible stain that forever gathered the consequences of its origins. It could not be shared openly, it could not become gossip for that would only serve to give it a strength of its own.

He knew it was imperative that she feel love immediately – the most gentle, nurturing love – before the hardness set in and robbed her essence of its passion. Instinctively he knew words and touch would only serve to push her further into her place of retreat. Already her face was turned away from everyone.

Instead, he sang to her – the song that Pauroseng had given him – waiting for it to curl its meaning into her shattered spirit. Andeysen and Freyora were embarrassed by the warrior's vulnerable offering. They too turned away.

He closed his eyes and let his voice stroke the child's pain

Edora tried to block out this gentle sound but it burrowed beneath her resistance. It sought her anger which, like that of a trapped animal, hissed and scratched inside her. It tore at her flesh and her body shook with its force.

She hated this man beside her. She wanted so much to strike him but to do so would be to reach out from her place of retreat. Slowly her anger slipped like a stain from her body and disappeared into the earth. From beneath its face there arose an ache so painful she writhed within its torment. It was her own fractured knowing of herself – that which she had known to be herself screamed in her like a tortured child until the sobbing began.

Finally she turned to face him. He gathered her in his arms and let her cry.

All these pictures and those of the morning's violence flashed before him. Each one he gave to the sunset and watched as they faded across the sky.

He had not yet spoken more than a few words to Ortarian and Pauroseng. That time would come. He had left them to prepare Osarien's body – a reverent ritual of grieving. There were questions within him – there was doubt. Again he asked himself what his actions cost others. Without his interference on that day in the market place, these events may never have occurred.

Then there were the men who, with Mercenta, had taken part in these heinous crimes. Three of them still lived and he must decide what was to become of them. There were those of Yeshotruen who would have them killed to satisfy their sense of justice and retribution. Then there were others who would believe that these men had sought their own justice and retribution for injury they had sustained.

In Imoshtan they would be delivered to Manon. Teilo had known of executions in the past for offences such as the murder of Osarien – for murder it was – an unarmed warrior – he sought only to care. Would Romarrah have executed these men? Teilo thought not but of that he was unsure. And Manon - what did he know of this place? There was a reason for its existence. There were always those like Mercenta who wreaked suffering – people like Myallon who plotted grand devastation for personal greed and desire. Yet there was something within him that recoiled at the thought of such banishment. What would it achieve for these souls, he wondered – where do they find peace for without peace they will continue to be as they are – fuelled by pride and anger – guided only by their avarice and hatred.

The dark gathered around him but he did not yet wish to return to the compound. He had left it in order. Andeysen and Freyora had all they needed. He must wait for clarity. Romarrah came to his thoughts again. Now he understood the Great Master's aloneness in his leadership. No decision could be made lightly. Intent must be studied so very carefully. It is all wrong, he moaned to himself – one man or woman should never bear such weight – have such power and control – it is doomed by its very own isolation.

A light moved through the darkness towards him and the sight of it nearly made him weep. There was only one person who would so selflessly come to him now and bring such perfect balance.

Pauroseng said nothing as she sat beside him. The light cast its warmth around them. This time it was she who took his hand. He felt her grief, mingled with the joy of who she was, flow into him and seek his own. He released at last the life of Mercenta that he had torn apart and lain to waste upon the earth.

From the balcony, Ortarian could see the glow from the lamp beyond the compound walls. He would not be returning to Imoshtan.

4

Syrath opened the small parcel bound with twine. Similar to the first it contained a letter, a drawing and a reading stone.

This is the stone of surrender and trust, Teilo had written. *It tells us that all for which we search is already before us, at all times within our grasp. Yet it is our grasping itself which denies us its flavour. It asks that we hold nothing; no claim; no fear or hope. It asks that we become blind; to use our knowing, that which emanates from the innermost chamber of the soul, as sight. In the very depths of surrender, when all of our life is offered back, only then is our sight opened to greater things. We must stay in faith Syrath; that faith which carries no falsity of knowledge or identity for this falsity only leads us to suffering.*

Dear friend, his letter began, *it is difficult sometimes to stay in that place of faith is it not, when faced with the wretchedness of inflicted sorrow. I pray you go to the orchard sometimes and that you hear there the song I so often send you.*

She smiled for it was here, in the orchard, she sat reading these words. Teilo had drawn a soft picture of a woman, dancing toward a flame – an achingly pure image – gently exposed and utterly compelling. Underneath he had written

> *Faith is vigilant;*
> *standing firm*
> *beneath the quaking shadows*
> *of doubt;*
> *until even faith*
> *is not needed;*
> *this riddle of separation*
> *dissolves*
> *when nothing is known*
> *and everything is blessed.*

At the very bottom of the page he had added; *Forgive me for keeping Ortarian; I know he speaks as your mentor and you value his tuition. Now we are both blind, my friend. May it give us the sight we need.*

♋

"It can never be easy with him," Romarrah sighed as he folded his own letter from Teilo – his irritation evident in his voice and his frown.

Syrath kept her counsel and her father continued.

"Perhaps I was wrong to send him there. Osarien's death was undeserved and quite possibly could have been avoided yet he tells me he keeps the attackers with him – he gives them that choice when in truth, they have forfeited this right by the sheer callousness of their deeds. I fear he will only court more trouble. Ortarian also has written describing the lawlessness of this place and his own doubt that it will rise out of its suffering. Would it not then be better to send more warriors as I first intended – to speed its recovery?"

He looked at his daughter. "You are very quiet, Syrath – what is it you are thinking?"

She rolled the reading stone in the palm of her hand.

"That you should trust him, Romarrah – trust him to do that which he knows he must. Surrender your own will and let it be."

The full weight of her words took a few moments to register. He laughed.

Syrath rarely saw her father's laughter and she greeted it with pleasure.

"I see that now you have lost your own mentor, Syrath, you have chosen to become mine – my gratitude to you."

♋

After the burial of Osarien, Teilo assumed fully the role of Master of Yeshotruen. Having given Osarien's assailants the choice of banishment to Manon or to stay at the compound under his command – offering their own lives in service for others, he was relieved when they readily chose the latter.

Without being requested to do so, Andeysen and Freyora commenced running the kitchens. The youths Teilo had met on his first day in Yeshotruen requested to train as warriors and they came prepared to listen and give of themselves.

But perhaps the greatest surprise was when Allencia, Mercenta's widow, insisted on an audience with him. The Master had already visited her on the day of her husband's death. He asked her forgiveness for taking the life of the man with whom she shared her own and offered his assurance that if in need, she and her son would be cared for. He had not expected a favourable response but she had merely bowed her acknowledgement and said nothing as he took his leave.

Now, when he ushered her into his chambers, he observed this woman more closely. He saw she carried a dignity beneath the burden of her suffering and that she was not of Yeshotruen born. Since Mercenta's death, Allencia had shed the dress of her peers, adopting instead a style similar to that worn by the women in villages south of Imoshtan. Instantly he knew her origins. There was a familiarity that he could not mistake. She was of handsome countenance with strong, well defined features. He smiled at her.

"What is it you wish to ask of me, Allencia?"

She looked at him fully, if not somewhat boldly. "Do you know who I am?" was her forthright question.

"I know you are from Athanan," he replied, "but your features are even more familiar."

"I am one of your father's cousins. My father was your grandfather's youngest brother."

It was a statement that obviously required a response, but if she expected to be greeted by Teilo with the warmth and affection of a welcome reunion, she would be mistaken. He remained unmoved by her declaration, waiting expectantly for the intention of her visit.

"You have no interest in your origins then, Master Teilo?" she noted his indifference. "You do not wish to know of your family?"

"My origins are what I carry within me now," he replied quietly. "I have no recollection of a childhood family other than Apheilio and Shimmera and no, Allencia, I do not need to know of those with whom I share the connection of blood – family is whoever stands before me."

"Do you know it is believed that because of you and your mother, Athanan was torn apart?" she pressed on.

He offered no comment. He was puzzled as to what this woman wanted – was there a claim she wished to make?

"It was a cruel life you were dealt in our village." She smiled at him as if to elicit his confidence.

"I do not feel any suffering from my childhood," he responded evenly.

"They were a deeply superstitious people," Allencia persisted, "but that did not warrant the course of action taken by Romarrah."

"I cannot change what has been done – what is it you want of me?" Teilo was aware of his impatience with this conversation which seemed to be meandering without connection but as he turned his attention to his own disquiet, he knew something crucial was going to occur – crucial to his plans in Yeshotruen. He became still.

Seeing that the Master had no time for her explanations, Allencia became more direct.

"Before I state my intent, I wish only to tell you that I harbour no ill will towards you for what happened to my family in Athanan, or for Mercenta's death – though the two are in a way connected. Had Romarrah not destroyed our village, I would never have been given to the trader. I was the same age as your youngest warriors."

Teilo chided himself for his impatience. This woman did not need his lack of compassion – she needed his support.

"Mercenta was a despicable man," she continued, "cruel and vicious. I cannot bear the shame of what he did to those children. For that reason I am leaving Yeshotruen. My husband was very wealthy and his wealth had bought him much property. By way of recompense for the suffering he caused, I wish to give this property to you."

She felt his imminent refusal and added quickly, "It may be of interest to you that some of it adjoins this compound. I would not be wrong in assuming your plans for Yeshotruen are quite ambitious – of that I am sure."

"Your offer is generous, Allencia, but what of your own future? Athanan no longer exists – where will you go?"

She was hesitant in her reply. "I will seek a home – perhaps I will find some of my family – perhaps somewhere that I may be of use."

She paused for a moment and he could see the struggle within her.

"There is something else, Master Teilo. I wish for you to take my son, Cencian."

Before Teilo could object, she hurriedly went on. "You yourself have admitted to being responsible for his father's death and therefore you have a debt to the child. I request, as is my right to do so, that you honour your debt by taking the boy into your care."

"I have seen your son – he is but a small child – it will be some years before he can train as a warrior. I would have thought that, at this time, he is still very much in need of a mother's guidance." She does not truly desire this parting, he thought, watching her face.

Allencia shook her head. "I cannot bear to lose another child and already he is lost to me. He is his father's son." Her words carried a brittleness that quavered sadly around her lips.

"What happened to your children?" Teilo asked softly.

It was a subject she never discussed. She resented his inquiry but there was also a need in her to tell this man her story. She steeled herself to give words to her pain. When she did speak her voice held little emotion.

"My first born son, Mealle was killed during an argument when he was fourteen. That is not uncommon in Yeshotruen but he, unlike Mercenta, was not given to violence – he was a gentle soul. His father detested him." A solitary tear escaped onto her cheek. She brushed it away.

"My only daughter, Mericia was traded by her father to a childless couple somewhere in the Land of Romarrah – I know not where. Perhaps she was the fortunate one. Cencian is Mercenta's heir. He kept him very close. What that child has witnessed does not bear thinking. He has learned to emulate his father's cruelty and contempt. I cannot bear to be treated by my son as I was by Mercenta. I thought you of all people might be able to reach him. I cannot bear to be with him any longer."

Teilo let the silence become strong again before he spoke and when he did his words surprised her.

"Stay in Yeshotruen. It is too soon to make this decision." His eyes had never left her face but she could no longer look at him.

"If you leave, Allencia, you will drown in regret and bitterness – you will not free yourself of Mercenta – in fact you will drag him with you every step you take – and Cencian as well – like a hollow despair that child will live – a constant gnawing inside you. Is this what you want?"

"I want this to be over," she almost whispered.

"Then stay," he urged. "Let that which entraps you become your liberation. Allencia, I have just seen you as you were in Athanan – an image I glimpsed from afar. You sat beneath a tree – a young girl – playing with the village children – reading to them. They were like your family. Look at the children of this compound – look at what they need – they could so easily be your family now. It is not Mercenta who has robbed you of your life. You have lost sight of that love you once knew – reclaim it – forgive him and let him go."

Her laugh was edged with bitterness. "I have only revealed to you the smallest degree of the pain that man inflicted. You yourself witnessed but a speck. It has tortured my heart every day. I wish he had died screaming in pain. I wanted him to know something of what he had done and you ask me to forgive him."

"If you cannot find it in yourself to do so, this will never be over and you will be Mercenta's accomplice in all he has done. You are the one who will keep it alive within you and around you in everything you see. If you do as I ask of you now and stay – if you help me bring joy and understanding to the lives of these children, you will place a healing balm over the pain Mercenta gave to you and the world. Who is it you wish to be – a beautiful, loving woman or a shadow of him? Did this man ever know love and joy within himself? Can you not feel his pain and suffering – that which kept him apart from his own goodness?"

"I cannot stay in this place, Teilo. You have no right to ask me to do so. It reflects too much of my own sorrow."

"It reflects for you that which you most need to heal. And I need you, Allencia – I need people like you who have such beauty and goodness in their hearts and so much love to give."

She could not stop the tears then. She had for so long been unloved and unseen. Now this man had probed the sadness she had learned to tuck like stray wisps of hair behind her mask. But she was a woman so private that it was too painful to her to be truly seen.

"I must go," she said hastily.

He rested his hand gently on her arm. She was almost fearful of that touch.

"I am offering you refuge, Allencia, but more than that, I offer you purpose."

He took his hand away. "If you leave Cencian with me, know that there will be a part of him that will always beg your forgiveness, for you have now deemed him unworthy of your love."

She left – unable to speak further – her heart and mind awash with conflicting thoughts and feelings that now seemed so tired and overgrown.

♋

Deshan's eyes smouldered with hatred. Each time he looked at the men who had caused his injuries, his resolve grew and hardened within him. They had beaten him with obvious relish as he had struggled to go to his sister's aid. He had seen Mercenta slam her body against the wall and he knew full well what that brute intended to do to her.

When the trader had finished with Edora, he strode to where Deshan lay beaten and bleeding and spat on him.

"You are but the excrement of a whore," he said grabbing the boy's hair and lifting his face from the dirt. "Know how little you are worth boy – you are nothing when there is no one to protect you. Let us see how much you will scream for your protector."

It was then he had hammered the stake through Deshan's hand and the boy had screamed in terror. The pain in his hand rushed into his body as if to feed on his flesh. He heard one of the men call in a loud whisper, *"he comes"*. Mercenta swore – he was not yet finished. How had word reached the warrior so quickly?

Deshan's body was so wracked with pain, he did not think to warn Teilo of the danger – he had done nothing but whimper when the warrior knelt beside him. He relived this scene over and over. Whenever he saw those men working within the compound, he again felt their fists upon him – he could smell their breath in his face and he wanted to hurt them. The only way he could redeem himself was to take his own revenge.

But now it was Teilo who inflicted the most pain. He too may as well have beaten him. Mercenta's widow and her son had come to the compound and the Master had taken them in. Deshan had seen Teilo walking with them and it filled him with despair.

Now he watched as the Master came towards where he sat leaning against a wall in the courtyard. Teilo was accompanied by Mercenta's men and the small band of apprentice warriors. Deshan knew they had been working on the water channels. These days Teilo was always surrounded by people. It was true, each night he came to see Deshan, Edora and their parents but he never came only to see Deshan.

The boy saw one of the men say something and the Master laughed. There could be no greater injury. How could he court friendship with these people?

Teilo farewelled the group of workers and walked over to join Deshan.

"How is your hand today, Deshan?" he asked, sitting beside the boy. He was weary – his body ached. He rested his back against the wall and closed his eyes.

Deshan looked down at his bandaged hand. How could he tell this man that it was not his hand that hurt?

"Talk to me, son," Teilo said without opening his eyes. "If you keep walking over and over this same path in your mind it will become so hard the earth beneath it will not be able to breathe. You are choking yourself."

Suddenly he was on his feet again. "Come – come with me now."

He held out his hand to the boy and helped him to stand. Without another word, he walked purposefully towards the building which housed the sick and the dying. Deshan held back.

"No," said Teilo, "come – I want you to meet some of these people – they too are friends of mine."

Before the boy could respond, Teilo had opened the door and gently but firmly guided him inside.

Although fragrant oils were burning throughout the room, Deshan was sure he could still smell death and decay. Pauroseng sat beside an old woman, holding her hand and speaking softly to her, as if she was reciting something.

Teilo went to the woman's side. He brushed back the hair on her forehead with his fingers.

The old woman smiled. "I'm not there yet, young Master," she said.

He bent and kissed her forehead. "I will be with you, Penoma – it is nearly time."

Dipping a cloth in a bowl of water, he gently wiped her face. Her lips stretched into a shaky smile and she opened her eyes. They were white and sightless. Deshan felt repulsed. He turned to leave but Teilo again took him by the arm and propelled him towards a young boy seated with his mother at the far end of the room. The boy's bandaged leg was resting on a cushion in front of him. He was several years younger than Deshan, very slight of build but with a face that begged excitement and adventure.

"How is your leg, Kestan?" the warrior asked.

"It hurts, Master Teilo. I did as you bid me – I breathed through the circle of colours and light – sometimes it takes the pain away, but sometimes I cry."

Teilo smiled at the earnest little face. "I must bathe it again, son – you will need to breathe very deeply for me."

The boy nodded but his fear shadowed his eyes.

"Here." Teilo poured some small black seeds onto the boy's palm. "Chew these seeds – they are very rare. They come from a tree that grows deep in the forest – a long way from here. It is a giant of a tree."

His voice droned on as he slowly undid the bandage. The sight of the boy's leg was too much for Deshan – he stepped back. Teilo looked at him and gave a small shake of his head.

"Kesten - this is my friend, Deshan," he said to the child. "He went with me to collect those seeds – perhaps he can tell you of his adventures in that forest."

Kesten looked at the older boy expectantly. Deshan could see the whites of his knuckles where he gripped the chair – the tears that glistened in his eyes as he looked at him. He was pleading for something to distract him.

"It was a scary place at first," Deshan stammered self-consciously. Little did he know that he had not only begun a story, but a friendship that would last a lifetime.

When they left the hospice, it was nearly dark. Teilo now made his way towards the kitchen. Deshan followed in silence. His family occupied a small dwelling attached to the main kitchen. Often Teilo would visit them there. Andeysen and the Master would sit together talking quietly – sometimes long into the night.

The sudden change in his father since his arrival at the compound had astounded Deshan. He could not understand why this man, whom he had so often feared, now took directions from his wife and prepared food for those who had attacked his children. He had done nothing to avenge their injuries. Deshan despised his pathetic cowardice.

Once inside the kitchen, Teilo greeted Freyora and Andeysen warmly. Edora was stirring the contents of a large pot – she smiled when she saw them. Teilo went to her and they spoke for a short time. Deshan watched his sister laugh at something the Master said then offer him a taste of the thick broth. Taking two bowls from the shelf above him, Teilo held them for her to fill with the steaming mixture.

There had been a time, before the attack, when Deshan felt as though his whole world was magically transforming. Teilo was the catalyst for this new life and Deshan wanted only to be close to him – no – more than that – he wanted to mean something to this new Master – to be someone of importance in his life. That dream was now crumbling. The Master suddenly belonged to everyone – even those who did not deserve his attention.

Deshan became aware that Teilo was standing before him, holding two steaming bowls. He handed one to the boy, took a candle lamp from a table and indicating for Deshan to follow him, said his farewells.

The stars had quickly spread across the sky and they retraced their steps through the courtyard and out the main gates.

Deshan was puzzled. He had no idea where the Master was going. Within a short distance from the compound Teilo stopped in front of a derelict building. Similar to most of the homes in the city, it was made of earth. Part of the front wall was crumbling, in need of repair.

As they entered through the archway, the warrior lit several lamps and the room came to life. Taking the bowls from the boy he placed them on a rough slab table.

"Sit down, Deshan – eat your food before it is cold." Removing his sword, he sat opposite his companion.

They ate in silence.

"Do you know who owns this house?" Teilo asked when the meal was done. Deshan shook his head.

"It belonged to Mercenta," the warrior continued. "Allencia, his wife, has now given this property to me to use as I see fit to help the people of Yeshotruen. This is the only way she knows to make amends for her husband's ruthlessness – and you would have me turn her out? You know nothing of this woman and what she has suffered. Deshan you must learn to look past yourself and at the same time you must learn to know yourself – to know what is really in your heart – what leads you into action. You despise your father because he did not avenge your suffering. Believe me, he tried, but I stopped him. He did not need to carry the burden of another man's death. That day in the market place when your father was beating you – do you know why he beat you?"

"Because I had failed – I had been caught. He was furious with me." The boy's voice was tight with anger.

"No, Deshan – he beat you in the hope that Mercenta would not kill you. He was trying to save your life and he knew he was responsible for placing you in that danger. Had I not intervened your father may very well have succeeded and then again, he may not – we will never know. So is it not I who bears some responsibility for what unfolded? Action is often fuelled by the wrong knowledge and it only leads to more misery. These men who attacked you – do you know anything of them? No, because you only see what they did to you – that makes you blind to anything outside your own suffering and that feeds your hatred."

The cold began to seep into the room. Teilo got up to light a small fire. Firewood was precious in Yeshotruen and Deshan was surprised by this luxury. Then he realised it was for him alone. The warrior continued talking.

"You have just met Penoma. She was the first person I greeted when I came to Yeshotruen. She was begging for food – not for herself but for her daughter's children. Do you know why she is blind?"

Again the boy shook his head.

"Her husband beat her so much that he robbed her of her sight. Now as she lies dying, would it be better to seek out her husband and tear out his eyes so that he too suffers blindness, or to love Penoma as she deserves to be loved – to bring peace to her heart? Is it not better to feed the children of her daughter and relieve her of this burden? Is it not fitting, as she takes leave of this world, to surround this woman with comfort and warmth?"

Satisfied the fire would continue to burn, he once more sat with the boy. "It was when your father let go of his desire for vengeance and sat beside you in the dirt that he knew he did not know how to give, how to love. He knew that he had never given you the better part of who he was. He would tell you this himself but he has not yet found the words and his own path to your heart. If you reached out to him now, you could ease his way. You want me to love you as a father loves his son, but I am not your father. I will love you for who you are, Deshan – you may be assured of that and of my protection for you, but it is your father who holds you in his heart."

The boy's eyes had filled with tears but he remained silent.

Teilo stood and taking a book from a shelf, he placed it before the boy, turning page after page of detailed drawings – gardens and forests – fields of grain – more buildings, drains and water channels. Deshan stared at this dream, fascinated by what he saw.

"All this is possible, son, but it will only be achieved when the capacity for love and goodness outweighs the capacity for loathing and hatred. Give me enough people who within them know this is so and this dream will live as surely as you do. Look well, son, for this is why love is so much more powerful than hate – one gives and creates that of beauty and joy – the other destroys life and all trace of joy. That is the choice you face right now, my friend."

Deshan raised his eyes to meet those of the warrior. For the first time he really saw Teilo, the man. He saw the weariness on his face – what each day cost him. He saw his capacity for giving of himself as he was now doing – giving the time he would normally spend in solitude and rest, preparing himself for the day to come, releasing the day that was now over. And he knew that during the night Teilo would go back to the hospice and be with Penoma as he had promised. This man was not indestructible.

"You are tired, Master," he said at last.

To his surprise Teilo laughed. "Ah, Deshan – your words show me that you have heard what I said. I am more than tired son, I am weary even in my bones but you have just lightened that weariness – do you see that? You have looked outside yourself to think of another. I will make us some tea."

"Is Kesten going to die?" Deshan asked as Teilo placed the pot of water over the fire.

The warrior shook his head. "No – I will not let the infection take hold in his wounds – he will mend well, but he will remain crippled to some extent."

Deshan thought for a moment of the young boy's shining eyes and expressive face.

"Could I visit him again?"

Teilo turned to face him. "The greatest part of healing is to stay in love within yourself – to keep freedom alive within. If you give your time to Kesten you will strengthen his will and his joy and you will take the burden from others like his mother who sits with him constantly."

They spoke no more and Teilo went back to preparing their tea.

Later as he walked the boy back to the compound gates, he spoke again.

"Tomorrow you will meet with your attackers – do not be fearful – your family will be with you and so will I. It is time for you to see who they really are. Each life has its own story Deshan – it is time to share your stories and then let us put this matter to rest for it only keeps us from greater things."

♋

"You are tired Teilo," Ortarian said some days later. "Why do you not ask Romarrah for more warriors to provide the labour you need?"

Teilo shook his head.

"These people must do this for themselves. They must hunger for this dream - they must own it. But you are correct, now there are more apprentices to train, I will send for two adept warriors to assist us in their preparation. It is also time these young men and women moved into the compound – their training is far too fragmented. Andeysen has found me several men who will extend this building – in time it will serve as the hospice. Then we may move the warriors into their quarters. Ortarian, I wish for you to begin teaching the children."

The Master's manner was very purposeful and Ortarian was slightly irritated by it.

"What would you have me teach them?" he responded.

Teilo noted the lack of enthusiasm in his voice.

"I do not so much wish you to instruct them – merely to open windows that they may see new visions – visions to which they can give their own understanding and interpretation."

"I do not yet grasp what it is you ask of me, Teilo. Do you desire that they study as you once did with Syrath – art, history, literature?"

Ortarian stopped – the Master seemed distracted – laying out plans for various buildings on the table before them.

"I wish for them to know of themselves and the world, without submission" Teilo replied without looking up. "Do not separate yourself from them, Ortarian – this I beg of you – or seek to bestow on them wisdom – they have the same knowing as your self. By observing this in them they will open new vistas for you also."

Ortarian heard these words as an affront. This was the child he had taught so carefully – with great compassion. Did the young Master now consider his tutor's ways of education somehow inferior?

"Teilo, these children of Yeshotruen are as wild animals – they require discipline and steadiness."

The Master frowned, stopped what he was doing and faced the chief warrior.

"Of what discipline do you speak?" he asked quietly. "Pray tell me."

"That which checks unacceptable behaviour," the older man sighed. "Why do you look at me thus?"

"That discipline, of which you speak, is an imposition. Do you not see – you seek to impose it upon them."

The Master's words only irritated the chief warrior further. His reply was abrupt.

"Discipline is training, Teilo – a foundation which enables children to make something of themselves."

"Make something of themselves?" Teilo raised his eyebrows as if inviting Ortarian to reconsider this statement. "These children are already whole! What is it you would have them make of themselves? You begin at the wrong end, my friend. The truth is, we fail them. In Imoshtan children are well loved and nurtured – here they are not so fortunate, but even in Imoshtan we still fail them. It is almost cruel."

The chief warrior interjected. "How can you say this? Is it not our duty to teach that which we know is the greater truth – to raise awareness? We have an organized, civilized way of being – why must you challenge that which is already good?"

"Because if we do not understand the child, we do not understand our self. To begin a relationship – with anyone and that includes children – we must first honour their innate intelligence – not dampen it with superiority!"

This argument – for it was now an argument – had crept up on them unexpectedly and both men became aware of the heat behind their words. Teilo released his breath in an audible sigh.

"We may stand taller, Ortarian, but we do not stand greater. There is no line between the ages – in every stage of life we are equal. Why then are children perceived, as you yourself have just done, as wild animals set on a course of wilful defiance? Such speech denigrates the child and also the animal for no creature displays such defiance – merely a will to survive. Can you not see the child as they themselves see everything – endless possibility – perhaps the key to all magic. In those possibilities there is expansion – for yourself and the child."

The chief warrior was silent. When at last he did speak, it was without anger. "Teilo – I cannot do what you ask – I am not sure it is possible. For you perhaps, but for myself I do not know."

"It is no more than a shift in perception – not to bestow but to share – that creates equality. If you believe in these children, you affirm their rightful equality and you do not displace them with judgement. Understand – it takes the greater effort to hold a door open for another's wisdom to step through, than to tell them your own. Forgive me, Ortarian – I meant no offence. I simply do not want these children to be discouraged. I want their education to be as an open forum where each of them is blessed – where they enjoy their gifts without comparison or expectation. If they flourish in a particular talent, let them feel the flourishing that they will also know gratitude. Our gifts do not elevate us above others – they elevate us within ourselves. You of all people must see this."

"I can see your passion, Teilo, but I question my own ability to meet your expectations." Ortarian looked at the young man. It was impossible not to feel the power of his presence – it flowed from him with such warmth – such sweetness – even in irritation.

The Master was now drawing his attention to the plans on the table.

"In the future we will erect another building for this purpose here – on Mercenta's land but until that time, I would like you to use the Great Hall at the compound – we have no need for it - it is but wasted space. The children at the compound number twenty-seven – such an open education shall see them with choices that until now have been lost to them. You will not be alone in this. Allencia has agreed to assist you when she has become more settled. Have you any thoughts on this matter?"

Ortarian's face softened with a smile. "Is there but one stone you have left unturned?"

"There are hundreds of stones still left to turn, my friend, and each day it would seem I unearth another. It tests me more than I can say to stay steady and contained without impatience – without taking my awareness away from that which is before me. Romarrah in his last letter asks me of my studies to be a chief warrior – that must be the last thing on my mind. I am grateful that Pauroseng does not even speak of it."

Ortarian frowned. "Have you not yet studied the rituals? Teilo you must be able to offer protection to these warriors."

"Do not fret – I can offer protection and I will study the rituals. This brings me to another matter. I wish to take Pauroseng with me on a short journey. I trust you are able to continue this work in my absence."

"You cannot be serious, Teilo – Pauroseng has not the strength to undertake a journey of any kind."

"Pauroseng has more strength than you think, but I promise you she will not suffer from our travel – nor shall we be a great distance from the compound. It is imperative that we have this time alone."

The chief warrior opened his mouth to argue but Teilo stopped him.

"Oh do not question me on this, Ortarian," he said, running his hand wearily across his forehead. "There are some things I know – there is no question and I can have no other way of being for anything else would be denial. It is what Romarrah resents most because I cannot give him what he wants."

Immediately he apologised for his words. "Forgive me, I have spoken in judgement."

Again Ortarian was caught off guard by the young Master's strong words. "Romarrah loves you as a son, Teilo – do you not yet know this? He sent you here because he believes in you. Do you think any other young warrior has ever been elevated to the role of Master such as you have been? He has shown you endless patience – are you sure it is not you who is resentful?'

"Ortarian, do not be vexed with me – Romarrah will always have my love and gratitude – I am fully aware of his greatness and I mean no disrespect, but when you look at Romarrah you see the Great Master - perhaps even the Great Wisdom. When I look at Romarrah, I see the man – wise and knowing that he is, but as fallible as you or I."

The chief warrior did not respond immediately. Both men needed time to be still again. Finally he said, "And Pauroseng has given her consent to this journey?"

"I have not yet asked her, but she knows it will be."

"So be it then," Ortarian, however reluctantly, acquiesced. "I will do as you request." Smiling he added sarcastically, "You are, after all, the Master of Yeshotruen."

"I will accept that as humorous shall I?" Teilo responded playfully but he felt the older man's distance. "You are still troubled. If we talk of resentment, perhaps we should speak of what you are feeling now.

It took Ortarian at least a minute before he spoke again.

"I did not come here to stay, Teilo – I came to visit my parents. I could feel their age slowly lengthening but, more than that, I had a sense of what was to come. I do not hold you in any way responsible for my father's death, but I simply cannot understand why he did not realize his own danger and protect himself. Why did his training desert him? Nor do I have an understanding of Pauroseng – she too does not stay in the training which has been her life. I grew up with these parents – both were mighty warriors. Pauroseng alone could easily stand against five men. It is true there comes a time for solitude and prayerful peace but she no longer practices the rituals, she does not teach the Great Wisdom to these people to elevate their minds – nor does she," he hesitated, unsure if he should speak those words which came to his lips. "Nor does she see me – her own son – as if I have no true reflection in her eyes." He looked away.

Teilo too waited – letting the words and feelings settle like dust around them.

"In Yeshotruen your father was used to facing danger without his sword," he replied at last. "He had the respect of these people. This last time it was not so. I think he knew for a long time the nature of what was to come, but I cannot speak for him. I ask that you not take offence at what I must say, Ortarian, but it is not Pauroseng who fails to see you – it is you who does not see her. You look into her eyes and seek there your mother, the great warrior. I look into her eyes and this time believe me, I do see the timeless knowing of a Great Master and even beyond. This is only hidden from you because you stand too close."

As Teilo spoke of Pauroseng, Ortarian observed the warrior had tears in his eyes.

"She does not need the rituals, Ortarian – she does not need the Great Wisdom – she is without need. She does not even need protection – her defencelessness is her peace – she is at one. Come, my dear friend – this talk leaves us unsteady – let us sit in stillness together."

5

The third stone is the stone of illusion yet it signifies also that which brings enlightenment. It is the stone of shadow and light and the illusion of both. When we stand deeply in the shadow we may not know how close is the light and when we stand in the light, the shadow is already upon us. It tells us of the duality that ushers delusion and the oneness of enlightened knowing.

"What are you writing Teilo?" Pauroseng asked softly.
"A letter," he replied, "to a friend."
"Ah," the old warrior smiled, "the one who holds your soul as you sleep."
The young Master looked at her and returned her smile. "You are correct – that is the one."
They spoke no more. The fire lost its brightness and he folded his letter and placed it inside a book.
For most of the day, they had walked slowly to this destination – a small copse of trees, aged and withered – the struggle of their survival in this barren land evident in their twisted forms – as if they bore a weight that would not let them stretch their limbs heavenward.
Although Pauroseng insisted it was unnecessary, Teilo had carried bedding for the aged warrior – a thin mattress filled with plant fibre. He wished for her to have no hardship.
"Tell me of this place, Teilo," she requested when they had eaten a simple meal.
"It is the last of the true forest that once covered Yeshotruen," he answered. "These trees hold the story of this land – in a sense they have lost their family and they alone now carry the burden of the earth's sadness. If the land is to be healed, it must begin with what still lives and gives life. That is why I have come here, Pauroseng – to seek their wisdom and fully understand this land."
"How do you know this?" she asked, watching his face in the firelight. *He is not yet aware of what others see and feel in his presence,* she thought.

He does not know his sweetness – he fears himself – who he is and what he can do.

"I do not know," he answered flicking a twig into the fire. "It is something my mother taught me – to feel the wisdom of the earth – to hear the voices of creation."

"Tell me of your mother, Teilo." She settled herself into a more comfortable position – like a child awaiting a story.

He was not expecting this request. Shimmera was forever with him but he did not walk in the past very often.

"What did you love about her?" the old master prompted.

"I was in love with her," he began but then waited a few moments before he continued.

"Shimmera was real – she was flesh and blood and yet, I often thought she was but a beautiful dream. Her hands wove a magical blanket of love and protection – they could take away pain and soothe fear. There were no sharp edges to her – no hidden barbs that could inflict injury. I loved to watch her – whatever she was doing, because her every movement was graceful. Her hands fascinated me the most – even at rest they spoke her love, her essence. So too did her eyes – they did not merely look at you – they held you – bathed you in her knowing of you. They let you glimpse something greater and deeper. As a child it pained me that the people of Athanan could not see her. She gave me beautiful stories and songs that would bring peace and sleep to even the most troubled heart. I could swear that all plants and animals turned towards her when she walked by them. More than anything, I loved to watch her dance for it was then she took the voices around her – those of the earth, the forests, the seas and heavens – of all life – even that which is beyond our sight and knowing and she danced its story. Her body became something outside herself and sometimes it frightened me because, as beautiful as it was, it was also when she was lost to me – she was not my mother – she was not of this world."

The warrior paused and looked at Pauroseng. "She danced your song – sometimes she hummed it as she danced – that was how she guided me to Yeshotruen – to you."

Pauroseng smiled. He has just described himself perfectly, she thought. Aloud she said, "And your father, Teilo – what of him?"

"Apheilio was a true man," he began slowly. "Strong, dependable – he lived life as if each moment was a source of wonder. His was a strong passion – a vibrant fire. He knew how to play and be joyful. When I was small, there was nothing more exhilarating than to be held in his strong arms and hear his laughter. He did not have Shimmera's knowing – he looked to her for his wisdom which is why he chose to become a warrior – to find his own way. He was so different from the other men in Athanan – he saw beyond that existence – he looked past the pettiness – he had time only for that which would elevate the spirit. He loved to watch the eagles soar and he would say to me – 'that is what we are meant to do'."

He paused as if lost for a moment in that memory.

"I loved the deep spiralling warmth between my parents," he mused aloud. "I could let myself fall into it and dissolve there. But I feared the unspoken pain between them – as if they knew they had borrowed something that was not to be held."

You are a beautiful statement of them both, Pauroseng thought.

"You were blessed with such parents," she said.

"I was – and I still am," he smiled, "it is a gratitude I hold always. There is something else you wish to ask of me." He had noted the perplexed expression that fleetingly crossed her face.

She nodded. "Do you know of Shimmera's origins?" Her words were almost abrupt. Teilo surprised her by laughing.

"Are you asking if my mother mysteriously walked out of the mist of Avarinsa and was therefore someone to be feared, as the villagers of Athanan believed? Then I can tell you no, Pauroseng, that was not so. On one hand Shimmera was my mother but I cannot deny that she was also an enigma. She simply did not need this existence. It would be easy to think she floated into this world and left the same way. No – I do not know her origins – they are indeed shrouded in mist. She told me only that she had passed through many lands to hold me."

"I believe she came from Yeshotruen." Pauroseng spoke with conviction. "Teilo – I believe I met Shimmera although this realization has only just come to me."

"Tell me," he replied, looking, not at her, but into the glowing embers of the fire.

"I had only just arrived here, ready for my new life as Master of Yeshotruen. O'Daewin was fired with enthusiasm for this new compound and Osarien and I also shared that dream. We believed we would bring change – create another Imoshtan. There was no shortage of men who stepped forward to become warriors but of course no women. It was not the custom in Yeshotruen for women to stand alone. I noticed the child because she had a manner about her that belied her poverty. I assumed she was an orphan – she was always alone and although there were many beggar children who gathered around the compound gates, this one was different. Whenever she saw me, she would fix her eyes on me. They were unwavering. In those days I was a very strong woman and although I could not explain or even admit to it, her stare left me grasping within myself for something to which I could hold. Osarien and I discussed whether or not to feed these waifs but we knew that once we started, more would come. We thought it better to continue with the chosen plan. Given time and patience it would eventually reach into their lives. Gradually they stopped coming – all except for this one child. She was tireless – day after day she stood watching. Then one morning, she came into the compound. I was training warriors. This was my calling and I loved it – it was always a joy in me to share with others that which elevates. The child walked straight to me. She placed the bowl she always carried, at my feet. Then she did the strangest thing. She took the sword from my hands. I did not even attempt to stop her, Teilo – such was her undeniable resolve. Carefully she laid the sword beside the bowl. Her every movement was soft and purposeful. When she looked at me I could not prevent the tears that rushed to my eyes. "*What is it you feed them, Master?*" That was all she said. The feeling of those words in my body and the sight of the bowl and the sword side by side in the dirt can never be justified by explanation and I will not try. The girl walked away and I never saw her again, but my life as I had known it was over."

Teilo was silent. He was lying on his back, eyes closed and Pauroseng waited for a response. When none was forthcoming she persevered.

"You are not surprised, Teilo?"

"No, Pauroseng – I am not." He appeared lost in his own musings and the old Master thought their conversation to be over.

"Nor does it hold meaning for me." He gave her a fleeting smile then rolled onto his side and resumed watching the fire. "That was your knowledge of Shimmera – it does not belong to me – although it explains more fully my being here in Yeshotruen."

"And what of Avarinsa?" she asked. "Do you believe the stories of this place of light?"

He raised his head, propping himself on his elbow, and looked at her.

"We are part of that which creates – therefore we too create. We create illusion in an effort to understand and make sense of what is until we learn to know nothing – only to see what is."

She frowned. "Are you saying Avarinsa is part of that illusion?"

"That which we think it is – yes – that is part of the illusion."

They spoke no further. After a time Teilo placed more wood on the fire.

"Let us sleep now," she advised. "I feel there is much ahead of us tomorrow."

♋

"Do you understand the rituals of the chief warrior, Teilo?"

They had begun the day together in quiet song and now Teilo had just finished his morning dance. Already the air was warm and dry. Pauroseng handed him a cup of sweet tasting tea.

"I do, Pauroseng," he replied, sipping the tea.

"From where does protection come?"

The old warrior was watching him carefully. He knew she wished to ascertain that he did have complete understanding of the powers of a chief warrior. He also knew he could not fool this woman – he could give the expected answers to her questions or he could tell her his own knowing but she would know the difference.

"It is taught that protection comes from the Great Wisdom, but I do not feel that to be so. The Great Wisdom is nothing."

He waited, anticipating a comment from his Master but none came.

"Protection comes through our own surrender," he continued quietly. "Not the surrender that merely speaks our acquiescence to life, but our surrender to death – that which fully renounces life. We must die to the world completely – only then will we go beyond the veil – beyond the illusion. In that state," he hesitated briefly then continued, "I align with the earth and the heavens and evoke the ageless form wherein we melt and gather the many strands of creation into the one vital essence. It then only requires a simple command."

Pauroseng's tea remained untouched. Did this young man fully realize what he had just said?

"Can you do that, Teilo?" she asked

"For protection?" he queried. "I have never done so for that purpose, but it is all the same."

"But you have done this?" she insisted.

"I have," he replied softly.

"You know fully what you are saying?"

He nodded.

"Why have you brought me here, Teilo?"

"That we may heal this land."

"But you do not need me."

He said nothing.

"Of what are you afraid?" she asked.

"Who am I to have this power?"

She was waiting – ready to catch his doubt – his own illusion.

"You do not trust yourself then?"

He did not reply immediately but when he did, it was with quiet deliberation.

"Shimmera gave me the warrior's stone. I did not know of its power or how to use it. I have used it to destroy and to heal. Twice I have stepped outside myself and used that stone without consciously evoking its power. I am not frightened to use it to heal, but I am frightened I will again use it to destroy."

"Did you use it to destroy Mercenta?" she asked sharply.

"No – I simply took his life, but I struggled with it, believe me. There was a point, when I saw his disdain in the suffering of those children and I felt Osarien's life fading – when I knew he was behind me – it was like fighting against a tide to stay present. Had I not struggled, I could have confronted him earlier for I knew he was there, but I didn't – I waited until my only choice was to kill him. Now do you think I should have this power?"

"It is so easy to have hindsight, Teilo – the past is distorted the moment it becomes the past – when we step outside of it. You know this – it is part of your training."

"We are also trained to recall each detail so as to be clear on what we have thought and seen – on how we have acted."

"Then tell me – when you knelt beside Deshan – when you saw the boy's shocking injuries – in that moment what was your choice?"

He frowned.

"You had a choice did you not," she pressed him, "to offer comfort to the boy or to seek negotiation with Mercenta? I know which choice I would have made in those circumstances."

"I waited, Pauroseng. I did not turn to face the man – I did not give him the choice. Had I turned to face him, he may well have surrendered – he knew he could not match my sword."

The old warrior sighed. "You have already told me why you waited, Teilo – you struggled against yourself. I will not give you absolution, my son – only you can do that, but I will counsel you for you walk a very treacherous path and I think you have been here before in the not too distant past. You are treading the same ground and it is not stable. The danger lies in forgetting who you are – your own fallibility and frailty."

"That is what I am talking about."

"No, it is not," she replied emphatically. "You are thinking you are something better than you are – that you should not suffer such ordinary, human frailty. This is the speck of blindness that gives rise in you to your own distrust and fear of yourself. I beg you be still, Master Teilo. You said to me moments ago that the Great Wisdom is nothing – well let me tell you – the warrior's stone is also nothing – it is but a tool. It is your power we speak of here – your power which you fear. I believe you have some contemplation to do. I will see to our food."

He watched her as she set about preparing their meal. Her words were strong in him and he spent a moment in gratitude for this woman with the lamp and the song.

♋

Pauroseng said nothing as he took the warrior's stone from within a folded piece of cloth. He held it in his hands – cupping them around its colour. It had a heat to it but also coolness. Ice and fire, he thought to himself. He waited.

She watched him. He slowed his breath. He stands within the silence, she thought.

Teilo listened for the command he must make – it would come – a whisper without words that promised the earth would no more be neglected – that all life would be sacred. A whisper that became clear and irrefutable.

The unknown words became colours. The warrior could feel the journey of the blood in his veins, then the blood of Pauroseng and that of the trees and the earth around him. Their pulse became one and he took it with him, beyond all awareness, gathering as he went the shards of light like strands of silken hair.

For an eternity there was nothing – then the light burst upon the earth. He was watching again. The ground rippled like waves. A sea was born beneath its crust. From the earth womb a single tree emerged – a giant whose limbs were clothed in the same silken strands. It spread a golden shadow, hungry for the barren space.

The images came – flickering – passing so quickly from one to the next. The gardens – the buildings – his own hands playing with the earth – the blood of Mercenta giving birth to a thousand star-shaped flowers, crimson and rich – the young Jemai standing before him a man – breathing with

Pauroseng her last breaths – Syrath opening a door beyond which a land, more desolate than Yeshotruen, hid from his sight. Before that door closed, he saw the face of Amis – the man with smouldering hatred masking his soul. One by one the images fell until there was nothing save his own breath and the rustling of the leaves above him.

Pauroseng had felt a rushing in her body – then the body was gone save for the beating of a heart – then nothing but yellow ecstasy breaking open until it too receded.

The young Master at last opened his eyes. He dug a small hole with his fingers in the earth. There he buried the warrior's stone and remained in stillness and contemplation until the sun reached the centre of the heavens. Unearthing the stone he replaced it in the cloth and tucked it inside his coat. Then he stretched his body and smiled at the old warrior.

"Now that my purpose here is done, we have an afternoon of pleasurable emptiness," he remarked.

"But my purpose here is not done, Master Teilo," his mentor returned his smile, "for I have a commitment to Romarrah to see your lessons complete."

She placed several small pouches in front of him. He knew they were filled with coloured sand.

"Now – show me the circles," she said. "The three stages of protection, the circle of healing and abundance and the coming of peace and harmony. Symbolise your command for me, Teilo."

As he let the sands fall through his fingers, he guided the colours into shapes interwoven with symbols from ancient times. He felt soothed and rested.

"All warriors should experience the softness of such expression," he murmured. "Their training must be balanced. Dance tempers the harshness of combat but this quiet play ushers such peaceful reflection."

"No doubt it will be done," she smiled. "There are not many wasted thoughts in you, my young Master." She watched the unhurried speed with which his hands fed the dance between the sand and the evolving pictures.

She studied his designs. Inside one circle was a golden warrior with the face of an eagle. "This is not one of the rituals. From where does this image come and what is its direction?"

"It was given to me." He carefully traced a finger along the edge of the sand. "It is protection also, but more than that, it is freedom."

"But why this image?"

"It reminds us that we too have wings – they are far more powerful than the sword. We were born to soar – even in death we must know this freedom. That which keeps us earthbound, is that which cripples our wings."

"What is it that holds us earthbound," she asked

"That which claims us – be it hunger or fear – is that which holds us earthbound."

"What then keeps you earthbound, Teilo?"

"I have chosen this life."

6

Romarrah walked purposefully through the compound gates. He was puzzled by the silence. Instructing the small patrol of warriors accompanying him to seek refreshments in the kitchens, he set off in the direction of Teilo's chambers. Yeshotruen had changed little. It was at least fifteen years since he last walked this land. The compound itself looked tired but there was a sense of quiet expectation within the walls – something was moving and there was definitely a feeling of sanctuary.

He had been surprised to find no guards at the gate but he was even more surprised when he knocked on the door of Teilo's chambers and it was opened by a surly faced child who showed little respect or courtesy. The child's mother appeared and it was obvious by her dress and features that she was from the south of the land. Even though she bowed to Romarrah, there remained a thinly concealed uneasiness about her.

"We did not know you were coming, Master," she said politely but without warmth. She was a very attractive woman but she held herself aloof – an attitude Romarrah sensed she had practiced for a long time. Aware of the Master's confusion at her presence, she put his mind immediately at rest. "Master Teilo does not stay within the compound at present. He has his chambers not far from the front gates. Would you wish me to have someone escort you there?"

"My gratitude to you, good woman," he responded, "but I will find my own way." He bowed to Allencia and left the building.

Once in the courtyard, he made his way to the kitchens. Freyora was there with her children. She had been a little flustered when the warriors arrived, interrupting her usual preparations. Now, on seeing the Great Master himself, her discomfort grew.

Deshan remembered all Teilo had taught him and bowed to Romarrah. Without being asked, he volunteered his services. "Master Teilo is away with Pauroseng, Master," he began, "but I can fetch him if you wish. Master Ortarian has taken the warriors to work on the water channels and garden beds and my father Andeysen has gone with them. I am Deshan and I am training to be a warrior also but Master Teilo said I could not do any work until my hand is fully healed."

Romarrah's eyes twinkled with amusement. "Very well, Deshan – perhaps you would be kind enough to escort me to Master Teilo's chambers. I trust there I will find food and refreshment."

"It would be best Master if you took some supplies with you," Freyora spoke nervously. "Master Teilo usually eats with us, in the kitchen."

The woman and her daughter hastily prepared a basket.

Inside the building that Teilo had obviously commandeered, Romarrah removed his sword and poured himself some of the tea Freyora had included in his supplies. So what is this young man up to, he wondered. He opened the book lying on the table. He too beheld pages of illustrations, diagrams and notes. The work was most admirable – even outstanding, but it made him groan to see what Teilo was proposing. It was nothing short of preposterous to think all this could be achieved. Why could he not simply train warriors?

Glancing around at the neat but sparse surroundings, he wondered to whom this building belonged. And where had Teilo gone with Pauroseng? No doubt all would be revealed in due course.

Deshan did not return to the compound but set off in the direction he knew Teilo and Pauroseng had taken three days previously. They would by now be making their return journey and he wished to be the first to tell Teilo of Romarrah's arrival. The Great Master's coming to Yeshotruen was cause indeed for excitement.

The boy ran and when he could no longer run, he walked quickly until he was out of breath. Resting in the shade of a large boulder, he viewed the land around him – a landscape of sameness – without interruption, except for the boulders strewn across its surface. It was so quiet away from the city. Not since the day he had been attacked had he ventured from the compound on his own – nor had he been alone. At first he felt quite content and peaceful but without warning, he began to feel anxious. There is no reason to be frightened, he told himself.

As Teilo had requested, the meeting with his attackers had taken place. They had begged his forgiveness and he knew they were sincere. He had to some extent been embarrassed by their remorse. They would not harm him again. There was no danger – he could see in all directions – nothing moved, but still the fear persisted. It was closing in – something terrible was going to happen – he could feel it.

He saw his family – murdered – their bodies cut to pieces. He saw Teilo lying in the dirt, blood draining from a large gash across his torso. Deshan began to panic and the panic seized him, constricting the muscles of his throat – turning his body to lead. He screamed. He curled himself into a rigid ball on the earth, as if to protect himself, and again screamed into his own tightened terror. When the terror subsided, he wept – his body limp and exhausted but the sobbing was uncontrollable.

Teilo was suddenly beside him – his arms were around him. The boy clung to the Master desperately. The warrior said nothing, waiting until the crying was done.

"Tell me they are not going to die, Master Teilo," Deshan's voice was distraught. "Tell me you are not going to die."

Teilo frowned. "Deshan death is a part of life – what has happened here?"

The boy told of his fear – the visions – premonitions of what was to come – the terror of them stalked his words. Teilo listened then offered him some water.

"They were not premonitions, Deshan," he said soothingly. "They were your fears."

"But I saw them," the boy insisted.

"I know you did son, but understand they were not real. No – wait," he said as Deshan made to argue, "let me speak. You were beaten, Deshan – by men – not by people your own age, which would have been bad enough, but by men – by those who should protect you. Such actions strip away our sense of ourself and our stability – they create their own fears in us by making us feel helpless, or even that we may have deserved such persecution – as if we are to blame. Here you found yourself alone – without the protection of the compound, your family or myself. Your fears became panic. Do not hang your head – there is no shame in what you feel. Your images were your fear of losing those you love – those who reflect your own goodness and who offer you protection."

"But you see things and you know them to be true – you have come to me now, Master Teilo because you knew of my distress."

"There is a difference. You will learn this difference as a warrior. You will separate your fear from your knowing. Be very clear on this, Deshan – true knowing does not arise from fear – it can only arise from clarity. It is your imagination that assists you in your knowing and yours is beginning to open. Be patient – in time you will learn to use it well. Now tell me – what were you doing out here?"

"I came to tell you, Master Teilo," the boy brightened as he remembered his mission, "Romarrah has come."

Teilo groaned. "Now it is my turn to sob. I do not feel prepared for this visit."

Deshan laughed. "I like it when you are like that."

"You mean miserable?" Teilo looked at him with amusement.

"No – when you are no different than I am."

The warrior smiled, then stood and extended his hand. "Come, my young mentor – I have left Pauroseng resting – we must go back to her."

Romarrah's presence at Yeshotruen did not surprise him – he had already experienced a sense of it but now he smiled to himself. The Great Master must have kept his energy tightly contained so as to give out no hint of his arrival – surprise is after all the first advantage of combat. Bless you Romarrah, he thought, I do love our friendship. He laughed and ruffled Deshan's hair. The boy looked at him puzzled. "It is nothing, Deshan – I am laughing with myself – I am glad you came to meet me."

♋

"My purpose in coming is threefold," Romarrah explained after he had greeted Teilo and Pauroseng.

They were all seated, Ortarian included, in Teilo's chambers.

"Of course I wished to see for myself your progress here and how all the materials and supplies that have been sent from Imoshtan were being utilized. Of this we shall talk later. Secondly, I desired to spend some time with Pauroseng and Ortarian. I was deeply grieved at Osarien's passing and the manner in which he died. My third reason, Teilo, was to present you with your sword myself."

"My sword?"

"The sword of a chief warrior," Romarrah clarified. "Pauroseng sent word some time ago that you had completed your studies and had full understanding of the rituals. You must therefore receive the sword as is the custom."

Teilo glanced at Pauroseng. Her face was a blank mask. Ortarian's eyes showed initial surprise. He briefly looked at Teilo with almost quizzical amusement.

Romarrah missed nothing. If there was one thing he excelled at, it was his perception of the feelings of others, reflected, however fleetingly, in their expressions.

It was clear to everyone in the room that the Great Master had arrived and he had assumed control.

"What is your own appraisal of your work in Yeshotruen, Teilo?" he asked when the two were at last alone.

Inwardly Teilo groaned. "It would be better if tomorrow you walked with me through the day, Romarrah – you will see for yourself how we progress."

"My question was - what do you feel you have achieved so far. You are not pleased with my being here. Do you think I am here to judge you – that I have come purely to find fault?"

"I am not displeased at seeing you, Romarrah. If I am to speak openly then I must say your visit is an interruption – it takes me away from where I feel I must be at this time, but I am not holding resentment. Nor do I think you are here to find fault, although I feel already that I will not have your approval of what happens at Yeshotruen."

"I merely wish, at this point, to have an understanding of what does happen here. Let us begin again – tell me of your perceptions of this land and its people – what has happened here since your arrival?"

Teilo related his first impressions of the city and as he talked Romarrah took time to make his own appraisal of the man himself – for it was a man who stood before him. The golden, joyful youth was still evident in the smile and laughter and he had not lost his gentle way of being, or the charisma that spread his presence into any room, into any crowd. But, he was a man – strong, independent, confident and knowing, but more than that, Teilo was completely willing to give of himself – to bear responsibility – to commit himself wholeheartedly. He was now briefly describing the series of events that led to the death of Osarien and Romarrah interrupted him.

"What has become of his attackers?"

"They remain here – at the compound – they follow my instructions and pose no threat."

"Do you think that wise? Do you not see fit to impose some form of punishment? They brutalized defenceless children and killed an unarmed warrior. I have seen men forfeit their lives for crimes such as these. Are you certain that such leniency will not be seen to condone the lawlessness of this place?"

Teilo shook his head. "That lawlessness of which you speak exists with or without my intervention – it is born of a brutality to which I have no desire to contribute further. No doubt you would have me send these men to Manon. I know little of that place but I do not feel that banishing those who offend us is of benefit – it is but convenient. It simply removes them from our sight – their deeds become the food of furtive gossip – the pain they leave behind plants its own seeds of despair and is rarely addressed. Everything is then hidden and the perpetrator becomes a victim of another kind. I have spent time with these men – they have their own stories of sadness and separation. They have openly asked forgiveness of those they have injured. Here we offer them a way to atone for their transgressions and they now give their time for the betterment of others. It is a solution with which I feel comfortable."

"That is all very well, Teilo, but what happens when you are no longer here? You have the ability to reconcile people with their feelings and actions – not everyone has your skills – nor can they invest the time you do in such matters – nor can you, I might add, sustain such effort – it becomes too much for one person. Laws are put in place for the good of all. If we adhere to those laws, we ensure the same standard for everyone. Do you not see that what is the right way for you is not the right way for another?"

"That is precisely what I do see, Romarrah, but be that as it may, these laws you talk of – do they not impose a limit on the depth of our understanding. If these men of whom we speak develop their own understanding, then I no longer work alone. When the people of Yeshotruen have a purpose whereby they glimpse a better way of being, then it becomes for them possible to embrace their wisdom. This in turn gives them the responsibility of their knowing – it is no longer mine. You have seen the proposed work," Teilo indicated the book containing his plans for Yeshotruen. "I know without asking that you believe it far too ambitious an undertaking. You wish for me to train warriors only – to introduce but a few to a privileged way of being, but I cannot do one without the other. I had hoped that by the time you chose to visit, I would have more order and structure in place and that perhaps you could gain a sense of what will happen here – for it will happen Romarrah – have no doubt of that. Pauroseng," here he suddenly stopped and changed the subject. "Forgive me – I have not yet offered you tea."

"I have taken refreshments," the Great Master smiled, "and you do not have to protect Pauroseng – I too know the grit of her remember – she is very capable of defending herself. I am aware of what she does here. You did in fact have my sympathy being the one charged with bringing change to Yeshotruen. First you and she would have to find a common ground. Seeing you both have difficulty adhering to certain laws and traditions, I thought this would unite you both. I trust you really have completed the rituals of a chief warrior?"

"I have," Teilo laughed.

"Then let us talk no more. Tomorrow I will walk with you as you wish and see for myself what happens here."

The following day, Romarrah accompanied Teilo. He asked no questions – he simply watched. Their day began in the warrior's sanctuary. He could feel the peace of this room. As it should, it spoke of prayer and the quietness of being. It therefore came as a surprise when not only the warriors but the women and children of the compound entered the room and found a space to sit. When Teilo began to sing men women and children joined in although there were some who remained silent.

At first the singing disturbed Romarrah – the mixture of voices – but gradually it flowed around him, guiding him back into his stillness.

After morning devotion the warriors assembled in the courtyard. They carried no swords. They had come to dance – there was no other word to describe their movements. They mirrored Teilo for perhaps an hour or more as if in a trance. There was no sound, save for the soft scrunching of the earth beneath their feet and even that was muffled. The movements became more vigorous, exacting and individual. It was obvious the more recent apprentices had difficulty keeping up yet, the overall impression was one of lightness, strength and purpose.

With the dance complete, the men and women strapped on their swords. Quietly Teilo gave directions to the new warriors from Imoshtan on how to conduct the remainder of the training. Deshan who had been with the group until this point now followed Teilo and Romarrah as they walked towards the hospice.

Within this building, Pauroseng moved quietly among her patients. She nodded to Romarrah and Teilo but she did not speak. Here she was completely absorbed in her ministry. Deshan went straight to Kesten while Teilo spoke with many of the ill and dying as he cleansed and bandaged wounds – sometimes laughing with someone – even, as happened on this day an old man who was awaiting death.

"We cannot be too serious about death can we, Master Teilo?" he spoke in a weak, rasping voice.

"That is true, Okara," the young Master replied, "it may put us off our living." Seriously he added, "Stay with your peace, my friend," and kissed the man's forehead.

The next building, also originally intended as warrior's quarters, housed women and children. The women had begun their day of cloth making but many were oiling and waxing very large pieces of coarse fabric. Teilo inspected their work. He explained to Romarrah that this cloth would be sewn together to form a large water resistant pouch. The pouch, attached to the end of a long beam, would be lowered on pulleys into the well. When the full pouch was raised, the beam, itself attached to a pivot, would then be swung away from the well and the sack of water emptied into a main irrigation channel. From here it would flow into smaller causeways and, finally, irrigate the fields and gardens. The Great Master could not help being impressed.

In the afternoon, the warriors and others from the compound worked on the same irrigation channels. Romarrah observed their work for some time then sought out Pauroseng.

The old Master was at rest in her room. The door was open. He noticed the pallor of her skin contrasting greatly with the darkness beneath her eyes. As he turned to leave, she spoke.

"I am not asleep, Romarrah – I am only resting – please come in and sit with me." She smiled at him as she eased herself into an upright position. She was very fond of this man – he could almost have been her son for he had spent much of his youth under her tuition and guidance.

They exchanged a few pleasantries and he shared his impressions of the day. She listened to the current of confusion that ran beneath his words.

"Romarrah, I will say this to you as an old woman who knows you very well. I am proud of what you did today. You gave Teilo your humility and that is the greatest gift you could have given him."

"He does not welcome my questions," he sighed.

"Nor does he welcome Ortarian's," Pauroseng replied. "You and my son are very alike – you both question Teilo with your doubt already on your lips. You would do much better to ask him of his own. This young man does not hide, Romarrah – his honesty is unpolished – like a child. Nor should you question his understanding of the rituals – he has moved far beyond that which we know, yet he is still a fledgling to his own power.

There will come a time, and I tell you this for your own safety, when you must let him go – you are not his Master – he will respect you always but he will not choose the way of Romarrah over what he knows in his heart."

He was momentarily stunned by her words. He grappled with their content.

"Pauroseng," he began, "I do not hold this young man. Already I have given him his own lead. Eventually I must choose a successor and at this point, no one comes even close to Teilo. Certainly there could be many years before this is so – much can come to pass in that time, but if I keep Teilo close it is for this reason."

"And if that is not his wish?" she queried.

"How could it not be his wish – he is born to lead? He is too powerful to stand back. I have seen his power – believe me it is a dangerous thing and must be guided."

"That may be so, but you cannot guide it, Romarrah. It is not within your own power to do so. It is not Teilo for whom I fear – it is you – all things must change." She stopped short of saying 'even the Great Wisdom'.

"Think on what I have said," she murmured. "You are a good leader – a good man. I know you have always doubted yourself – this in turn gives rise to your withholding of your self. Imoshtan has flourished under your rule as I knew it would and it is largely because of you that this young man stands where he does today. He loves you, Romarrah, but not as a father, which I think you would like, and not in the way the aspirant loves his Master and this, I feel, is what you really want from him. He loves you for the man you are – not in spite of the man you are but because of the man you are and that is far more honest."

"It is you who should have been Romarrah, not I," the Great Master shook his head.

Pauroseng smiled. "That is not the way of the Land as we both know – perhaps one day that might change but that kind of change usually comes at a cost. Give Teilo your friendship and support – it will be what is best for both of you."

"I am grateful for your counsel, Master," he bowed. "There is just one other matter. I can see your health is frailer now and I would urge you to come back to Imoshtan where you will have more comfort and peace. Why is it a stranger lives in the Master's chambers while you have this room which is far from adequate?"

"Because it is my wish – just as it is my wish to stay in Yeshotruen. I am in peace here and I am in the very best of hands." She smiled. "But do take

Ortarian with you. He stays because of his loyalty to his father and myself and because Teilo asked him, but it is not his place. Master Teilo may be a little put out at his leaving but Ortarian is not here for the right reasons. Teilo will compensate for his absence."

Ortarian returned to Imoshtan with Romarrah – relieved of a burden that was not his to hold. Teilo challenged this change to his plans.
"You cannot have everything the way you wish it," Pauroseng was quick to point out. "You knew Ortarian did not belong here, Teilo – do not tell me you could not see that. It was your need that kept him here, not his. You will still have Allencia to teach the children and you will give her what she most needs – her freedom."
He did not question her judgement – he simply bowed to his Master's wisdom.

The third stone arrived with Romarrah. He handed the parcel to his daughter without a word. Immediately she observed his sober mood – his pensive air. What part of himself had he left behind in Yeshotruen, she wondered – something which now haunted him and stole his harmony.
Her pleasure at seeing Ortarian was also tempered by the sombre feeling that part of her father was lost – the part that had no name – an intangible spark that spoke of things noble – almost consecrated – and it was crumbling within him.
She had so many questions about Teilo and Yeshotruen but she knew better than to ask them at this time. She took her letter into the peace of the orchard. There she read of the third stone – the stone of illusion and gazed upon a beautiful painting of a lone tree, surrounded by desert, hung with strands of golden, flowing hair. It was a symbol of feminine essence, bleeding its fertility into the earth. Above the tree a sword hung suspended and below the earth, coiled among the roots of this giant, lay a sleeping serpent.
Syrath looked at the picture for a long time – it gave her equally a sense of joy and awe. This time Teilo had written her a letter so bare and touching it was almost too painful to read.

My dear friend, sometimes the thought of you leads me to peace and I am almost fearful to go there. There is a sadness in giving love and hope to the sick and dying;

of raising the spirits of those who know only despair and persecution; for by the actions of one hand, the other hand delivers a blow to those who live with such love and goodness in their hearts. I cannot be other than who I am. If I allowed myself to be fully absorbed by that which is – therein I would no longer exist; therein there is no purpose, no history, no obligation. But that is not yet to be and I am given this which is before me.

I know of you in the quiet times; you are as that soft flower which floats upon the water in my dreams and you give your peace softly, without desire for return.

I see the days before me as being long. I do not say this in despair, it simply is and I shall not return to Imoshtan for many years. In your letters you speak of your work there with such contentment and I take pleasure in knowing of your quiet, graceful existence.

Here he had left a space after which he had written:

> *Shadows are unknown*
> *in darkness*
> *as a flame is unseen*
> *in the bright light of day*

Can you hear the laughter in these words? Is it not the irony of life? All life oscillates between the two until we see through the illusion. Know this stone well, dear friend, feel its secret. Stay within your peace. May it continue to refresh my dreams.

She sat for a long time, nursing his words and the third stone, when suddenly a vision shattered her stillness. It was of a hand – casting the stones upon the ground – pointing at the third stone as if there she might see something. But it was the hand that captivated Syrath – meek, unresisting – a life hidden from the world. She longed to touch it – just this once, but as her heart reached out to take it, the vision disappeared. She knew it was her mother's hand – speaking to her through the stone – not a vision that was lost in time – it was of now. Syrath's sight had returned. Teilo had known something in these stones that she had not felt until now. Her mother still lived and breathed on this earth. The air rushed into her lungs – fresh and tingling.

Daylight had faded but still she sat waiting until all of what she had seen was absorbed in her. This must be her mystery alone – she could not share it with Romarrah or even Ortarian. Teilo would keep sending her the stones and she would read her answers within them.

Closing her eyes, she sent her peace and gratitude to her friend – watching it travel the distance between them like a bird carried by the wind.

7

"That is unfair, Deshan – I cannot move with ease as you do."

Kesten was frustrated. His leg only hindered his practice.

Deshan stopped reluctantly. "I will go slower then."

Teilo smiled at the conversation. Both had changed dramatically in the past three years. Deshan was taller and although he had always been lean, now his leanness was strong and athletic – his body was shaping itself towards manhood. Kesten had also grown taller and no doubt stronger, but he was still a child and too young to train as a warrior. Nevertheless, he had pestered Teilo so much that the Master finally permitted him to train with Deshan of an afternoon, when the day's work was done.

The young Master enjoyed this time of day for it brought with it a sense of peace. He was free to work in the gardens or wander further afield planting seeds. The children from the compound would play in the water channels, often having mud fights which the Master would sometimes join in for the sheer joy of it. Their delight each time they managed to hit him with a ball of mud erupted in a chorus of squeals and laughter of which he never tired.

On very hot days, he would indulge them by emptying a sack of water into the channel – the novelty of so much after so little never staled.

The rains had at last come back to Yeshotruen as he knew they would. The seeds he had planted were now young trees – some saplings as tall as he. The gardens within the compound thrived, producing enough food for those within its walls and at the hospice. Whatever remained, the women traded at the market place.

One hundred and sixty men and women lived within the warrior's quarters – five of those had come from Imoshtan to assist him with training.

"Kesten," Teilo spoke from where he was working in the garden. "Your opponent will not make allowances for your lameness. You must learn to use it to your advantage."

"That is impossible, Master Teilo – I cannot move fast enough – I have no advantage."

The Master stood up, washed his hands in a trough of water, and strapped on his sword.

"Deshan, come – let us play. Kesten watch and tell me what you see."

Deshan loved to spar with Teilo. The Master made it so much fun. He played a game but through that game, he lifted the trainees to another level of expertise. The pair bowed to each other and raised their swords.

Deshan fought hard and he worked at co-ordinating his moves – being light – allowing his breath to guide him and hold him steady. He was a good student. But this time Teilo played the game differently. The moves were the same but tighter and he dictated the range of his opponents movements. His body still danced but the dance was contained.

"Well played," he said to Deshan, calling a halt to their play. He turned to the boy. "What did you see, Kesten?"

"You were quieter," the boy replied.

"And?" Teilo raised his eyebrows.

"You made Deshan work harder."

"What else did you see?"

"You worked mostly off one leg?"

"Correct – I mimicked your lameness. Did it seem to you that I was disadvantaged? You must move to your own body – not try to emulate those around you, when for you, that is impossible. This part of you that is maimed, is every bit as whole as the rest of you – it is only different – remember that. If you perceive it as a disadvantage then that it will be forever more – it is only the body and the body is guided by the spirit. Spend more time in dance, son – with your eyes closed. Practice feeling where movement comes from in you and where it needs to travel in your body – that alone will make you stronger and more powerful." He ruffled the boy's hair. "Be gone the two of you – it is late – the warriors will already be in the kitchens."

He watched them go – their voices flowing back to him in the stillness of late afternoon. The sun was almost gone and the soft colours graced the earth with a feeling of calm.

There are moments in the tide of a lifetime that hold perfection for no longer than one can hold breath, he mused watching all around him. The breeze just touched the small forest of trees and the smell of fresh turned earth spread its dampness into the evening air. He delighted in that smell for it replaced that of the tired dryness which greeted him when he first came to Yeshotruen. The earth was breathing deeply again. When he dug his fingers into the soil, he felt life begging to play and his hands did play. Something shifted in him when he caressed the soil – something moved aside to make way for a communion between his body, the air, the breath of the plants, the earth spirits – combined they formed a rhythm that kept beat with the sacredness of all.

For some weeks now he had allowed himself, the warriors and other willing workers, a time of rest. The first stage of his plans was complete and functioning well. Everyone had worked hard to ensure its success. There were now enough people working at the compound to spread responsibility and lighten the burden for those who had shouldered it for so long.

The hospice had been built on Mercenta's land. Not far from this building was another where Allencia lived with her son, Cencian. It was here the children learnt to read and write – to understand their way of life and explore their own knowing. Between the two buildings, Teilo had planted groves of fruit trees and gardens of herbs.

The Master again lived in his chambers within the compound. He spent more time than ever with Pauroseng. They prayed and sang together, discussed the threads of each day and sat in contemplation. The old warrior daily visited the hospice for several hours and that was her only duty. Teilo prepared her meals – as Osarien had done – combining different herbs and foods to hold her health as steady as possible. Even so her frailty grew with each passing year although the life force within her stayed strong. Teilo knew she would be with them for some time yet.

"You are restless," she said to him that night after they had shared their meal.

"Pauroseng I have not moved," he laughed, but he knew she did not refer to a physical restlessness.

"What is it you are planning now? Or is it that you wish to visit Allencia?"

He looked at her fully then. There was no mistaking the inference of those words. That is better, she thought, now I have your complete attention.

"What is it you are questioning," he asked quietly, "my integrity as a man, or as a chief warrior?"

"I thought they were one and the same," she replied with a smile that he had learned preceded a challenge of some kind. She sat with her hands on her lap – one folded over the other. When he looked at those hands he was reminded of infinite patience – the kind that never tires of waiting.

"That would depend on one's perception," he answered. "A chief warrior is a title and with that title comes certain conditions – and in some cases impositions. A man is not his title and therefore must follow what he knows to be right in his heart, rather than that which is dictated."

The old Master interjected. "Some men have wrong intentions in their hearts."

"No," he insisted, "they have the wrong intention in their minds, Pauroseng – our essence is all one and the same – it is one of goodness. It is the mind that places intent. If there is no clarity, intent usually arises from fear or desire – longing or loathing."

"So it is not loathing that takes you to Allencia's rooms of an evening – one might then assume it is longing."

"One should never make assumptions," he retorted.

"I have not made an assumption, Teilo, I am merely assuming – there is a difference. One implies the truth of a situation while the other merely considers the consequences of a possible situation."

He smiled at her sharpness.

"She is a beautiful woman," Pauroseng continued. "She is also intelligent and older than yourself. That gives her a most beguiling quality but her own longing is for the love and tenderness of which for so long she has been deprived."

"Do you think I am unaware of all this?" his voice betrayed irritation.

Good, she thought, now I have rattled you.

"Forgive me, Teilo – I intended no condescension but you are a man and that has nothing to do with being a chief warrior. Nor do I have judgement on your relationships with others, regardless of Romarrah's decree – that is for you to decide. I only ask that you be very clear on this. It is times like this, when all is well, that we need to take care – you have too much at stake."

Teilo had no intention of leaving his chambers that night but he reflected on Pauroseng's words and his relationship with Allencia.

Their friendship had begun slowly. When Ortarian left it fell entirely to Allencia to be with the children. The Master met with her often to discuss such matters. At first it was Cencian who commanded his attention. Never had he met a child with such wilful hatred and disregard, but it was a hatred that was learned rather than truly experienced. The boy would call his mother insulting names and spit at her if she requested anything from him, or did not immediately supply his needs. He treated the Master with contempt and whenever the warrior came to their chambers the boy was surly and unresponsive.

Apart from an initial greeting, Teilo did not engage with him – he neither reprimanded him for his appalling conduct towards his mother, nor spoke to him of his angry brooding.

"I would have thought a Master such as your self would not tolerate this behaviour," Allencia said one night after her son had behaved disgracefully in Teilo's presence.

"Would you have me chastise the child, Allencia? Engage him in a battle of wills? To what purpose? You cannot force anyone to behave as you would have them behave. How can you break down aggression with more of the same? If you beat him, you will add to the scars he already carries."

"I do not know what else to do," she answered tearfully. "He refuses my love – my affection."

"He simply does not understand his own love and affection," Teilo responded. "It is not refusal – just as he does not even understand his own anger. If, as you have told me, Mercenta guarded him jealously and took him everywhere with him, then he has learned Mercenta's way of being – that is all – but beneath that crust there lies the innocent child you suckled. Have no fear – that child still exists."

He would watch Cencian and the boy was aware of the man's eyes upon him. Whenever he met the warrior's look, it never held frustration or disapproval, yet it silenced him.

One evening as the boy was nearly asleep, the Master sat close by and sang him a song. Cencian pretended to be no longer awake but he was listening to the words and they gathered him – they took him flying over mountains and valleys – through forests and oceans. The next time he visited, Teilo told a story of the forest.

Again Cencian feigned sleep, but he was there – among the trees. He heard the earth spirits as they played – he felt the heart-beat of a giant tree and a feeling of excitement stirred in him – an excitement for something he did not yet know.

There came a night when the Master gently ran his hand through the boy's hair. Cencian felt the tightness of his skin soften. Warmth spread through his body – nothing stirred in him – everything went quiet inside.

Gradually the relationship expanded. They would exchange words – Teilo would draw pictures for him. If Cencian conducted himself badly, especially towards his mother, the Master would say nothing – he would simply withdraw himself and watch the boy, as if from a distance.

Soon it was not unusual for Cencian to fall asleep in the Master's arms.

"You have endless patience," Allencia had commented one recent evening as he covered the sleeping child with a blanket.

"He deserves no less," he smiled at the sleeping face. "The child's world is one of wonder which we are privileged to share. We have no right to rob them of that wonderment. Forgive me, Allencia," he added when he looked up and saw her tears, "I intended no judgement of yourself.'

She shook her head. "It is the pain of the life I brought my children into – that is what grieves me. I do not know how to heal this pain – nor the dreadful ache of loss. You have spoken to me of forgiveness, but does that take away the numbness which lives within me? I think not – how can that grief ever be dissolved?"

"Only you can make that choice," he replied gently. "It is a matter for your own willingness and knowing the right time. I beg you – do not treat yourself so harshly – it is undeserved."

Spontaneously he had held her and straight away he knew he had been caught off guard.

Their friendship was one of ease. Allencia was not a warrior and she was at once, from their very first meeting, familiar to him. He had allowed himself the comfort of her presence. At the end of a long day, he could sit with her and talk. There was a peace in her company. Perhaps, in some part of him, there was a vague, nostalgic connection with his own childhood – the evenings of togetherness with Shimmera and Apheilio – the quiet conversations spun like soft webs around their isolation.

So occupied had he now become with the shaping of the compound at Yeshotruen – the constant details, requests and duties to which he spent his day attending, he failed to notice this soft attachment curling its tendrils into a strong coil around the framework of his daily life.

Now when he had called this period of rest, when he allowed himself a small reprieve to take in where he now stood, he did not expect to become present to such strong feelings.

That night he had gently disengaged himself from their embrace. He could see Allencia struggled with her emotions but she quickly retreated into her privacy. Composed, she resorted to formality so as to stay hidden.

"It is late I fear, Master Teilo – I must see to my work for the morrow."

As he walked back to his chambers, he could still feel the heat of her embrace within him. There were too many frayed threads of conflict in this situation. He needed to be alone – to sit in contemplation and let his vision clear.

He had not been back to her home since. A week had passed since Pauroseng had once again opened the door on his dilemma. He had looked at the situation from every different perspective – his, Allencia's, Cencian's – from the view of a chief warrior, a man – the Master of Yeshotruen. There was not one angle he had left unexplored. Romarrah's decree meant nothing to him – it was but a human law and it served to mask the Master's own pain and helplessness at the loss of Tharease.

This physical knowing of another meant something different in Yeshotruen than it did in Imoshtan. Here it held some form of possession – it implied dominance or power of a man over a woman. It could be an aggressive and, at worst, a demeaning act. Yet the women of this land also used it in a similar way to gain some sense of status or identity. It gave rise to jealousy and mistrust.

In Imoshtan, physical knowing of another had different layers of meaning. One was mutual light-hearted play that was nevertheless based on respect and understanding. Another was born of mutual love and commitment that could signify the welcoming of a child – for a child could only be welcomed into the world – there could be no regret, no resentment present at its birth. Both man and woman would offer this child love, protection and guidance. They need not live as a family but the giving of themselves to the child was unconditional. There were those who believed that any physical knowing would give rise to suffering and this form of love or expression was best mastered and its essence given to contemplative devotion.

There was another path of which Teilo was aware. When two people used this knowing to replenish the colours of one or each other's existence. It was not play – nor was it the love that seeks continuity. It came from the purest essence – not within, but without – summoned like a prayerful song from the depths of creation. It was used to elevate, to heal, and to restore but it carried no longing or desire being born only of surrender and humility. He understood this – he had first known it in Maurapin – in the love Syrath had given him. It was true that at later times, he had experienced a more physical desire for her, but that path would have destroyed what they held of each other.

With Allencia he must not create longing or attachment – herein lay the greatest danger. Her spirit was already too bruised to hold the pain of such impermanence. The moment he had held her he had felt the crying of her soul – like a beggar pleading, not for food, but for a tender knowing of herself – to heal that part of her woman that had been torn and cast aside. At first he was confused by his own sense of desire but that was fleeting – it did not torment his thoughts with visions and fantasy. It was but a physical reaction to something much stronger.

In his heart the voice urged him to go to her. Still he hesitated. He did not want to feel even a whisper of unwanted sorrow hiding in some grey, burdened picture that he had failed to truly see.

♋

In that space,
between the many quarrels
of dislike and longing, 'tis empty;
but perhaps for the smallest tension
which hangs like a spider's thread;
attached, a quivering leaf awaits;
it knows the flight must come.

The fourth stone, my dearest friend, is the stone of choice. We fail to understand the play of human existence. We place our understanding on ancient teachings and myths. We become lost in debates and philosophical discourse. Such teachings are written mostly by those wise people who would seek to give us guidance, yet they cannot give us knowing. That comes from the choices we make; the steps we take; the silence we court. This stone tells us we are at a crossroads and must become steady. We must know the treasure of waiting. This is not the choice of instinct and survival; it is the choice that takes us beyond instinct, beyond survival. Not a choice that creates separation, loss or gain but the choice that realizes complete union.

Stand in the sun, Syrath, and look at the colours of this stone; they gather light just as all the choices we make must gather light as a consequence. This stone tells me there is in you the longing to find freedom; for yourself and the mother who is within you. My love for you could not be stronger than now when I hold this stone and feel your origins upon it.

The picture Teilo had drawn was endless. It depicted a man and a woman – naked – at one with their purity. Between them flowed a stream but it did not separate them. Around them a forest grew and at their feet were the crumbled ruins of a city over which the water flowed joyously. From the ruins a child was taking an overflowing cup and in the distance, barely discernable, stood a figure holding a lamp.

She smiled. Now Yeshotruen was nearly independent from Imoshtan, he had not written to her for such a long time and she saw instantly how different their worlds had become.

The afternoon sun was weak but brought such mellow tones to her surroundings. Here in the orchard it leant the softest yellow light to a verdant green background. She could hear the stream – it always seemed quieter of an evening – as if it too was subdued by the restful tones around it. How effortless to stay in peace.

Suddenly she frowned. All was not well in the Land of Romarrah. In her heart she knew this to be so. Should she send word to Teilo of her concerns? The conflict within the villages along the western border was a growing aggravation. Sometimes she felt as if the earth shifted beneath her – yet all remained still – the cause of her trepidation was indefinable.

Romarrah was not overly worried. "There are always small periods of unrest, Syrath. If it will set your mind at peace we will increase patrols."

But it did not set her mind at peace. A cloud still hovered – lonely and dark.

She must wait – Teilo had enough choices to make.

♋

In the end it was Allencia who came to him.

When he opened the door she stood before him with a host of questions in her eyes.

"Allencia," he began but she interrupted.

"Forgive me for coming unannounced to your chambers – I fear it will be considered improper but you have avoided seeing me and I must clarify what may be your mistaken perceptions of my self." Seeing the amusement in his eyes she added, "You laugh at me, Master Teilo?"

"I do not laugh at you, Allencia," he said, shaking his head. "I was wondering when you would draw breath. You have no need to seek my forgiveness – there is no impropriety in your being here. I am indeed happy to see you. Nor have I been avoiding you – I have simply been giving myself time to seek clarity regarding my relationship with you."

His candour – the fact that he could speak without evasiveness, surprised her.

"It is not something to be hidden, is it?" he asked, noting her surprise. "Pray tell me of my mistaken views."

He gave her that look that made her shiver. There would be no masks with this man – not his own or those others hid behind. He looked straight through them. He himself was so bare of disguise. Sometimes it was all she could do to hold his gaze.

She felt more at ease now. This was not a battle. It was as it always was with him – calm – without secrets.

"Teilo, I fear you see me as someone who wishes to cling to your kindness – someone who is lost and far from their own understanding. You have met me at a time in my life when I am at last free to feel my grief – to search for a way to restore my dignity. That I struggle with this is not because I am perhaps incapable of doing so – of mending the brokenness of my life – but because at times, I feel so bereft and alone. You may think of me as damaged because I allowed you to see the depth of my pain, but I was not asking you to heal it. Nor do I want from you pity, or enduring commitment. I will stand alone – I only longed.."

She faltered. This time he did not hesitate to hold her – to let her feel the love of his arms around her.

"Let me tell you my perceptions of you, Allencia," he said softly. "I am certain that they are not mistaken. You have never lost yourself – your understanding or your dignity. It is that which has held you so that you could endure unspeakable suffering. I do not look at you and feel pity – I look at you and feel love. I admire your courage and strength."

He lifted her face that she might look at him. "Your struggle does not demean you in my eyes, nor do I see you as damaged – to the contrary. I see you as having the same beauty and wholeness as my own soul – as any soul and the only commitment I will make to you, is to honour you – and that is enduring."

He felt her body surrender its lonely agony and he took it from her. When they lay together, from him she knew no claim or demand – no expectation – only the most sacred, tender love of all human expression.

"You have mastered your quandary, I see," Pauroseng spoke some days later as she watched him preparing their evening meal.

Teilo said nothing. There was a weight in the space between them.

"Is there something else you wish to say to me, Pauroseng?" he asked, still concentrating on the task before him.

"No," she responded slowly.

He frowned to himself – what am I hearing, he thought and turned to look at her.

"Do you wish to reproach me?"

"The world does not turn around you, Master Teilo," she smiled. "No,

I do not reproach you – I have no doubt where your intent lies and that is not my concern at this moment. I have a feeling that something is not well and yet I find no cause for it. If you do not share my apprehension, then perhaps it is that of my own fear which disturbs my quiet."

"No, Pauroseng – I too have felt it – even before I left Imoshtan. Then it was only a faint disquiet, but now it is stronger. There is an uneasiness in the land – it comes from many sources, I feel – as if they all conspire as yet unknown to each other."

"This will be your battle," the old warrior spoke looking fondly, if not a little sadly, at the young Master. "I will no longer be here. But there is something else – something more pressing. Perhaps I am being anxious – perhaps my body is over tired. You are taking some of the warriors on a patrol tomorrow are you not?"

"I am – it is time they walked the borders of this land and knew different horizons. We will be gone but seven days."

"They are young and inexperienced, Teilo."

"I will take two of the warriors from Imoshtan. Pauroseng, what is it?"

"I do not know and if you have no concern then I must be losing my sight - but protect them, Teilo – hold them safe – although it is around you that I feel death hover."

"Nothing is lost to you, Pauroseng, and I bow to your knowing. It does not come to me this more immediate unease, but I do not discredit your feelings. I will be cautious."

He turned his attention back to their meal.

"Which path will you take?" she asked.

"We will walk directly to the western border and follow its lines until we reach the edge of Manon – after which I intend to continue south east to find the source of what was once a small, but vigorous stream, which flowed through this land. The dry bed tells me of its story and I would conjecture that there was, at some time, a shaking beneath the earth that caused this water to cease. I have a hope that we can bring it forth again. Although the rains have brought great healing, to unleash that hidden current will make this land truly sing."

She smiled at his enthusiasm – it was always boundless, but in his own innate way – one that held his energy close rather than let it spread too far and become lost.

8

The western border of Yeshotruen was a mountainous region. In fact the entire land of Yeshotruen was wedged between two mountain ranges. There was only one small opening on this western side and that led into Manon.

There had always been rumours that some of those who had been banished to Manon escaped into Yeshotruen. No doubt this was one of the reasons the compound had been built.

It was to this opening that Teilo led his band of enthusiastic young warriors. Why he had chosen such a course he was not completely certain. He was curious to see this region – to know something of its nature and to read the seams of the land that were always visible to him. He had known them since his childhood – those unseen lines that carried their own life force and like the trees, held stories and songs that were immortal. He felt their talking in his body as he walked. But there was something else calling him to this place and for once he was unsure. He had taken Pauroseng's words very seriously. He held his senses fully alert.

The young warriors were in high spirits. Of an evening, around their fires, they talked of all they had seen during the day, of other places they would like to see and their lives as warriors.

When they did reach the border and the gap in the mountains it was still early morning. The scene before them was breathtaking. They beheld the most spectacular chasm – as if here the mountains had suddenly subsided deep into the earth creating a dramatic canyon. The sun was sending shafts of light bouncing off the rocky sides, spraying their colours into the shadowy depths below.

This striking disruption in the landscape was known as The Longing of Tharseywon.

Teilo did not know who Tharseywon was – there was no mention of him in any of the history books or legends – no doubt he was a warrior but his memory had been erased – another mystery for which no one sought explanation.

He gazed across the ravine into the land of Manon. There are too many secrets here, he thought. He felt disturbed and that in turn gave rise to disquiet and a vague anxiety and apprehension. Pauroseng's words returned to him – *'it is around you I feel death hover'*.

"Master Teilo, are you unwell?" It was the soft voice of Edora, standing beside him, watching him.

He smiled at her. "I am well, Edora – my gratitude for your care."

He looked at her for a moment. Her broad face and dark eyes framed by a mane of chestnut hair which she wore lightly bound. How strong she had become – there were no shadows anymore of her ordeal. She was different to her brother and she had changed perhaps more dramatically. No one will ever injure this young woman again, he thought. She possessed an unwavering confidence – it carried with it no scars or bitterness, only the surety of who she was and where she stood.

"That is better," she returned his smile. "For a moment, Master, I thought you looked pale."

"You are very astute, Edora – tell me, what do you feel as you stand here?"

She closed her eyes.

"Death,' she said simply as she looked at him again.

"That is so," he replied. To himself he thought – death and much, much more.

He bid the warriors to set up camp, intending to stay in this place for the remainder of the day and into the next. The warriors from Imoshtan were surprised to see the Master then take the small pouches of sand from his coat and commence the ritual of protection. The young apprentice warriors had never witnessed this before. They were intrigued.

Softly speaking words they did not understand, Teilo let the sand run through his fingers. Finally he completed the ritual by surrounding the picture with a golden circle.

"Are we in danger, Master?" It was one of the warriors from Imoshtan.

"There is no danger," he replied, "do not fear – I merely wish to leave for a short time and desire to give you protection. I will return if you need me."

He went in search of a way into the ravine.

No one would wish to escape Manon by this path, he thought when he had descended but a short distance – it is by far too treacherous. He took great care and several times had to steel his nerves. He had fallen down one mountain already – he had no wish to repeat the same mistake. Testing each foothold and where he grasped with his hands, he slowly made his way towards the bottom. Halfway down the precipice, he came upon a ledge that offered a narrow walkway to the base where, thankful the descent was over, he sat and rested.

He felt like an intruder but something, or someone, was calling him to this place.

There was a still heat in the ravine – nothing stirred – the air was oppressive and close.

When he sensed which direction he must take, he resumed his mission reluctantly. He smiled, noting his avoidance, but he could not shake off the sense of dread. The only consolation was that it carried no threat.

He came upon the bones without warning. At first there was a scattering – almost unrecognizable so that he paid them little heed, but suddenly, around a bend, was a mountain of bones – old and brittle – deteriorated with age.

Who were these people – what had befallen them here? This is but a place for the dead, he thought.

It was common practice in the Land of Romarrah to inter the dead. The earth was the mother's womb to which all life must be returned. This was not the custom in all villages. He knew there were those who left the bodies exposed to be devoured by beasts – to rot and return to the earth in that way. Was this then where the people of Manon left their dead – cast into the ravine? If so what had taken place in Manon a long time ago to create this mountain - obviously a catastrophe of large proportions.

A little further along the bones became more scattered, varying in age and the state of decay, confirming that this was still used as a place for the dead. From the tattered remnants strewn about, it was apparent these corpses had been swathed in coarse cloth, indicating some form of reverence and ceremony. Many of the remains had been spread by animals.

The part of him that did not wish to experience pain, urged him to turn back. His sense of anxiety and sadness intensified. Still he walked on, knowing he was close to that which reached out to him. He came to the last, more recent bones – strewn upon the ground, picked clean – bleached by the sun. He knew before he touched them and his body was shaken by the intensity of the grief he felt. He had at last found Orphaele.

The warrior sat, slowing his breath – allowing the initial force of his feelings to subside. Then he placed his hand on one of the bones. The tragedy he felt there sickened him. He knew he had not been mistaken. A surge of emotions struggled for space within him but it was his rage that surfaced like a silent demon and for a short while part of him became lost in its swishing fury. Then it too became still.

Why was Orphaele here – he puzzled. It was at least seven years since he had last seen her. An image of her shy friendliness crept through his sorrow. He had asked for her in every village through which he had passed. He had looked for her when he first came to Yeshotruen. It was always his hope that the life she lived was a good one – that she was loved and did not endure unnecessary hardship. Yet, in his heart there was always a deep sadness when he thought of her. If this was Manon's place for the dead then so many questions remained unanswered. Did she belong to Manon? Had she been taken there against her will? Even more frustrating – why was he never aware of her? His sense of others was not diminished by distance.

He knew then that it was Manon itself that was hidden from him and all that lived and breathed within that place.

Now as he sat in this valley of death, he knew the story of Orphaele's death – the release of this gentle life that had once held his own. He lay beside the bones and gazed up at the narrow stretch of sky above him. Softly he sang the song he had always longed to give her.

The warriors were settling for the evening – lighting fires, preparing food. They had spent the day at rest. He did not join them once he had completed his ascent. He had no desire for food or talk – he wished his body to be free of all disturbances so as to be in contemplation. Quietly and unobtrusively, he again took up his position on the outskirts of the camp.

The sun was setting. It offered a desperate beauty to the sharpness of the landscape. Closing his eyes, he slowly released the feelings and images of the day.

How long he sat, he did not know, but when the vision came it carried with it a force so strong that the earth around him shivered.

He was standing, in blinding light, at the edge of the abyss. No longer clothed as a warrior, he wore but a single robe. Below him lay the rotting corpses of all the warriors he had trained – their lives over – the beautiful children with their eager faces – their aching honesty – their hopeful dreaming. His own body was there and Syrath's. The more he looked the more he saw – all those he loved – they were but decaying flesh – nothing more.

He took himself above the earth – no longer entrapped in his body – and defiantly gathered the strands of all those lives.

The voice spoke then – a solid command. *"You will not touch them – though it be your power it is not your right – let them be!"*

He did as he was bid – he let them go – everyone. Immediately he again stood contained, upon the earth.

"Who are you?" he heard his own voice.

"We are the seeds of creation – would you see us in you?"

He gave his assent and again the earth shivered. Again his body fell away. He became the shivering of the earth – he contained the earth – but more than that – he went beyond the earth and all its lands – beyond other worlds – through all light and dark – he spread until there was nothing and everything and he was the eye of creation – watching.

The sound of feet softly striking the earth reached out to him. He remained motionless – absorbing this place to which his senses had returned – the smell of a fresh day scenting the air – the sound of the warriors at their morning practice – the breeze as it brushed his skin and moved the strands of hair against his face. Life was again touching him.

There was a peace in him unlike any he had ever before experienced and it radiated from him. Unknowingly the warriors felt it also. Their movements flowed without hesitation as though something had released in them a common music. They moved as one – a dance of life beside a valley of death.

He watched until their dance was complete. This time we seek to fill, he thought – the human struggle to give purpose to the space between birth an death – the consuming attachment to that purpose. He smiled – everything is but the flesh and blood of our existence and it too will rot. Nothing compares to that which is boundless in us.

The warriors strapped on their swords and began their combat training. Would that I could take it all away, he sighed.

From that time onwards, death became his constant companion. In as much as his feet kept pace with life's patterns and rhythms, in him life and death became as lovers – inseparable – merging as the seasons merge, as water flows to the ocean, as the heavens meet the earth. He no longer belonged to the world – it breathed in him like a tide and he did nothing to hinder its reaching and receding. Nor was there anything he would change of it except that which he was given to change.

9

Jemai stood before the Master's door – a mixture of apprehension and excitement rising within him. He took a deep slow breath, preparing himself. Before he could draw his second breath, the door opened. He beheld Master Teilo looking straight into his eyes.

"Would you stand there all day, Jemai," the Master said laughing. He embraced his guest with great fondness and genuine pleasure at seeing him.

Jemai had not known what to expect. He had wondered how changed the Master would appear. Had he become more like Romarrah – powerful yet distant – leaving no question of his being the Great Master? Yet here was Teilo with the same joyful laugh – the same infectious warmth and energy.

But there were differences. His skin was darker from hours in the sun. The muscles of his body were even more defined from the constant physical labour though his movements remained light and measured. Apart from the physical changes, he appeared the same – vibrant, charismatic without effort – just as when Jemai had last seen him – except, and here the young warrior grappled with an elusive sense of something beyond his comprehension. The only word that would come close to describing what he felt in Teilo, was quiet – a deep quiet. There were no questions in him. Only a still surface that was host to the reflections of all around him – undisturbed and clear, it was looking at him now.

"Jemai," the Master was saying, "I left you a boy and now you stand before me as a man – a strong, fearless man. Come – let us sit together – I will make tea."

Jemai's appearance had of course altered in the years since they had trained together in the orchard. His face, once pinched with sadness and uncertainty, had broadened with openness and confidence. His physique was now that of a powerful warrior. He removed his sword and sat quietly, observing his surroundings.

In comparison to Romarrah's, these chambers were bare – simple without decoration. The only luxuries were books and a shelf stacked with pots of inks and dyes for painting.

Teilo placed the tea in front of his young friend and sat facing him, waiting. Jemai laughed – his Master had not forgotten.

"Containment is without effort," he said, "just as a vessel contains water without effort. Restraint requires effort. One is about control and the other speaks to us of grace. One denotes struggle – the other compliance. One means to hold on – the other asks us to allow. Is that enough, Master?"

"It is more than enough, Jemai," Teilo smiled. "I cannot tell you what a delight it is to see you."

"My gratitude to you, Master, for your letters. They kept me steady. At times when I longed to speak with you, your letter would miraculously arrive."

Jemai took some pages bound with twine from inside his coat and handed them to Teilo. "Master Syrath asked me to give you this."

"Tell me of Imoshtan, Jemai – what happens there?" Teilo placed the pages to one side, giving his full attention to his guest.

"It is much the same, Master. It is indeed the most wonderful place – still as beautiful and peaceful as always, although we have been called upon much more to settle disputes in the border villages."

Teilo frowned at this disclosure. "Do not the warriors stay in the villages to ascertain from where this unrest arises?" he asked.

Jemai shook his head. "The Great Master does not think it necessary."

Teilo noticed his hesitation. He pressed him further.

"Tell me – what do you see?"

"When I first went on patrols, the children of those villages would come to greet us – as I myself did when I was a child. The warriors were important in our lives – they were inspiring – they kept us safe. Those children do not come to greet us anymore. In the villages closer to Imoshtan, all is as it should be, but in the border villages men and women look at us suspiciously – as if they have been poisoned against us – yet we are as always without aggression."

"What do the Masters say of this?" Teilo asked quietly.

"Master Syrath says little, although she has, on occasion, engaged the villagers in conversation in an effort to show them our support and protection – and also our respect for their way of being. Master Prisheed has told me on occasion that he too has a sense of uneasiness and yet nothing is defined."

"When you say disputes in the villages, Jemai – describe these to me – where are their origins?"

"That I cannot tell you, Master – one village will rise up against another for crimes of theft and in some more serious instances, physical attack, but the accused always deny such transgressions. Villagers have been killed yet no culprit can be identified. Blame and suspicion are scattered in all directions."

Teilo was thoughtful for a few moments. "Jemai," he spoke at last, "I sent for you because I know who you are and I need someone whom I can trust completely."

The young warrior looked slightly confused.

"Master, I have gratitude for this honour, but you could trust any of the warriors of Romarrah."

Teilo smiled. "We have a lot to talk about. In the coming days I wish to spend time with you as my intention is to train you to be Master of Yeshotruen – if you are willing."

"But – I have not even commenced my training as chief warrior."

"I am aware of that. You do not have to be a chief warrior – you need only the understanding and insight and the ability to guide – that is all. You remember that day in the warrior's sanctuary at Imoshtan, when I took your hand – I will tell you what I felt. Your touch told me of your sadness at the loss of your parents, your loneliness at Imoshtan – your insecurity and lack of confidence. But beneath all that and above all, what led me to seek you out, was that your heart was crying out for someone to recognize who you were – you yourself could not – someone to guide you to your destiny. Believe me, that destiny is to lead. You saw yourself as one who works with the land – a simple farmer – but it is precisely because of this that you understand things about the earth – about life – even if you do not fully recognize them in you. The earth is now alerting us to danger, Jemai – to what ails us. To ignore it will be at our own peril."

They were interrupted by the sudden arrival of Cencian. He came running through the open doorway as one who is confident of being welcomed.

"Teilo," the young boy shouted as he entered then stopped abruptly on seeing Jemai.

"Do not be concerned, son – this is Jemai – he is a fine warrior from Imoshtan and he is a friend of mine. Do you wish to see me?"

Cencian bowed respectfully to Jemai then turned back to Teilo. His eyes told of an excitement in him. The Master smiled fondly at his joy.

"Well – what is it, or do I have to guess?"

"The stream is running, Teilo," the boy was beaming with this epic news. "You must come and see."

"That I will, Cencian. Come, Jemai – this is cause for celebration. We will talk later."

Jemai followed the Master and the boy. From the moment the latter had entered the room it was evident this was a close relationship – almost as a father and son would relate. Cencian addressed the Master in a most familiar way and now as they walked in front of him, the young warrior saw Teilo place an arm around the boy's shoulders. It was a gesture that spoke many words.

Other people were walking in the same direction, carrying with them an air of anticipation. Jemai was fired with curiosity. He could see at a glance what had been achieved in Yeshotruen since Teilo's arrival.

The land within the compound was like an oasis, but it was a recent oasis. The land beyond the compound was in recovery – all growth was new – the trees could not be more than a few years old. But what excited Jemai was the feeling of change which bathed this place – the earth was all but singing. No, he thought, it is singing. This land is giving birth.

A large crowd had gathered to witness the water once more flow through Yeshotruen. Teilo and his young warriors had spent many months – the best part of a two years – toiling to free the stream from its rocky bed – to once more let it inhabit its ancient course.

The Master watched the water – brown and stained – carrying with it the layers of tired apathy and dust that had been its discontent. It would take time to clear but when it did, it would once more bless the land as only clean flowing water can. It would reflect life and joy to these people – already he saw it on their faces. He knew his time in Yeshotruen had nearly come to pass. All that remained was to train Jemai to step into his place, ensuring continuity, and to farewell his dearest Master and friend, Pauroseng.

The sixth stone speaks of that which we hold or contain. The least understood stone for its meaning has several layers. It represents all that has been; all that is; all that will be. It is the stone of death and transience; just as light and shadow are one and the same, so too are life and death. It tells us that all we hold cripples our ableness and all that we truly contain is our uncreatedness. The human struggle is our failure to distinguish between the two. It tells me that the joy of our power is that we are powerless. I cannot give this stone the right words, Syrath, yet it is imperative that you know it now; you must understand it for your self. My

gratitude for your letter and what joy to see Jemai a grown man. He too has told me of the unrest but to know that some of the ancients of Maurapin are dying tells its own story. The time fast approaches when we will stand again against forces that do not know their own pain; it will require all our strength. Do not give of yourself to fearful thoughts; they only serve to feed that which we wish to heal. Be steady, Syrath, all change must come.

Why had Teilo sent her the sixth stone and not the fifth, she wondered. Had he forgotten – no he would not forget – he would have a reason. His words were cryptic yet he was so insistent that she understand. She sighed and looked at the painting he had sent. It was an enlarged section of the previous one – the child holding the golden vessel – sitting beside death and ruination – yet with such peace. The child's face held an expression of innocent awe – unaware of the devastation – intent on the vessel which overflowed with life.

The image moved her deeply. Her tears spilled freely. The unrest that had at times shivered within her these past months instantly became quiet. She had felt like a ship without a rudder. Romarrah had retreated from her and for the first time, she questioned his leadership. Ortarian also seemed unperturbed. Did they fail to see and feel what she knew – that this was but a symptom of a greater disease? She had witnessed herself the failing life in the oldest trees of Maurapin. The waters of the land were not as vibrant – as though some unseen parasite was insidiously sipping the life from the earth. The conflict on the surface was but an ominous warning.

How alone she felt. Although there were others who shared her unease, no one ventured to name it. She longed for Teilo to come back to Imoshtan.

Jemai became as Teilo's shadow. His first week in Yeshotruen had been confronting. He had trained as a warrior – a very exacting training, but he did not expect the duties of Master would be so extensive and not within his education.

"Be with me only to observe," Teilo instructed him on that first morning. The Master had insisted Jemai share his chambers and had roused the young warrior earlier than his usual waking time. Jemai had followed Teilo to Pauroseng's room, adjacent to which was a small sanctuary. Immediately he felt the atmosphere of this place embrace him – as though all he need do was be here and his soul would be clothed and fed. That

Pauroseng and Teilo sang their morning devotion gave rise in him to an initial discomfort but that was soon lost as their song stole from him all defence – all resistance. I did not know my lessons after all, he thought before he surrendered to the lament of his own mute voice.

Jemai said nothing to Teilo of this experience – there was no need – the Master already understood. Their early morning devotion complete, they went to the courtyard to commence training. Jemai already felt that in the hours since he had arrived in Yeshotruen, he was a different person. He had made the journey from Imoshtan with childlike anticipation and the lively anxiety of one who desires to be seen for who they have become.

Teilo had acknowledged him and taken nothing from him but in the Master's presence, Jemai felt all he had learned was shallow – a hollow echo of something he had not yet grasped. Suddenly he felt a sense of dread at training with the Master.

Abruptly Teilo laughingly turned to him, took his face in his hands, and kissed his forehead. "I am glad that you have not changed, Jemai – you are still the same beautiful soul you have always been. Your doubt will dissipate in time – it is but a shadow that plays in your thoughts." He touched the young warrior's chest. "It is not what I feel in here. Here you rise above all doubt. There are moments when you know everything, Jemai – you reach out to grasp those moments – to preserve them, but they cannot be held – let them go – they will not have words – they will be as the water which holds you as you float upon its surface."

The warriors were making their way into the sanctuary. Teilo did not join them. Instead he led Jemai away from the courtyard, past the gardens and into the orchard – not an aged and fruitful orchard as in Imoshtan – this was but a promise of what might be.

Jemai could hear the song of the warriors drifting across the still morning air. It brought with it a breath of unity – nothing was out of step.

He was not expecting Teilo to draw his sword.

"Come," the Master smiled, "I long to spar with you, Jemai – I feel you have a lethal sword."

He had. The young warrior had practiced relentlessly. He was a powerfully built young man and the Master had to work harder than he was used to. Jemai allowed himself a fleeting sense of gratification.

It was just then, that Teilo seemed to step into a different rhythm. Jemai could not find his footing – his dance became erratic – he began to falter.

With the speed of a viper striking, Teilo reached out and grasped the young warrior's wrist.

They were standing very close. Jemai tried to fathom how the Master had done what he just did. Still Teilo did not release him.

"You have put your trust in this sword – you put your strength in this sword – where is the dance in you now? There is no surrender in this hand, Jemai."

His words were not forceful and they were softened by his smile.

"Tell me what just happened."

Jemai looked at his Master. "I felt as if for a short time I was in control and then you led the contest into another place where I could not even begin to match you – it was," he shrugged, but Teilo waited. "It was as if you were no longer here. Master Teilo, I feel as if I have trained so hard and lost that which I once knew – or thought I knew."

"No Jemai – you have not lost it – you have just found it. Do not give yourself up in deference to me. Make no mistake – I'm asking you to be fully that which you are – not emulate something you think you should be. That is why I asked you to tell me what happens when you truly surrender to the dance – do you not remember? You have trained so hard to be something and now I do ask you to lose that for which you strive and that which you think you have gained. Everything must yield in you, Jemai – everything – even that which you guard so privately. But we have talked enough. I cannot tell you anything that is not already yours. It is time I was with the warriors."

♋

Jemai had many revelations in his first weeks at Yeshotruen. To see warriors who danced, sang, painted and also grew trees and gardens, would be unheard of in Imoshtan, where they had but their study and training on which to focus. There were of course those who, once adept, had adopted a life away from the compound – many were farmers, but that was separate from their practice as warriors.

Here there was no separation and Jemai could immediately see the difference. These men and women saw life move through them and just as water finds its own course – this life stream found its own expression in them. They knew a deep joy and grace. It wasn't merely an acquired discipline – it was a practiced knowing. It was not the giving of the Great Wisdom, it was the rising of their own.

Teilo's guidance was never dictatorial and this, to Jemai, was fascinating to watch – as if the Master cleared a space and invited those in his care to step into it. Whether they be a warrior, a child, a mere acquaintance – if they harboured anger or ignorance – if they were in wonder with life or if they were releasing life to the softness of death – it made no difference – it was always the same. Teilo was totally present to each face and he fed them – sometimes a mere sip – sometimes an ocean. There were times Jemai felt tears in his eyes as he watched – when it was all too open – too bare.

And then, there was Pauroseng. Teilo was devoted to her and she, in a different way, to him. They knew each others' words before they left their lips. They shared an invisible mirth that played in their brief conversations. But it was their morning devotion that cast an aura around each day – touching everyone. Jemai was sure their song travelled on the air – permeating all in its path – breathing within people as they slept, then lingering in empty spaces – like dew remains, slowly evaporating into the ether.

The hospice itself astounded him – a place of peace and nurturing to which the warriors also gave their time, nursing and caring for those who sought refuge there. Three warriors in particular moved about the compound and hospice with great energy and enthusiasm – Deshan, his friend Kesten and Edora – Deshan's sister. Jemai did not know their stories, but it was obvious to him that they were in love with their life at the compound.

Deshan was a tall, slim but well-built young man – perhaps in his nineteenth or twentieth year. His features were well defined and his laugh was strong and hearty although at times he appeared too serious. His friend Kesten was possibly four years his junior – he had only just commenced training. Jemai had questioned the Master on this matter.

"He is lame, Teilo – would it not be better for him to give himself to something other than the life of a warrior – surely he will fall behind and therefore despair."

Teilo had merely smiled but his eyes laughed with a hidden mirth.

"Remember your words, Jemai, when this young man becomes a most accomplished warrior."

It took only a few days for Jemai to realize how mistaken he was. Kesten was slight of build and his face was dominated by large, luminous eyes. That, and his noticeable disability, gave him a look of vulnerability that disguised an enormous will and determination. This boy would take on the greatest challenge – he would pick away at it – he would persist until every obstacle gave way to his insistence. He was also an incorrigible tease and prankster. As the youngest warrior and the one with the most infectious personality, his ruses were tolerated with good humour although on one occasion Jemai witnessed Teilo draw the boy away from his mischief.

"Consider first the appropriateness Kesten," was the Master's only comment as he passed. It was enough – nothing more was needed.

But of the three, it was Edora who captivated Jemai. Her features were soft and kindly yet, like her brother, she was strong and capable. The bond between the two was evident. Deshan sometimes looked to his sister for guidance – his was the more unstable foundation – there was something in him that needed reassurance – it was only slight but it was there. Hers was a quiet, steady enthusiasm. She was diligent in all she did and quietly self-assured.

These three were always present – familiar faces – never doubting their welcome. He deduced that Teilo had given much time to them. Their love for him was easily discernable.

It was during his second week in Yeshotruen that Jemai accompanied Teilo to Allencia's home. The Master had already introduced him to this woman. Jemai knew the role she played as mentor to the children and in the hospice yet it was with a faint sense of awkwardness that he went to her home. It was not a familiar experience for him to visit another's dwelling to share a meal. Warriors ate together at the compound. He could not imagine Romarrah indulging in such a social outing. The thought of it made him smile.

Allencia bowed to them both respectfully when they entered her home and they returned the courtesy. At once Jemai knew it was a customary practice for Teilo to visit as he was completely at ease in these surroundings. In fact, it was as if in some way, he belonged here. Cencian greeted him with tidings of his day as one would engage with a parent.

Jemai was uncomfortable with this familiarity. Allencia was very kind and charming. The eloquence of her speech, her calm, yet friendly demeanour – her graceful movements – all made her quite enchanting.

He saw Teilo unabashedly reach out and take her hand as she moved past him. He caressed it for a moment, looking at her fully, then smiled and released her. Obviously this was a most natural gesture but, to Jemai, it was laden with implications, some of which he did not wish to contemplate. They may lead him to doubt his Master's integrity. He kept his counsel but within him the matter begged to be addressed. He could not stay in Yeshotruen if his faith in the one who was his beloved mentor was compromised.

"We will spend some time on the rituals soon, that you may offer protection," Teilo spoke to him some days later.

"Master, I do not wish to be a chief warrior," the young man responded vehemently.

"You do not need to be a chief warrior to understand these practices, Jemai, but tell me why it is you are so adamantly opposed to this direction?"

"A chief warrior is obliged to honour their vows, Master. It is my understanding that through this discipline they deem themselves worthy to perform the sacred rituals. I see myself as one day having the comfort of a family life – it would therefore be dishonest of me to take vows I had no intention of honouring."

"Very well," Teilo responded and said no more.

Jemai felt frustrated – he wanted the Master to account for himself.

It was Pauroseng who shifted his focus. "You are a troubled young man, Jemai," she said quietly when they were alone. Teilo had left their meal prepared but he himself was not present.

Perhaps he has gone to visit Allencia again, Jemai thought irritably as he ladled the food into bowls for himself and the old Master.

Pauroseng smiled at him. "Ah you warriors are far too immutable. Now you are at odds with the Master, my son, but he is not at all vexed with you. Speak to him, Jemai – tell him your fears."

"My fears? Forgive me, Master Pauroseng, but it is not my fears that give rise in me to a disaccord with Master Teilo's ways."

He stopped – hearing the rashness of his words.

"Oh but it is," she said gently. "You must ask yourself why it is that you wish to find fault with him. Take time to be with your self and when you know your fear – speak it to him. He was not wrong in choosing you – I can see that."

She bowed to him as he placed her food before her.

"He is in the hospice, Jemai – with one who is leaving this earth. He is not given to frivolous pursuits as you would imagine – that is definitely not his way."

Jemai felt his face colour at her words.

Later he walked beyond the compound gates – further than he had ever gone before. He made his way among the confusion of pathways that linked this overgrown village. He allowed his thoughts to travel and watched from a distance their stumbling race. A fear sprang from behind a shadow – was he safe here? Some night wanderers such as he glanced at him with suspicion. He let the fear find its release. Would he trade the peace of Imoshtan for this – this uncertainty – this fragile, foundling peace? Within the next few steps, he had his answer. He had become a warrior – it was his chosen path – he was not born to it – he had wished to know it. Imoshtan had provided refuge, until he could once more take up his parents' land and live that simple life to which he had been born.

Now he had been called to this and he came because he loved the Master. He had nursed for years a silent hope of seeing him again. He knew the parallels between his own early life and that of Master Teilo's. Here in Yeshotruen the Master welded his knowing of the land with the ways of a warrior. He had taken what he knew and let it find its own expression. In the same manner he had trained the warriors and, in doing so, had allowed his knowing to spread and gather and absorb more. *'Do not give yourself up in deference to me – I'm asking you to be fully that which you are'*. Jemai gathered the meaning of those words as he retraced his steps towards the compound.

Outside the hospice he hesitated for a moment and then entered. In the dim light he could see Teilo seated beside a man, his hand resting lightly in the centre of the man's chest.

The Master did not open his eyes to acknowledge Jemai's presence as the young warrior sat opposite him. The dying man was of a similar age to Jemai and the sight of his wasted body was unsettling. Jemai was surprised at his own reaction. He had only known death to come quickly. His parents had been murdered by the warriors of Lemarron. Death was final – he did not see it as a process, nor had he experienced the waiting that precedes it.

The gurgling breath of the young man dominated. Jemai's unease intensified – but he did not turn away. He stayed present, watching the scene before him. He witnessed the struggle until it no longer appeared a struggle but rather a journey and he, by his presence, was part of it.

Suddenly he saw something beyond this physical form which lingered on the earth, not yet released from its burden. For the briefest instant, he saw there the unified soul – its sacred beauty casting a blessing – like a small flame illuminating the darkest room. He knew so much in that moment, yet as Teilo had said, it did not come to him in words.

He stared at the hand upon the chest and remembered watching it scrape the wax off the statues in the sanctuary at Imoshtan. It was constant that hand – regardless of its industry; it remained steady – stroking life, stroking death – as if there was no separation.

He had no idea how long he sat absorbed by that knowing. He became aware the breathing had stopped and when he looked up, Teilo was watching him. The Master said nothing – he stood and walked to the entrance. There he rang the small bell that announced a death – its clear, strong vibrations resonating into the night.

To Jemai's surprise, it was two warriors who came to prepare the body as he and Teilo left the hospice and walked in silence.

Once back in the Master's chambers, the young warrior finally unburdened his confusion.

"Teilo – I cannot do as you do – I am not up to this task. My fear is that I will fail you for I cannot give what you give. Nor can I take the vows of a chief warrior only to dishonour them."

Teilo looked at him. "Do not lose me, Jemai, because of something as inessential as a man-made decree. It is not the breaking of vows that is the depravity – so often it is the vows themselves that are morally corrupt. I ask nothing of you but that you be fully yourself – then you cannot fail me. You do not offend me with your judgement – you offend yourself. Nor will I offer you justification for my own actions. Tell me why you came here."

The young warrior frowned. "You summoned me."

"No – tell me why you came here – to Yeshotruen – what was your intent Jemai?"

"I wished very much to see you again."

"Take all of that away – why did you come here?"

"I knew in my heart it was to be."

"And that is precisely why I asked you. I would not give this to you had you not already asked for it in your heart. Nor will I abandon you – my intention is to stay until I am no longer needed. Until that time I am here to give you all you ask of me – to ease your way. What say you now?"

Still the young warrior hesitated. He had trained as a warrior of Romarrah – the teachings were solid – they formed a close to unshakeable foundation. Teilo did not adhere to the law – he would teach the rituals to those who were uninitiated. Was it not folly to give such power to the ones who had not the awareness to use it well?

"You grapple with words, Jemai – a title is nothing but a name given – your laws are but invented words. I have been in villages that honour an anointed healer – all healing must be done by them alone. There are others, in those same villages, who also have the power of healing, but to use it would cost them dearly. Their gift to the world remains unknown. Why? Tell me why we continue to limit ourselves so that but a few have control. Do not confine your vision with teachings that come to you already ruminated. Have gratitude for the foundation you received in Imoshtan. It gave you steadiness, but now let yourself expand from your own heart – beyond those limitations – for limitations they are – they are only meant to hold us for a short time until we find our wings. We all fear that step, Jemai – we fear who we are."

It was with those words that Jemai felt an enormous release in him. Seeing the emotion on the young warrior's face, the Master smiled. "Why do we wait for permission to be who we are – who we have always been?'

The days spread into months. Jemai became a familiar figure within the compound and beyond. He slowly gathered knowledge and understanding of the ways of Yeshotruen.

What Teilo had achieved in such a short time to him was inconceivable but because of it, the man was revered. His warriors did not simply respect and honour him, they loved him. They went beyond the compound assisting others to heal and work the land. They planted forests.

In time Yeshotruen will be unrecognizable as the place it once was, he thought – and I will be given the task of maintaining its state of flourishing. He felt a mixture of fear and passion. It was essential his observations were clear and unclouded by his own opinions – he must understand what happened here and why.

"How is it that the warriors are responsible for attending to the dead, Teilo?" he asked one evening.

Their evenings were quiet – mostly spent in contemplation or study, although occasionally they wandered into conversation. Teilo looked up from his writing.

"Only for those who have no family to do so. It is for the family to prepare the body, but if no kin exist then the warriors are given that honour."

He saw Jemai's doubt. "It is an honour, Jemai – the warriors have reverence for all aspects of being. Death is a most significant aspect of being – it is the one constancy of our living. When the warriors prepare a body, they honour life – they give gratitude for that life but also, they live their own death – it speaks to them, prepares and comforts them. It teaches us how to live. These warriors truly know the goodness of all souls. It is an irony that most people are not fully known until they die. To those bereaved the goodness of their loved one becomes fully apparent again – no longer shackled to an acquired way of being. These warriors will not wait for death to know the dance. Their hands have tilled the earth – given birth, tended the frail and honoured the dead – they will live the dance well."

After this conversation Jemai spent more time in the hospice. He learned to give of himself in a way he had never done before. He saw the honesty of this place – where the world's cares fall away and words are clear and not wasted.

It was here he learned that the fullness of life can only be realized through death. Slowly his own life revealed itself. He gave himself completely to the song, the dance and finally one night, as he walked from the hospice to the compound, he surrendered. He truly gave up himself.

He sat against one of the earthen walls that lined the road. It was still warm from the heat of the day. Looking up at the scattered disarray of the evening stars, he suddenly saw the perfect order of everything. His joy seemed infinite.

When he did return to the compound, the evening meal was over, Pauroseng had returned to her room and Teilo was sitting in quiet contemplation. He observed the Master briefly and again recalled his words before he left Imoshtan – *'tell me what happens when you surrender to the dance'*.

Jemai had no words to give him. Quietly he sat beside the Master.

Teilo's hand reached out and touched his arm. "I dread trying to match your sword on the morrow," the Master said softly.

Jemai laughed. What joy to share his life with someone who never lost their own humour and joy.

"I am blessed, Master Teilo," he said blissfully.

"That you are, Jemai – that we all are. Yeshotruen will be safe in your hands."

10

Pauroseng knew her time was close. No longer did she attend the hospice and minister to those lives to which she had given so much of her own. Her days were spent in the peace of her sanctuary. At times when her health permitted, Teilo would accompany her to the orchard or the forest. The old warrior was in wonder of this new life and liked to sit and gaze upon it. They spoke little – there was no need – there was nothing more to be said.

"So precious what you have given, Teilo," she murmured one day, looking at all around her. He remained quiet knowing she was saying her farewell.

"My gratitude to you, son, for walking with me – I have not much further to go." There was a long silence before she continued.

"I know you are returning to Imoshtan – it will not be easy for you."

She paused again.

"There is nothing I can give you to ease your way. I know in my heart what you face, but I can give it no words and Romarrah," .

He stopped her then.

"Pauroseng, I wish no harm to Romarrah – at Imoshtan I will bow to his leadership – I go only because I must."

She smiled fondly at him.

"Teilo – you speak with sincerity but we both know the land is failing. Be prepared – your intent is one of willingness and allegiance but your heart will tell you otherwise – of this I am certain. It will take all your strength and wisdom to find a path through the maelstrom that I fear awaits you. How you will do so and stay in your peace I do not know. It is a heaviness in me that I must yet release."

Once more she smiled at him and added, "That and other things."

Briefly she went back to her watching.

"No matter how at peace is our compliance with death," she murmured, "it is an uneasy farewell, is it not. It is the simple things that hold us – not of the mind but our belonging – the breeze – how perfect, Teilo, is the breeze?

No words can do it justice – its music speaks to us – so soothing to the soul. And then the leaves – sometimes the music takes them and they are never out of step – but at other times they wait – they hold their breath as if they too are in amazement of their humble belonging. It is true," she sighed, "no matter our knowing, it is a difficult farewell. We both face a death, Teilo, and we both step beyond our sight."

He had been watching her as she spoke – there was not a line on her face he did not know. He loved her age – the same age as in the new-born's eyes – when the spirit still lingers outside itself – before they are absorbed by life. Now it returns again – rich with the promise of release.

He loved her dearly – this joyful spark that was Pauroseng. Taking her hands in his, he did nothing to hide his tears from her.

"What remains of my life, Pauroseng, I give to honour you. It is the steel I first saw in your eyes that will hold me strong and steady. It is the love you have given me that will keep me safe, no matter what my fate."

That was the last time Pauroseng left her room. In the following days her body became weaker. Teilo began tending to her day and night. Ortarian again arrived from Imoshtan and together they kept vigil. Allencia came often, bringing food and comfort.

Pauroseng made certain she left Ortarian with his knowing of her as a mother loves her child – she was as self-less in death as she was in her living.

The night before she died, she sent for Jemai. When the young warrior sat beside her, he suddenly felt he was in the presence of a timeless pilgrim – an eternal goodness.

"I am pleased to have met you, Jemai," she said simply, "to have seen your open, honest face. Have no fear, son – your destiny here is strong. You will continue to love those you serve and they alone will give you all you need to know."

Her words moved him in a way he did not think possible. In that short exchange she gave him something he did not fully know in himself – his own love, like hers – like Teilo's, was boundless and infinite.

It was to Teilo that she gave her last words. She turned her eyes to his and looked at him fully.

"Now, my son," she whispered, "you may calm my restless spirit."

He placed his hand upon her chest and softly sang their song. Then he breathed with her each breath as all else faded quietly beyond the curtain.

Jemai walked into the night. He was aware of the warriors standing within the courtyard – a silent vigil of honour, but outside the gates he was surprised to see a much larger crowd had gathered. How many lives had this woman touched - so quiet in her way of living – so magnificent in her way of being.

Instinctively he went to the hospice where her spirit lingered and rang the bell. He felt enormous gratitude for having known her, however briefly, but more than that, he was grateful he had come to Yeshotruen – to honour his calling. He now knew the difference between Yeshotruen and Imoshtan. He understood why Teilo encouraged the young warriors to rise up out of their conditioning – he didn't simply train them or give them a new conditioning, he showed them how to heal their past knowing and become present to themselves.

Jemai understood why the Master bid him – *'be fully yourself'*.

His thoughts turned to Teilo and Allencia at this moment – preparing the body of Pauroseng. They would bathe it and anoint it – Ortarian had asked them to join him in this ritual. Soon, they would open the earth and lay her body to rest. As was the custom, nothing would mark her grave – there was no need – her gift to life was immortal.

♋

Pauroseng's death marked the beginning of Teilo's withdrawal from Yeshotruen.

Ortarian had come to him and requested he be allowed to stay.

"Teilo I wish to remain here, in Yeshotruen, and I seek your permission to do so."

When the Master made no reply, Ortarian presumed Teilo was not in favour of his request. He quickly sought to justify his intentions.

"I am aware that I was not content to be here when you first asked for my assistance," he began. Teilo stopped him.

"Ortarian, you do not need my permission to be here – if that be what your heart dictates." He saw the older man's relief.

"Tell me," he encouraged. "You hold a sadness in you. Do you wish to unburden this grief?"

For a moment Ortarian bowed his head.

"You were so right, Teilo," he spoke at last. "I did not truly see Pauroseng until her death approached. Only then did I see her – that love – the light it cast – and my grief groaned in me. I myself did not know that love. That which I thought love was but a lesson I had learned – it did not have life. I want to stay here – not to know that love, but to be it, as Pauroseng was. And no – my friend – I do not wish to be with the children but to work in the hospice. That is all for which my heart now weeps. I am past books and study. I know you soon will leave. Perhaps you feel I may not settle here with young Jemai as Master and the difference between Imoshtan and Yeshotruen – that which once I could not bear but believe me, Teilo, it is Yeshotruen that calls to me in my sleep – it lives in my dreams."

Ortarian stopped. There was no more to be said except for a faint stirring of unease and he placed his hand upon the Master's arm.

Teilo read the feeling of that touch and gently reproved him.

"I have no promise to leave you, Ortarian – what will be, will be – but do not think there is between Romarrah and myself any contest, and before you ask, I do not know what will come nor will I look for that future but I will tell you that destruction is not always an intent to harm. There is that which must end because its time has come. Nor is it the destroyer we fear – it is but the fear of our own annihilation that grips our peace as we both know.

The older man nodded. "Forgive the fear in me, Teilo – it is but an old one. In truth I am fast losing sight of that world – there is little before me now."

Teilo smiled, "My gratitude to you, Ortarian."

Jemai wondered how he himself would fare without the Master's guidance. Surely Romarrah would not allow this transference of leadership – it left the compound without a chief warrior. Although Teilo had instructed him in the rituals of a chief warrior, he knew Romarrah would not approve. The Great Master would surely appoint a new Master if Teilo were to announce his departure.

But Teilo had already foreseen this obstacle and, unbeknown to his young successor, he had taken steps to ensure a seamless transition. Now with Ortarian choosing to stay in Yeshotruen, regardless of his industry there, no argument would be forthcoming.

The fifth stone is the stone of birth and renewal; a cleansing stone and thus of water, it washes away the pain of who we once were; like spring rain washes away the longing of winter.

This is your stone, Syrath. I can feel in its voice the journey you must make. It tells us to wait, and in that waiting to remain still; to hold humility as our beacon; not the humility that comes with effort but the humility of our birth; that which accompanies us before the separation of our knowing.

It is not easy this waiting. I can but tell you the time is close, very close; a moment that reaches out to you; that brings you to yourself. It is important that you listen with great care to the belief in you heart, for this is the key. Do not lose yourself in the teachings you have been given, Syrath; this I beg of you. Hold only this belief that you do not yet understand or dare to speak of or deny.

How did he know her turmoil? It was but a gentle seething in her – like a rash one is fearful to scratch lest its irritation become unbearable. Why did he not come back?

A year had passed and grown into the next since she had sent word to him of the trees in Maurapin. She had thought he would return.

The unrest in Imoshtan increased but only in the smallest of increments – as if to make its escalation go unnoticed. But she did notice, and her frustration grew. Were others blind to this darkness? Did it disguise itself so well that they did not see it slip past their watchfulness? Did not Teilo feel the urgency that paced in her? Of course he did – he bid her to be still.

She breathed slowly and studied the painting he had sent – again it was part of another. This time it depicted the young forest but now, clearly visible through the trees was the figure with the lamp. It was that of a woman – around her was an intricately woven wreath – not of flowers but colours – almost a rainbow though softer. It was comforting – as if a mother's love reached out from it, to stroke and forgive. But it was more than that of human succour – it encompassed all of the earth and all sentient beings. It was an eternal mother essence – that of giving birth – honouring life – holding the lamp of renewal. This was the belief that ached in her heart – that she would know this woman in herself.

Beneath the painting he had written:

> *Your song took my sight*
> *deeper*
> *into the forest;*
> *no longer a tree before me*
> *but patterns and stains of colours;*
> *they lose their names*
> *in the wonder*
> *of gently threaded music.*
> *There is nothing here*
> *moss and lichens*
> *grow across the mottled bark*
> *but all I see*
> *is your song;*
> *like a blessing,*
> *it leaves me quiet.*

He too had found it hard to wait and yet harder to leave – to be caught between an ending and a beginning – the limbo between death and birth. For this past year since Pauroseng's death, he had stood back and let Jemai take the steps that would once have been his. The waiting had been made bearable by the gardens where he spent hours playing in the earth, feeling the gift of its growing richness.

He remembered Shimmera doing the same – letting the gardens of Athanan be her comfort. She needed such solace because she was shunned and mistrusted He needed it because he was surrounded by love – by people who had put their faith in him – who would give their lives for him. May it not come to that, he prayed.

He needed to release them all, so that his leaving left not the slightest tear in the fabric he had so carefully woven. He had prepared them for this separation, taking the time to talk to each one – to leave them the right words – but more than that, to let them see that they did not need him.

Jemai required his guidance less and less and he knew he could not delay much longer. The greatest irony was that he would leave the budding peace of Yeshotruen for the growing unrest in the Land of Romarrah.

Cencian walked with proud contentment. From the moment he knew Teilo was leaving, he had nursed this hope that he dare not reveal. But his mother had read it – in his eyes – she had known what it meant to him.

It was on Teilo's last night, when she thought her son was asleep, that Allencia gave voice to his request.

"Teilo, I beg you to take Cencian with you – he longs for it – he dreams of it – he loves you and I cannot bear his loneliness without you."

"And I, Allencia, cannot bear yours," he had responded. "To have you parted from this child you love – and that love carries with it all the anxiety of a mother. I do not want to think of you alone."

Cencian watched them from beneath his blanket – the Master, sitting on a rug – leaning his back against the wall, and Allencia, sitting beside him – her legs tucked beneath her. He liked to listen to their voices – the quiet, hushed tones carried a peace that settled around the walls and sent him to sleep. But not this night – this night his secret aspiration beat its own pulse against his tiredness.

"I am not alone," his mother argued. "You were so right to make me stay in Yeshotruen. The people here have become my family. I wish for nothing more than to be here – to continue Pauroseng's work in the hospice."

"I did not make you stay in Yeshotruen – I simply gave you a choice." Teilo spoke with mock indignation.

She smirked. "You know very well, Teilo that most people do precisely what you ask of them."

Silently Cencian laughed too – his mother was right.

"But not you," the Master countered light-heartedly, "you are much too wilful. You stayed here because you loved your son," he added seriously, "and you had no wish to be parted from him."

"Of course I love Cencian and I will be sad to farewell him – but what is sadness – it is but a part of life. I know he is safe with you. He will embrace the Land of Romarrah and Imoshtan – it will become his familiar – and I will nurse the joyful dream that he will one day return to Yeshotruen. Then I will see the man he has become."

Teilo looked at her and said nothing. He gently brushed a few strands of hair from her face. Cencian held his breath.

"Do you not wish to have the burden of this responsibility?" she queried taking his hand. "Have I asked too much of you – forgive me, Teilo – I forget you go to Imoshtan for a purpose and that your time there may be difficult."

Still he did not answer. The boy could feel the tears prickling his eyes.

The silence seemed interminable.

Suddenly the Master sighed then spoke very quietly, "Go to sleep, Cencian, or I swear I will leave in the morning without you."

Cencian was sure his heart would burst it pounded so strongly. It had taken him an eternity to go to sleep such was his excitement but sleep did come. He was not awake to see his mother's tears or Teilo take her in his arms or the sadness that reached from one to the other as their time together unravelled into a memory.

♋

Edora watched from the balcony until she could no longer see them, and then she turned and walked inside. She looked at the sword where she had placed it – the sword of a chief warrior. Master Teilo had given many hours to her training.

"I will teach you in this way, Edora, because I must, but hold only to that part of it you know to be true. Trust your voice – it speaks no falsehood. It is the same voice which spoke to you at the Longing of Tharseywon – when you felt my fear – for fear it was. You knew also that it was a place of death. That is the voice to which you must pay heed."

He had wished her to be the chief warrior at the compound, and Jemai the Master. Edora had been astounded by his request – that he would regard her as so worthy. "You do not see what I see," he had smiled. "Your spirit carries with it will and compassion in perfect harmony with each other – a rare combination."

Two nights before his departure, Master Teilo had revealed to Jemai that Edora was now a chief warrior of Romarrah. The three of them had spent the entire evening together discussing the future of Yeshotruen. Teilo advised them to be each other's counsel.

She had shed tears then, knowing his departure was imminent – how could they be without him.

When she thought of her own journey to where she now stood, she knew it would not have been possible without him. And she loved him – they all did. He had coaxed them all into a life of which they would not even have dared to dream. Such honour he had bestowed upon her, she thought as she basked in the stillness of this room. It was easy to feel Pauroseng's spirit, especially in the sanctuary.

Never had she felt so satiated with contentment. Her hands wandered around the walls, rested upon the simple furnishings – her own blessed space wherein she could be without disturbance. How well Master Teilo knew that part of her which so needed to be alone – the part that was her guiding strength.

Deshan and Kesten had farewelled the Master with light hearted banter and promises of future encounters. He had laughed with them, hugged them both and walked away. Only then did they stand in silence and blink back their tears.

"Do not be sad, Kesten," Deshan comforted, "we will see him again – of that I am sure."

"I wish it was I who was going with him," Kesten muttered.

"No you don't – you know he wants us to stay. We have been here from the beginning and he has left us the task of keeping Master Jemai steady."

It was unusual for Deshan to joke and Kesten laughed.

"He did no such thing – that is almost disrespectful." Thoughtfully he added, "He wants us to keep ourselves steady – though it will not be easy without him"

Deshan reflected on this for a moment. "He always had plans for Yeshotruen," he said quietly, "from the very beginning. He would just watch and let those plans take shape. Some part of me believes he's still watching us, Kesten. Yeshotruen remains part of his plan.

There had been few words between Jemai and Teilo in those last weeks. Jemai had simply watched the Master – watched him take his leave quietly – purposefully – giving of himself to every person within the compound and hospice. He was unhurried but even so, Jemai sensed an urgency – not in the man himself, but around him.

On the morning of Teilo's departure, the new Master watched him strap on his sword – the sword Romarrah had given him – that of a chief warrior. Jemai had never seen him wear it before this day and somehow that action alone made him aware of how much it cost his Master to return to Imoshtan. He went only because he must.

"Something threatens does it not?" he asked as Teilo placed his few belongings into his sack.

"More than threatens, Jemai – it has already begun."

Teilo stopped and looked at his young friend. "Do not fear – Yeshotruen is safe and protected and you will keep it so - nothing outside it will harm you."

He waited for a moment and Jemai glimpsed something he had never seen in him before. It was only a brief flicker and then it was gone, but he was in no doubt – it was fear. The Master knew something of what the future held that, for whatever reason, he would not reveal.

"Jemai," again Teilo looked at him, "keep the warriors strong and ready. I pray I will have no need of them but it may come to be that I must send for you if I am left no other course."

"We will be ready, Master," was all he said but his look told Teilo all he needed to know – Jemai was with him.

He walked at a steady pace – considerate of the young boy by his side. With every step the warrior let Yeshotruen fall from him – the people, the gardens, the forests – he watched them go. Each footfall was like a tear drop shed but it would take until he reached the mountains before all that remained was Pauroseng's song and that, when it was not in his thoughts or on his lips, was forever in his heart.

He looked at the boy and was reminded of himself – walking alongside Apheilio to Imoshtan. At the time he had been numb with silent despair whereas this child beside him was fired with enthusiasm. It made Teilo smile. Cencian was nearing his fifteenth year. Teilo would beg Romarrah's indulgence to allow him to commence training. He knew it was right for Cencian to accompany him, as did Allencia, but there he wished the similarities between their lives to end. He did not want this boy watching him die on some futile battlefield that contained only remnants of meaning for the living to gather and piece back together.

When they reached the top of the pass through the mountains and beheld the land below them, the warrior's eyes went straight to Maurapin. Even from this distance he could see the dying canopies and their tacit grief was like a dry wind on his face. Teilo had returned to the Land of Romarrah.

PART THREE

MANON

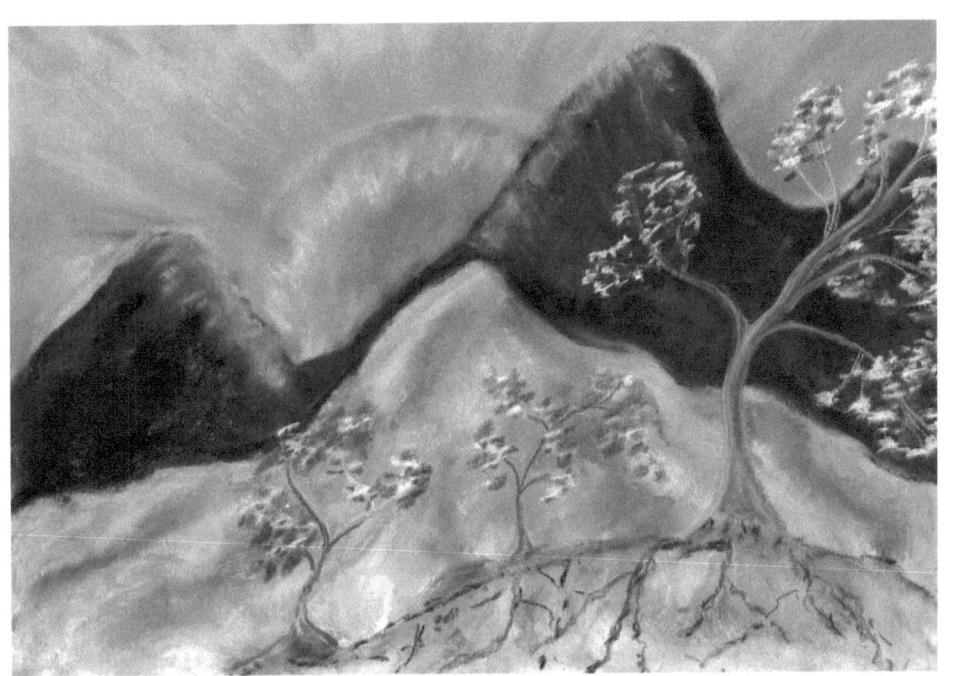

1

She knew from the moment he took his first step that he was coming, though he had sent no word of his arrival. It lightened her heart to think he would soon be with them again.

Romarrah had tried to allay her concerns for the Land but to no avail.

"Syrath, I have sent warriors to every corner of this land – even to Manon. I have sent them beyond to Lemarron and further and I can find no threat. It is true that the unrest continues but I can ascertain no cause. What more would you have me do? I could send warriors to each village as you suggest but if by now there exists resentment towards them, what would be the benefit?"

"Romarrah, we need to know why these villages harbour such animosity towards us – we have done nothing to deserve this and though I have tried to converse with them on many occasions, it is as if they are too fearful to speak to me."

Romarrah sighed. "We can but remain watchful, Syrath. I do not have the answers but in time we will understand this riddle."

The chief warrior and the young boy stood before the compound at Imoshtan. It was late evening and all was quiet and settled. The two guards at the gate did not know this stranger although they could see he was a chief warrior of Romarrah.

"What is it you want, Master?" one asked.

"We have had a long journey, my friend, and the young boy is in need of food and rest. Master Syrath will be expecting me."

Teilo smiled at them and turned to Cencian. "One of these warriors will take you to the kitchens, Cencian – if Riata is there still, tell her Master Teilo sent you and she will serve you a feast."

"Forgive me, Master," said one of the guards, bowing respectfully, "we did not know of your arrival."

Neither had seen this man before but they knew of him – his legend still lived in Imoshtan.

"Do not be concerned, good man, Teilo spoke kindly. "If you could just see to my friend, I will take myself to Master Syrath's chambers."

Nothing had changed in the compound – the same quiet peace pervaded – the same aesthetic beauty. It was at once so familiar and completely foreign.

He quietly mounted the steps to Syrath's rooms and momentarily the ghost of the child and Apheilio walked with him. He knew she would be expecting him and he tapped softly on her door.

When it opened, neither spoke at first. Then he took her hand and placed the last stone in her palm.

"The seventh stone is the stone of realization and completion. It denotes the end of a cycle – that something is over – either within us or without. With completion there comes realization. The essence of our journey is understood. Without this realization, the cycle remains incomplete and it will return to offer the same path again until our knowing is unbroken. Completion only brings us back to where we started – everything is as we left it and yet nothing remains the same."

His eyes looked straight into hers. They both needed time to behold each other – that their image of each other could become flesh again.

For Syrath there was an awkwardness to this moment. The man before her was not the man she knew – as if he had taken a journey of three thousand days and she had just stood still, holding a faded picture. He was a stranger to her. He had come from another world and she could see the colours of it – an invisible cloak around him. Now nearly all of him was hidden from her and it was like a pain that seized her breath.

"Tea would be welcome," he said with smiling sarcasm, aware of her bewilderment. The awkwardness fell away. She laughed and hugged him close.

In that moment of tenderness, he could have wept, as all the grief of leaving Yeshotruen that he had so patiently laid to rest, came flooding back. He breathed deeply and let it pass but it was there long enough for Syrath to know it. Imoshtan had never been his home – it had been his refuge. It was in Yeshotruen that he had let the earth claim him again – he had found home.

"Have they removed your tongue, Syrath," he said, holding her at arm's length. "I came expecting a barrage of questions and I am greeted with silence."

She saw him then – he was calmly waiting for her but even so, she could not speak. She hugged him again – just to feel the warmth of him – the inimitable, joyful core of him – so real – so unwavering. The words would come later.

♋

> *Why weep for all that is lost;*
> *is it not yet down another path;*
> *a song waiting to be sung*
> *by a voice that knows its suffering?*
> *Why weep for love*
> *that is never forgotten;*
> *washed away on a day of endless rain;*
> *its life carried where the heart needs it most.*
> *Why weep with the burden*
> *of grey skies;*
> *is it not but one moment's fullness*
> *that takes the breath of sorrow*
> *and presses it sweetly into a quiet caress?*

His painting was that of a hand – holding the same flower from the first painting he had ever sent her. In the background was a distant mountain range above which shone a bright full moon. Underneath the painting he had written the words – *the last flower brings us back to where we began.*

He had stayed only long enough to let her see him, leaving the poem and painting to complete his journey.

By morning, everyone in the compound knew Master Teilo had returned. Prisheed sought him out in the warrior's quarters early in the day and greeted him warmly.

"The Master awaits you, Teilo – he did not know of your arrival."

Teilo smiled. He heard the rebuke in those words. For an instant he felt trapped – suffocating in a small, confined space.

"Come, Cencian," he said smiling to himself, "the Master will want to meet you too."

When they entered the Master's chambers, Romarrah had been writing in a large tome. The ink was not quite dry and the book lay open on the table. Placing a cloth over the pages, he rose to greet his visitors.

Although Teilo had only glanced at the book, every nerve in his body knew what it was – the one volume that had always been missing when as a child he had studied the history of all the villages. It was the book of Manon.

There was a moment that begged explanation as Romarrah saw the recognition in Teilo's eyes but he let it pass and turned his attention to Cencian.

"Why did you come back, Teilo?" Romarrah asked. Prisheed had taken Cencian on a tour of the compound and to give the boy the clothing of a warrior. The Great Master was watching his visitor astutely. "Your heart is not here. Did Syrath summon you?"

The chief warrior smiled. "Not in words – no – and whether she did in her heart, is not the reason I am here. I came because this land is failing."

"What then is your intent here?"

"To ascertain what happens for myself," Teilo responded with blunt honesty.

"Is that your place?" Romarrah's tone was uncommonly stern, his eyes never leaving the young man's face. "To come back to Imoshtan, unannounced, with the intent of conducting your own inquiry? Do you forget yourself? Your responsibility is to Yeshotruen."

"Romarrah, I do not come here to usurp your authority – everything is as it was but I can take no other course. I have not neglected my responsibility to Yeshotruen. I have honoured it by leaving it in the most trustworthy of hands. It is the Land of Romarrah that falters – do you not wish to know the cause?"

"I can see no evidence that we court danger. Both you and Syrath talk as if doom is already upon us. Where is your proof of this?'

"Come with me to Maurapin and I will show you."

"Everything has a finite life in this realm, Teilo – forests included – it is all but a cycle of birth and death."

"No, Romarrah – it is not their time – it," he stopped abruptly. At the mention of the trees of Maurapin he had felt a wave of panic rise like a frozen tide within him. The future was pressing its vision upon him but he would not give it entry. "What ails you?" Romarrah's irritation changed to concern.

"It is of no concern," Teilo shook his head. He looked at the Great Master and continued with care, stepping his way across the raging torrent between them.

"Romarrah, I come to you without claim or desire. Do you still not trust me? Every task you have ever set me I have honoured. The warriors of Yeshotruen stand alone – their numbers steadily increase. Was this not what you asked of me? I wish to take nothing from you. Why must I constantly justify to you that which I know to be true? To deny this peril – and I have no doubt of its existence – would be to deny who I am. You of all people know I cannot do that."

The Great Master was silent. He heard Pauroseng's words clearly – '*there will come a time Romarrah, and I tell you this for your own safety, when you must let him go*'.

"Very well," he said, "What is it you wish?"

"I ask for nothing but to be here and to have the freedom to go where I must."

"I will have rooms prepared," Romarrah began but Teilo shook his head.

"There is no need – I am content to stay in the warrior's quarters. I ask for nothing else except to keep the boy with me."

"Ah – the boy. Am I to understand that you have a responsibility to this child?'

"I took his father's life – that in itself is responsibility enough. I will treat him as my own son."

The interview was over.

After Teilo had taken his leave, the Great Master considered what had just occurred. It is true, he thought, I do not trust him. Even now – when he has proven himself time and time again – when he stands before me and declares his allegiance – why do I not trust this man? All others easily fall under his spell. He draws people to him like bees to the hive and yet, although I feel his sweetness, I remain unsure of him. The boy who had defeated Myallon was cold – without mercy – devoid of feeling.

It had been a chilling display that Romarrah had never forgotten.

Teilo had thought Yeshotruen would pass quickly from him but it remained like a mist that, from time to time, clouded his sight. When alone, he was silent – refusing all visions of what might be so that nothing would turn him away from his purpose. The sadness that came was like the blackness of old – the approach of something that called for its own death – something the earth could no longer hold.

Romarrah had insisted that, while residing at the compound, he must assume the duties of a chief warrior. To Teilo, the training was colourless. It taught a method – a technical precision – a much digested philosophy while the nameless essence slipped between the cracks.

Nevertheless, he trained the warriors accordingly but his humour brought a colour to the rituals. His own joy coated his words and actions.

It was to Cencian he gave the opportunity to find freedom and understanding – taking the young warrior to the orchard as he had done with Jemai – letting him dance and discover the strength of his own spirit.

Romarrah observed it all. He remembered the laughter and love he had also witnessed between Apheilio and his son. Teilo was certainly keeping this boy close to him.

The first time Cencian saw Teilo leap naked into the icy waters of the stream and sink below the surface, he shook his head in disbelief.

"You suffer madness, Teilo," he scoffed as he watched him climb out of the water.

"It is the madness that keeps me sane," Teilo laughed, splashing the boy playfully.

The seasons passed quickly from one summer through to the next and beyond. Cencian became settled in his new life. The way of a warrior came easily to him, not only because Teilo was his mentor, but because it gave him a platform from which he could see far beyond the tired shapes of the world he had known since birth. From that first moment when Teilo had sung to him of other lands, he knew that he wanted to soar. This was his opportunity to learn his own song.

His personality was one of openness and friendliness with occasional bursts of rashness and impatience. The surliness of his childhood rarely surfaced in him and when it did, it lasted but a short time. He was not overly confident and rarely assertive in the company of his peers but he possessed great physical strength. He often entertained friends with his ability to lift heavy weights – often his friends themselves.

Cencian looked to Teilo for advice in all matters both personal and social. Their afternoons in the orchard or forest were often occupied with intense discussion on aspects of life.

"What of passion?" he asked suddenly one afternoon. He had been telling Teilo of his friends and their ventures into the forest and nearby villages in their time away from training.

"Your passion is something that you give to everything you do, Cencian, but I feel what you are really asking is of the passion which accompanies a physical knowing of another. Does something trouble you?"

"It is different here," the young man mumbled. "I know the teachings on this matter and it does not pose a problem, I simply wish to understand it more. I know it is private – a relationship between people with which they are in accordance. I know that love and compassion is our first duty in this matter as in all others. Yet here this relationship reaches beyond what I have known it to be. Here I have known men to share with other men and even women with women. In Yeshotruen this was wrong - it met with punishment. Here several of my friends sometimes spend time in play in the forest. In Yeshotruen behaviour of such nature was considered that of beasts."

How much this boy had seen in the very early years of his life, Teilo thought. He knew of the punishments inflicted on those of Yeshotruen – especially the women. They were often extreme – even fatal.

"Everything in nature is but colour and pattern, Cencian. The human form is simply part of the one expression. Make no judgement on the patterns others choose to create in their lives. If, as you say, there is love and compassion – if there is no harmful intent and awareness of action, our expression of love is the pattern we choose and should be allowed its peace within us. It is when we identify ourself as being that colour or pattern that we separate our self from others and we see others as being separate from ourself. It is this separation that creates turmoil. If you would understand this relationship more fully, then love and compassion is not enough – there must be an even deeper awareness of intent – not just your own but also your companion's. For yourself, be very clear that all aggression be released before entering into such a relationship."

"Teilo – I have no aggression in this matter. Aggression is something we take into battle not into matters of love." Cencian shook his head.

Teilo smiled at him and continued. "The male form by its very nature of being, is aggressive – have no doubt of that. If there exists in you a desire, no matter how slight, to claim, possess or dominate, then there is aggression. It may be coated with higher intentions but look carefully. If there is one lesson a man must learn, it is surrender. If you will enter into a relationship of this kind, be it with a man or woman, do not do so while there is lust in you for gratification. Your longing will make you blind to the true power of this union. When you surrender your will, you open your heart to the other's glory and that is what elevates you – not your own feeble desire. And, make no mistake Cencian, we surrender to that which is feminine – that which contained us and still lies within us."

Cencian remained silent, pondering.

"What then is the lesson for a woman?" he spoke at last.

Teilo looked at him in a way that caused the young man to feel uncomfortable. The Master held him there for a moment before he answered.

"From where does that question arise in you, son? Be very careful – already you struggle for dominance. Wheresoever exists that struggle for power, aggression is also harboured. Nor will I answer for another, but the female form, by its very nature, is one of giving love and nurture – not only does it bring forth life, it nurtures life and therefore it already knows within itself that which is the heart of existence. Theirs is the passive essence of unfolding."

"But woman is aggressive also – are they not trained to fight beside us in battle?"

Inwardly Teilo sighed. He remembered how much his own questioning had rankled Romarrah even though the Great Master always appeared patient and attentive.

"Anyone may be aggressive, Cencian. We are merely discussing the nature of the form, but there is a difference between aggression and the act of being aggressive. One is of the mind and is that which harbours destruction and hostility. The other is physical. This dance we perform is not aggressive yet when used in combat it becomes so. Be clear on this – when we enter into conflict, we do so without aggression – without hostility to those who threaten us."

Teilo suddenly glanced up. Syrath was walking through the orchard towards them.

"Perhaps if there is one lesson for woman," he murmured, "it is true compassion."

Cencian, unaware of her approach, frowned. "You contradict yourself, Teilo. You have just stated that the female essence is one of love and nurture – how then can their lesson be compassion?"

"For their own self," the Master responded quietly. Then, more firmly, he added. "Enough talk, Cencian. Take your questions into your own stillness."

He smiled as the young man stood up. "Already you are nearly as tall as myself. Allencia will not recognize you on your return to Yeshotruen."

He turned to greet Syrath.

Unwilling to accept the amiable distance he had placed between them, she had at last decided to follow him and Cencian to the orchard.

"Teilo, I wish to dance also," she stated by way of explanation for her presence.

Her eyes were asking him to let her back into his life as before but he could not do that – not now – he needed to be without distraction.

"Of course," he nodded agreement.

She joined their practice.

He watched her. At first she could find no freedom in her body. It held tightly to its expectations.

"Syrath – in the beginning the dance is imitation. That imitation allows the mind and the body to feel and understand. When that understanding penetrates deeper than the flesh, then the dancer becomes the dance. Do not try so hard to find something that is already there.'

Slowly she shed the skin of habit. He saw her tears when the movement unearthed a stolen memory and set it free. Few words passed between them until, late one afternoon when they had finished their practice, she requested to speak with him.

Cencian left them, bowing respectfully to Syrath. She watched him walk away. "You are very careful with him," she said, observing the young man as he strode confidently through the orchard.

Teilo smiled – he knew exactly what she meant.

"His foundations were not of goodness – he witnessed things no child should have to bear. It is like removing a thousand splinters – one must go slowly lest some are overlooked."

"You have chosen to be his father then – to take on the fullness of this responsibility?"

"I have," he replied. "Is this what you wished to discuss with me, Syrath – my responsibility to this boy?"

It was her turn to smile. "You do not change – there are no wasted words with you. I wish to know why you have placed this distance between us when I need so much to talk with you about the land and my own sadness and fears."

"I have placed no distance between us dear friend," he replied gently, "only a stillness. I cannot risk my own silence – it requires all my will to be where I must. Come, walk with me in the forest."

Without hesitation, he took her hand and led her across the bridge. They walked for a time without speaking. It was dusk and the forest was cool, hushed and restful. The aged trees always offered comfort and privacy.

"Do not fuel yourself with impatience, Syrath," he said as he sat beside a fallen log and waited for her to do the same. "What is it you wish to ask me?"

"I want to know what is happening in the land, Teilo – is that not why you returned? I want to know what is happening within myself."

"You already know these things – what is it you are really asking?"

"I only know one layer – as if I look through a window that is but partly open."

"Perhaps that is all you are meant to see at this time."

Her frustration intensified. "Do not riddle with me, Teilo. You know the truth of this and I can see even in you there is a fear where I never expected it to be. In myself, it is as if I want to flee far from this place before I choke. Why will you not tell me what it is you see, that I may prepare for that which is to come?"

He did not answer her – he just closed his eyes as if he needed to be alone. She wanted to shout at him but all that came was a sigh of resignation. As she made to stand up, he reached out and took her arm.

"Be still will you – your agitation will not bring you what you ask."

He had not opened his eyes and so, she did as he, and became still. The warmth of his hand still resting on her arm brought calm to her being. The vision, when it came, was frightening – a river of blood – on one side stood Romarrah – on the other Teilo. Between them floated the bodies of many warriors. The blood flowed from a wound in Teilo's side colouring the water with its deadly stain. He bowed to Romarrah then turned and walked away. It was the look on his face that frightened Syrath the most – the look of one who calmly faces death – one who is already beyond the world.

Then she saw herself – no longer a warrior – alone on a mountain of bare stone – a landscape that was so utterly unknown to her and yet so familiar. She was aware of an immense freedom. It was in the wind that teased her hair and the sense of joy that wrapped itself around her.

When the vision faded, she opened her eyes. It was nearly dark.

Teilo turned to face her.

"Do not ask me any more, Syrath," he said before she could speak. "Have no fear – you will one day know that freedom I promise you. No matter what happens, your destiny is strong. The only preparation you can make is always the same – be fully who you are and see clearly whatever is before you. You know you are holding onto turmoil – it damages you on all levels – it robs your essence. Can you not let it pass?" He smiled at her. "Perhaps you should dance more."

"And what of your fear?" she asked.

He raised his eyebrows.

"Believe me Syrath, my heart does not fear. You are frowning – do you doubt me?"

"Do you see your own death? Is that what you hide from me? Teilo, do you propose to turn against Romarrah? I cannot bear to think of such a divorce."

He kissed her lightly on the forehead and rose to his feet – offering her his hand.

"I am privileged am I not – to be the one with whom you share what others do not see. When that quiet, unshakable composure gives way to Syrath – the child you have always been from the moment I first saw you – calmly watching me walking behind Apheilio – probing me with your eyes in case I had any secrets hidden from you. Syrath, when my death is imminent you will be the first to know. Did you not know of my struggle on the way to Yeshotruen? Why do you ask me these questions – they are not mine – they are yours. It is not I who will have the answers. What your vision showed you was the gravity of what we will face and I need so much to stay still – I need no emotion other than that which arises in me. I entreat you to let it be. Did we not promise to hold each other? Then know that we do – be at peace with that – all else will be as it will be. If my need to be alone places a greater burden on you, forgive me, Syrath, but that is for you to carry – I cannot."

2

Maurapin was dark. As always there was the gloom of a world lost in shadow only now, the shadows seemed deeper and longer. No one confronted him. At times he was aware of being watched. He sensed those with ill-intent – their wrong desire pressing itself like a faint odour into the air. But not once was he accosted. He walked with assurance and listened intently as the earth gave up its secrets.

The chain that linked the lands had been broken long ago. He sighed when he felt this damage.

"They do not know," he said aloud to himself, "they do not feel it – the more they separate themselves, the more they cast aside what holds them."

"But you know – don't you warrior?" said a familiar voice. "You know what they do."

The tree man stepped from the shadows. He did not immediately come to the warrior – there was an uncertainty about him. Teilo sadly noted that his friend was ailing like the earth.

"Why do you not come to me?" he asked softly.

"I will take your strength, Master – my body will beg to borrow it and you must keep it all – you must not give it away – not now."

Teilo walked to the once ageless man who now stooped with the weight of time and despair and wrapped his arms around the frail form.

"If I give my strength to you, it only enhances what I come to do, dear friend," he said, holding the other man close and letting him feel his warmth.

"Come – I will make you some tea – you are wasting – but no more of this – I need you to be strong. Do you understand? If you choose to die now – like your brothers and sisters – you leave me too great a sorrow and a far greater need. I must have someone who stands in the forest – my eyes and ears to the earth."

As he had been speaking, Teilo set about making a fire. He was grieved by the state of the tree man. The beautiful and the innocent suffer, he thought - love and compassion have become words which indulge rather than bequeath. He snapped a branch with unnecessary force.

When he was assured the fire would burn, he placed an earthenware flask in the coolest part of the flames and once more spoke to his friend – sitting beside the sorrowful form and stroking him lightly.

"I will bring the life back to Maurapin – that is why I have come – you know this. Why have you relinquished hope?"

"There is none that can assure me of your success, warrior – it is but a prayer we hold to and I have lived too long. I have seen it before – the change we seek rises and hope soars – then like a tide it sinks back into blindness – not of the eyes – of the heart. That is when the human form becomes but a plague again. No longer humble it seeks to be greater – to spread – it courts its own displacement. I am too brittle and bitter, Master, to be of any good to you."

He wept then – a soundless weeping – turning himself away from the one he called his child.

Teilo stayed silent. He made the tea and placed a small bowl before his friend. The truth of the tree man's words was perhaps the saddest thing. To some extent, the warrior knew what lay before him. For this reason he was aware of what he was given to do – he measured every step of his actions so that they would match his purpose but even then, he could not say what would follow. That was not his to know or seek to manipulate.

"I give my life to this, tree man. Is it too much of me to ask that you not lose your own life in sorrow but that you give it to me that I might use it? If then we both die, we die as one."

Saying this, he stretched his body out on the ground. He had walked far and was in need of rest.

The tree man came to him – peered in his eyes – felt the pulse of the blood in his veins.

"Your destiny stays strong, Master," he said gruffly. "You have the stone – why talk of your death?'

"Death may become the choice I make." Teilo replied evenly.

They were both silent. The warrior closed his eyes – he could feel sleep stealing his weariness. By day and night he had walked with quiet resolve to this place. To travel by the fullness of the moon is to know the beauty of a tender night, he mused and the thought was like a smile – he drifted into it.

"What is it you want of me?" The tree man shook him, banishing any sweetness of sleep.

"I want you to stand by me," the warrior replied opening his eyes and looking straight at his friend. "I want to know you are here for me – that I do not walk alone."

"You have others to stand by you – many – you have gathered them around you."

The tree man sipped his tea. Teilo smiled at him affectionately.

"That is different, as you well know. You hold me to this earth, my friend – even when I lose my footing, remember – it is our bond." He paused. "There is something else," he chose his words carefully. "The boy who walked with me to Imoshtan – I want you to be for him what you have been for me – as long as you are able."

The tree man frowned then, to Teilo's surprise, he spat.

"He is not like you, Master – his blood is not beautiful – you cannot cleanse his blood."

Teilo laughed. "So you have already sensed him and judged him to be part of the plague? I have faith in him, tree man, and my faith is not misplaced – it is that faith which will live in his blood – do not doubt that. I have taken him as my son. Tell me that I have your faith to hold me and I will sleep in peace."

"I am not bound, warrior – yet this is what you ask of me – to bind myself to this cursed race – to give my life for theirs?" His eyes darted from one shadow to the next, avoiding the warrior's gaze.

"It is," Teilo replied, feeling the tearing of the fabric they had woven between them.

"You have my life," the tree man said simply, "but do not ask me to be like them – never will I enter their dwellings or eat at their table. He stroked the warrior's head. "Sleep, Master, in the morning I will show you what it is you wish to see."

♋

"The water beneath the earth has become stale," the tree man spoke as he guided Teilo through the maze of Maurapin – the thickest part of the forest where it is said no man treads. Here the earth's moaning was loudest and constant – rusty with the age of its aching.

Teilo did not speak, he just followed his guide absorbing all he saw and felt. Suddenly the small man in front of him stopped, sniffed the air and placed his ear to the ground.

"Here," he nodded, "this is where the line begins."

Without another word, he set off at a trot expecting the warrior to follow. Teilo understood – his friend was tracing a line beneath the earth – the broken chain. As they moved through the trees, the forest closed behind them, guarding its secrets.

For hours they ran until the forest of Maurapin came to an abrupt end. The tree man rested – the last hour of their travel had been steadily uphill.

"Do you know where you are, Master?" he asked

Teilo was marvelling at the endurance of this frail little man.

"I do," he replied, "beyond this rise is the land of Manon. Do you propose to lead me there? You know it is forbidden for me to enter without permission from Romarrah."

The tree man's face crinkled in a cheeky grin. "That will not stop you, will it, Master Teilo? I will show you the only way to enter Manon that is safe – come."

To Teilo's surprise the tree man slipped back into the trees. He could only follow. They did not retrace their steps. Instead his erratic guide led him through a complex interlacement of pathways. The warrior was puzzled. Was his friend deliberately trying to confuse him?

The clearing opened up unexpectedly before him. He recognized it instantly – the Pit of Maraka. He gave the tree man a look that said – why here? The little man laughed with glee and clapped his hands, satisfied he had, just this once, confused the warrior.

"My secret, warrior – no one knows because no one is brave enough. Are you brave enough, Master – of course you are because you know something. No one can touch you is that not so?"

He was teasing and he danced around as he spoke. Teilo laughed at his antics.

"Now that you have confused me hopelessly – kept me running for hours so that I am wet with the sweat of me, are you going to share your little secret or do you merely wish to help me fill my day?"

The tree man stood still and cocked his head to one side as he sometimes did when he was thinking.

"This is where I will leave you, Master."

He looked around as if to make sure not even the trees were listening. Walking closer to Teilo, he took him by the arm and led him to the edge of the Pit.

"You will not like this place, warrior – you are not that sort of creature. Yours is the face that turns to the wind and the sun – that drinks moonlight and shares the mysteries of light and colour. But if you would know what is hidden from you, give yourself to the world beneath us – here is the only way to Manon that is safe for you – give yourself to the pit, Master."

Teilo looked into the narrow black hole and frowned. He could see no way to climb down – how deep did it sink into the earth? One thousand breaths, he thought – I pray that is but myth. He shook his head.

The tree man, seeing his expression, laughed again. "You must jump," he chortled, "that is what you must do – jump – you will come to no harm unless you land on your sword."

It was obvious he found this thought amusing. "Give it to me – you must not take it to Manon. Do you not trust me, Master?"

"I will give no consideration to that question," Teilo responded, removing his sword and placing it on the ground. "And I will do as you bid although the thought of it makes me shiver." He relaxed, steadied his breath, then lowering himself into the Pit, let go.

"Now you will know," he heard the tree man whisper above him as he fell.

The piercing cold shock of the water robbed him of his breath and opened that momentary void which precedes the rush for survival. He drifted there – sucked into numb silence until his body vigorously sought the surface.

When he had taken a deep breath, he quietly cursed his friend. There was no visibility – just a black cold, leeching the warmth from his flesh. He did not have time to give way to fear or indulge his thoughts. The part of his brain to which he was not listening, was trying to tell his body that he could not survive in this freezing water. He swam in what he hoped was the right direction.

It did not take long before his feet touched the bottom and he could stand and an even shorter time until he walked out of that frigid pool and onto a loose rocky surface.

"You are right, tree man," he muttered to himself shivering, "I do not like this place at all."

He gave up peering into the dark and instead closed his eyes. That is better, he thought – much easier to not look rather than to not see. As he walked, he listened. Even here there were sounds – the occasional dripping of water – a gentle scurrying – the almost inaudible creaking of the earth – forgotten whispers. The more he listened, the more he saw in his blindness. The earth above him again became visible within him. He felt the breathing of the tree roots deep into the ground, bearing the light from the heavens. He knew when the forest ended and he entered Manon because here the earth was dry and restless. Like Yeshotruen, he thought at first, but then he sensed the difference – the land of Yeshotruen had ached – a lonely wasteland of indifference. Manon seethed – as if it wished to spew forth a long held venom.

Yet there was also peace deep in this earth – thirsting to be known – a peace that he could not challenge. There was light in that peace.

He opened his eyes – there was indeed light. He hastened towards it and the warming touch of the sun.

The hole was barely large enough for his body. Sure that he could sense no presence beyond it, he pulled himself out of the earth and lay on the ground, relishing the warmth – allowing himself a few minutes to enjoy such simple pleasure. He waited – watching his feelings – curious about this hidden place. Everything that was broken in the earth had its origin here – in this land.

Knowing had become an ease in him. No longer needing to seek his answers, he let the earth tell its story – more truthful than any recorded history. He listened to the voices of a people – their stories seeping into his flesh. What had happened in Manon had occurred countless times before on the earth and would no doubt continue. He felt the displacement of a people and their absorption into another land, another way of being – not by choice but through desperation – governed by force and fear. Even Apheilio's roots – though distant, were buried in this land and still lamented in the earth.

Displacement splinters the firmness of our being, he thought – that woven cord that held us in place once frayed carries a deep hurt that is seldom healed. Assimilation rarely offers a conciliatory compromise. He sighed, rolled onto his stomach and looked around him.

The sight of Manon was a shock – a place of rock and stone – more than desolation, it was an eroded anguish. This land had not merely changed with the passing of time and the whim of the seasons. It had been slowly and deliberately tortured. Who would wreak such devastation upon the earth, he wondered.

Seeing that he was completely alone, he sat up for a better view. He could see no buildings, no people, no creatures. Cautiously he stood. He was on the side of a large outcrop of rock at the foot of a small mountain. He hesitated. Already he had sensed the greater part of what he would see – he had known and felt it for a long time and he had done nothing. There had been moments when this knowledge in him was almost on his lips but he would not give of it. With whom could he share it? *"Tell me so that I may prepare,"* Syrath had begged him but that preparation would have been for war. The fear and sadness of the Great Battle had become welded into a hallowed memory. No doubt there were songs written about it – heroes emerged from it and, as always, lessons were learned, but those lessons always fell short of the truth and those who knew the truth did not speak it. They tasted the futility of their words and left them unspoken.

He crouched and moved carefully around the base of the mountain. That old familiar churning was stirring in him but he paid it no heed. The view from the other side was like an illusion. In the valley below him, were faceless stone buildings woven into a colourless walled city. From the activity taking place within those walls, it was obviously a city of warriors – a large army in a land that was forbidden identity – a land whose history had been erased to ensure its voice would never be heard.

If Romarrah had sent his warriors here only recently to ascertain that no dissent would come from this place, how had they missed an army of this size? Teilo knew the answer before he had posed the question. Manon was no longer aimless – it was organized – very organized. These people would have known before the warriors of Romarrah entered their land – all entrances would be covered, except for this one, and all trace of their activities would have disappeared beneath the ground leaving above only a desperate, shuffling wretchedness. They hide within the earth, he mused.

As if to verify this fact, a man suddenly appeared a very short distance from where he stood. Teilo quietly slipped behind a large boulder. The man was not a warrior – his clothing told of poverty but his demeanour spoke of his contentment. He was not young but he carried his age youthfully. His long hair was as grey as smoke.

"I know you are there, warrior," he said without looking in Teilo's direction. "You walk a dangerous path, young man, and you carry no sword which tells me you are either a fool or," here he turned, looking towards where the warrior was hiding, "you are very sure of yourself and your purpose here."

Intrigued, Teilo stepped out from behind his safety to face the man. There was not a hint of aggression here, only calm.

"Good man," he said, "tell me who you are."

The stranger smiled. "I am one of the few who once were many."

"You are of this land," Teilo returned the smile and walked closer to him. "They are your roots that probe this earth – your peace that breathes below the surface. You were not banished here – you belong here."

"You see well, warrior." The man nodded and glanced over his shoulder. A small patrol of warriors were leaving the city and making their way up the slope.

"If you value your safety you must leave now though what you take with you will bring only pain."

"I come only to prevent suffering," Teilo replied.

"A noble sentiment, friend, but only words - those of Manon do not rely on words to give them understanding."

Teilo bowed, acknowledging the elder's wisdom. "It would appear I need your help, kind sir," he said.

Again the man smiled. "I will show you a passage to safety for you cannot return by the way you came – I doubt any have entered by that course. Come."

He led Teilo into the cave from which the warrior had seen him emerge.

"The patrols come often to see we harbour no enemy," the man spoke. "They cannot understand that we have no allegiance – be sure of that, warrior – not even to you or any of the warriors of Romarrah. I help you only because they may tear you apart like dogs their prey if they find you, though I have no doubt you would have found your way."

Here he turned to face Teilo. "What is it you really seek?"

"A way to avoid carnage," the warrior replied.

"There is more than that – your eyes ask something beyond what you see. You are complete in yourself and yet you wish to be finished with something – perhaps it is your own peace you seek."

They had been walking steadily and Teilo marvelled at this underground world – connected by tunnels. How long had it taken to carve rooms and pathways into this rock? There was no answer he could give the man and so he stayed within himself. There were few people who saw him but this stranger knew how to look – perhaps too well.

His guide stopped abruptly. "You will have to stand on my shoulders," he said. "This vein above will take you back to the Land of Romarrah. It will not be guarded."

Crouching, he took the warrior's hand to assist him upwards but quickly stood again and looked fully at this intruder.

"This is not the hand of a warrior – it is the hand of a great healer. No wonder you are torn, son. Would that you could heal the rift that carves a valley through your own soul. Forgive me," he resumed his crouching position, "you do not need to hear that which you already know."

Lightly Teilo sprang onto the other's back and disappeared into the cavity above.

"I know who you are, Master Teilo," the man spoke again, "and I bid you a safe journey."

Teilo's face reappeared at the opening. "And I know who you are, good man. I honour you but I cannot speak of our meeting. That part of our lives must be suspended for a time – there is a greater play at hand. You have my gratitude." With that he was gone.

The tree man turned to greet him. He had made a fire and prepared a broth.

"The smell of that food will make me feel no kindlier towards you," the warrior said as he entered the clearing. "Did you wish me to perish down that hole so you were no longer bound to me? How long did it take for your laughter to subside?"

The tree man gave a little skip. He so delights in mischief, Teilo thought with great fondness.

"Another might have perished, Master," the little man replied, "but not you – you have done it all your life – your body knows it – it knows the water. Your mind cannot use its fear to penetrate that which your heart keeps warm. Did you not see what you needed to see?"

Teilo smiled – helping himself to the food. "That and more, my friend."

"What will you do then, Master?"

"Nothing – I will wait."

"I do not like what I feel about this," the tree man muttered. "You have a plan – I know you have a plan, but you are keeping it so close I cannot even smell it on you. I do not care if people destroy each other – the earth would breathe easily without them. Why must you love them – let them war with themselves and be free of this curse. In time the earth will heal the sickness they leave behind."

Teilo looked at him.

"You forget yourself, friend – I will not remind you of your own origins. Their sickness is that they have forgotten they belong – yours is the same but in reverse. This disunion corrupts as surely as rust defaces iron. Do not be offended, tree man – I would ask you to be no different, and I love you for yourself, but you cannot separate yourself from them or your folly is not dissimilar to their own."

His companion blinked rapidly. "Diseased flesh is best cut away before it spreads its infection," he mumbled sulkily.

Teilo laughed. "Stop now – you desire to provoke me but you forget I already know your heart and there is enough love in you to fill that icy pit into which you sent me. Do not lose your joyful enthusiasm for it is that alone which counters the spread of infection. Come – sit beside me – I need your warmth for I swear I am still chilled to my bones."

They sat together beside the fire, seemingly at peace, but between them they felt the wisps of unrest that warned them to savour this loving friendship fully – their time was slipping away.

3

Cencian was quiet. The fire had died down to a hearty glow and Teilo had left to collect more wood leaving him to digest their conversation. It had not been an easy one. Cencian himself had avoided it, but Teilo would not let it be – he wished to lay the ghost of Mercenta to rest between them.

Cencian had always known that it was Teilo who killed his father, even though this truth was shielded from him – it was never discussed within the compound. His mother did not speak of her husband but she had not forbidden her son to do so.

Perhaps what Allencia had never understood, and what Cencian now knew, was that he had loved the man. Mercenta had indulged him – like a pet to be pampered and rewarded – that was his way of loving.

Cencian had seen his father beat people – even his own mother – but he himself did not fear him because he knew that Mercenta saw him as special. He would be the one who would keep his father alive by continuing the same life pattern.

As a young boy he had seen how people feared this man – their eyes would give them away every time. Mercenta had power over them. They would grovel to him – beg his mercy and he would hold them – suspended – helplessly dangling – until he cut them free, or crushed their miserable lives. Cencian knew he had enjoyed his father's power.

He had only witnessed one person face Mercenta without fear and that was Teilo – in the market place – defending that cowering boy. He had never forgotten the look on the warrior's face. There was no emotion written across that countenance – it was clear and strong.

Even though he was only eight at the time, Cencian knew – this was real power. How he had hated that man who made his father appear small and diminished.

Nor had he forgotten his father's anger afterwards. It was not hard to imagine what had ensued. Mercenta must have carefully plotted his revenge. No doubt it carried with it an inhumane ugliness but Teilo would have walked right through the middle and ended it without fuss.

Still he wished the Master had not told him – that it could have remained unspoken – that he would not need to confront it in himself. But now, what hurt most, was that he feared Teilo did not really see him.

When the Master first entered his life, Cencian hated him – more than he hated Allencia, for that hate was only a contempt inherited from his father. He dreamed of how, as a man, he would take the warrior's life and avenge his father's death. Even when he began to feel drawn to Teilo, he told himself he would only let this man come close enough so that, in time, he could lure him to his death. He kept his plan alive and fed it constantly – embellishing the details – waiting for it to ripen. He did not notice when it lost its passion and became lifeless. He had lived it so often, he kept it breathing from habit rather than desire.

He smiled now as he recalled his loathing. When did he actually realize it had changed to love? When had he really forgiven Teilo? He knew the exact moment – it was four years ago when he had run into the Master's chambers and seen Jemai there. Instantly he sensed the bond between the two men – he knew that at some time, Teilo had stood for Jemai as he now stood for him and he felt the sharpness of jealousy.

But on that day, Teilo had put aside his business with Jemai and had walked beside Cencian to the stream. He had felt the warrior's hand upon his shoulder and there in front of so many people, he had stood by the Master's side as if it was the most natural place for him to be – and the one place he wanted to be always.

Once I wanted more than anything else to kill him, he thought – now I would gladly give my life for him. It pained Cencian to think Teilo did not know this. Why else would he have sought out this conversation? Teilo did not seek out conversation.

Cencian glanced around him. It could be seen as eerie, this place – the empty cottage – like a ghost – the shell of lives once lived. The dark looming forest and, even though he could not see it from where he sat, the mist of Avarinsa, curling around the nearby shadows. But it wasn't eerie – it was strangely soothing.

In the past two days Teilo had told him everything – his childhood in this now deserted village which had also been the home of Allencia. He had talked about Shimmera and Apheilio and the fate of Athanan. Cencian learned of Apheilio's death and Teilo's own struggle with the blackness of hatred and self doubt.

They had walked in the forest and the warrior described his childhood escapades and the evenings he spent with his parents in that same soft darkness. Never had Teilo talked like this. He was a quiet man who spent time watching, only speaking that which needed to be said.

It was now, out of the darkness, that the truth came bounding in homeward haste. Teilo had sought this time for one reason. He did not doubt Cencian – he was giving him his life – as a father would a son – passing on a history – trusting him with his memories. Teilo had brought him home.

The joy of this revelation was short lived. There was a fear attached to it – a blemish upon his glowing contentment. Why now? Why had Teilo disrupted his training and brought him here now?

So absorbed was he in this thought that Cencian did not notice the warrior return and stand to one side watching him. When he did look up, he startled.

"I wish you wouldn't do that."

"What did I do?" Teilo placed more wood on the fire.

"You scared me – I didn't know you were there."

"Oh you knew – you were just unaware of your knowing – in time it will come to you."

"Will it? I do not know. Sometimes I think such gifts will not come to me – that I will not grasp the teachings – that my blood holds too much adversity. I have just now, this moment, become aware of how much I loved my father. Does that shock you, Teilo? Even when I saw his cruelty? And part of me loves him still."

Cencian stared at the fire almost embarrassed by his disclosure.

"It does not shock me, Cencian – it pleases me," Teilo responded quietly. "It tells me Mercenta died knowing your love – it will hold him in good stead."

"I always knew it was you who killed him."

"I know," the warrior replied.

"Did you despise him?" Cencian had not meant to continue this thread of their talk but now he had started he could not stop.

"No – I did not despise him. He was a man who lived the way he had been taught to live – he did not know another way. Disdain was a solid habit in him."

Cencian's next question caught the Master off guard.

"Were you without aggression when you killed my father?"

Teilo remembered their recent discussion in the orchard about aggression. He shook his head. "No – I was not."

Cencian nodded. It suddenly didn't matter. "You would have done your best, of that I have no doubt."

Teilo smiled at this kindness.

"You talk of the blood in your veins, Cencian, as if it will prevent you from knowing your own goodness, but that is now impossible. You have seen a world open up within you – much bigger than the one you knew as a child. This knowing alone prevents you from going back. That blood has already given you Mercenta's strength and physical power – he has bequeathed you his will and resolve – he has left you the goodness he did not know in himself. Your choice is now how to use these gifts."

"Do you trust me, Teilo?" Cencian asked. Before the warrior could answer he continued. "I am not sure I trust myself – that at some point in my life I will become Mercenta – as if an evil will rise up in me that I cannot control and I will inflict it on others – that I will never be perfect."

Teilo walked over and sat beside him.

"None of us is perfect in this life. You must learn to see the perfection of imperfection. Give me your hand."

Holding the young man's hand in his own, he asked, "Do you trust me, son?"

"In every part of me."

Again the warrior smiled at this earnestness. "Then let me tell you what I know in you. Your heart is strong and pure – it harbours no ill-will and the love in you is as sure and steady as the beating of that heart. You have patience – even if it is not yet strong in you – a gentle humour and a strong imagination. Wherever you direct your effort, you will be powerful. It is fortunate for me that you no longer dream of killing me."

Cencian laughed. "How did you know?"

"You wore it – every time you looked at me it was in your eyes. I am glad you had your dream – for a time it sustained you when nothing else would but be very clear in this truth, Cencian – you are not your father. Tell me – with what were you struggling just now when I returned?"

Cencian was doubtful he should voice his concerns but to not do so would now place a smear of doubt across this open threshold between them.

"I was frightened, Teilo – there is something happening around you – something almost secretive. It unsettles Romarrah for I see him watching you sometimes – he looks at you as if he is trying to fathom some deep mystery. There is talk among the warriors that the land is ailing but no one knows what is wrong."

"What do you feel, son?"

"That we are waiting for something to happen and Romarrah is looking at you as if you hold the key. I am frightened this is true – that you know what is happening and that places you in danger. Why else would you give me your memories to hold if you did not sense such peril? But it is worse than that, is it not? None of us is safe."

He was expecting Teilo to dismiss his fears but he didn't – instead, for just a few seconds, he looked away as if gathering his words from the darkness.

"You are correct, Cencian. All of what you have said is true. I cannot tell even yourself what I know to be but I will tell you what is wrong with the Land. If I am wounded in battle, it is not only my flesh which holds that wound – it is also my mind and my heart and they too must be healed if I am to regain my health. When one people rise up against another, the consequences go further and deeper. People forget that they belong to the earth and that the earth is part of our unified mind and heart – the earth holds these greater injuries like a wound and that wound is the weeping of our injury to our self. For us to live in rightness, this too must be healed. Without healing, we feed a cycle of discontent and unrest. This is what ails us now."

He paused. "I want you to understand this carefully, Cencian. If death comes to me and it appears to be by my own choice – it would not, on my part, be a rejection of life – of those I love. Apheilio said as much to me in fewer words before his own death. The time is coming closer when this unrest will rupture. I cannot prevent that happening – my hope is to contain it so that reconciliation will come before yet another carnage erupts upon us. If that results in my death then so be it. I too am concerned for those I love. I question my actions in bringing you to Imoshtan – in Yeshotruen your safety would be assured – at least for a longer time. You must promise me that when I send you to Yeshotruen, you will go without argument."

He watched the boy struggle with this request.

"Your staying will not serve me, son, but your going will serve to alert those of Yeshotruen as to what happens here. Do I have your word?"

"You have my word, Teilo."

The warrior looked at the young honest face and the sadness his words had placed there. What do I ask of him, he thought – I cannot guarantee his safety, nor will I use my power to know his fate but my body already feels the pain of carnage.

"Know that I love you, Cencian – as I would my own son. Come – I wish to show you something."

He walked towards Avarinsa – letting the mist reach out to curl around their bodies. He felt the young man's fear.

"Let it go, son – what is it you fear? Is it life or death – the living or the dying? Once you fully know your fear laugh with it. Do not laugh at it, for that would be to deride yourself and only serves to make you small and diminished. When you laugh with your fear you give it your joy until it can no longer contain its own shadow – then you expand. If you stand here long enough, you will feel the magic of this place."

"It is a magic that disturbs me," Cencian responded still holding back.

"It is simply the magic of life and death – that which people forget and then spend a lifetime trying to recreate in some form. It becomes a spectacle – something to be manipulated. Yet all we need to know this magic is to be fully part of it. If we forget we are part of it, we delude ourselves into thinking the magic actually comes from us - we lose it and forever try to reclaim it. Place yourself in the centre of life and death – do not fear it – trust it – give yourself fully to each moment and all magic will occur of its own accord in and around you."

The quiet voice of the Master brought calm to Cencian. He let himself relax and absorb the words and the mist.

"This, which you call life," Teilo continued, "is but a dream that has no beginning and no end – it is forever unfolding – an endless adventure. This passage through time – this path you walk that you call your own life is the same – it is no different. Know this, Cencian, for I have been there – in the eye of Creation and have witnessed that unfolding. This I cannot give you – it is nothing and everything but be very clear on this – do not waste one breath on that which gives rise in you to grasping or loathing for to do so robs your life of vibrancy. Give of your passion to every moment – live it as vividly as is possible and your knowing will be complete. This is your choice – it has always been your choice. Come – stand with me on the edge and feel this power. We both need its strength in us now."

They stood, side by side – the warrior's arm resting lightly across the young man's shoulders while the world fell away into white emptiness.

4

"Why have you taken this path, Teilo – it is unfamiliar to me?"

Syrath was perplexed by the deviation. They were leading a legion of warriors on a regular patrol but Teilo, giving no explanation, had suddenly changed their direction.

"Does it present a problem for you, Syrath?" he asked genially.

"No," she replied, "but you do – you are perhaps too watchful. You persuaded Romarrah to give you many times the warriors necessary for a patrol such as this. I feel you are waiting for something to happen."

She stopped when she realized her friend was no longer present to her – he was instead gazing intently at a lone figure standing on the pathway ahead. It was that of a beggar woman. Even from a distance her poverty was evident yet poverty was something that was seldom seen in the Land of Romarrah. Although the woman's hood was pulled forward over her face, Syrath had the feeling she was watching them – that she even expected their arrival.

"What do you feel?" Teilo nodded in the woman's direction. Syrath frowned.

"I can get no sense of her," she puzzled.

"Nor can I," came his surprising reply. "She is well folded within that cloak. It would appear we have a mystery."

Involuntarily Syrath shivered – a reaction that did not go unnoticed by her companion. As they neared the woman, Teilo addressed her, bowing courteously.

"Are you in need of something, good woman?' he inquired.

At first there was no answer – the stranger kept her head down and her face hidden.

"Do the warriors of Romarrah come by this path for a reason?" she asked at last in a soft, almost lilting voice which could have been soothing were it not for the slight edge of a challenge.

"We come only in peace," Teilo responded, "you have nothing to fear.'

Even as he spoke he knew there was no fear in this woman – nor was her poverty that of destitution but he would maintain the pretence as he endeavoured to know something more of her. When she spoke again, her words almost carried a visibility of their intent and seemed at once threatening and yet enlightened.

"Fear," she said, "does indeed destroy peace, but my good friend, the absence of fear does not mean that peace will be your conclusion."

He tried to meet her words but no sooner had she uttered them, than they, like her face, became invisible.

"Let me see your face, kind woman, that I might honour you." His voice matched her tone.

"I am not ready to be known by you," she countered, "and you do not need to see my face to honour me."

"That is true," he smiled, "but you would honour me by showing me who you are." He had begun to feel more comfortable in her presence – in fact he was enjoying their exchange – there was indeed a sense of something familiar.

"We must continue on our way, Teilo." Syrath's voice was commanding and she offered the woman some coins. It was a dismissal and the beggar woman showed reluctance to accept the alms. After a moment's hesitation, she took the alms and walked away.

Teilo turned to Syrath, his eyebrows raised in question.

"I did not feel comfortable in her presence," she offered, almost embarrassed.

"Then why did you give her the coins? She will know of you now – be sure of that."

He said no more and they walked on a short distance each in keeping with their own thoughts.

"We must stop soon" he commented noting she had quickened their pace. "The younger warriors are tiring. There is a river nearby where we can make camp."

"How do you know of this – have you been this way before? It is not our usual path and there is no village anywhere in this part of the land – which makes the beggar woman's appearance even more disturbing."

"I have come this way before – for my own curiosity. The land by the river is very beautiful. It is true there are no villages here – this forest you see gradually thickens into the south western edge of Maurapin. And I concur with you – the beggar woman is a mystery but did you not hear the clever play of her words?"

"I am not sure what she meant Teilo, or why her words were so clever – they held nothing of her self."

Syrath's irritation gave a sharpness to her words which she tried to soften. "I doubt we will ever really know peace – that is why the warriors of Romarrah give their lives to that cause.

"Which is precisely why there can be none,' Teilo all but muttered.

No longer could she hide her annoyance.

"Do you seek to discredit the warriors and what they hold sacred, Teilo? You talk as if we are at fault – as if we are the cause of war."

She was unable to keep the frustration from her voice.

"You have trained as a warrior of Romarrah – you know the goodness that lies at the heart of all that we do. Why do you heckle me thus? Why do you wish to sow seeds of doubt in my own heart that would only serve to deepen sorrow and discontent?"

She had slightly raised her voice at him and some of the younger warriors glanced at each other and smiled. No one would speak to the Master in that tone. It broke the pattern of their walking. Teilo waited until they resumed their rhythm.

"Forgive me, Syrath – but those seeds of doubt already exist in you and your discontent grows stronger with each passing day. I watch you try to smother it, for it speaks to you a treacherous path – it scares you – you see it as ingratitude, which it is, though not for your privileged life as you would see. It is ingratitude for your struggle – your blindness – that which rankles your peace that you may see its lack of substance. The warriors of Romarrah only exist because of war and unrest – do you not see that? By the very nature of their being comes an acceptance of war as part of that existence. It is all so futile. By the time the warriors go into battle to offer their protection that which gave rise to the conflict is already dying. War is the death of discontent – we are killing that which has reached its end. We slay something that is dying and it will be born again because we fail to heal it. Listen to me, Syrath, if you would have peace go to the heart of your own discontent and know it fully – and once you understand it, know that your duty is not to protect, but to heal yourself. When you can heal yourself, you can assist others to do the same – to heal their bitterness and disappointment – to heal their loathing and fear – to heal the blindness that prevents them from seeing their own goodness. Not by placing over it a balm of some acquired knowledge but by understanding it within themselves. Only then will they protect themselves through the living of that very understanding. We have grasped a sword, my friend, when we could have grasped a hand."

He turned abruptly and walked away. Never had he spoken to her so forcefully. It was as if his words tore through her clothing, shredding her skin and exposing her own wretchedness.

The warriors had reached the clearing beside the river and he instructed them to make camp. When they were settled in their tasks, he slowly returned to where she still stood trying to steady the shaking of her constancy. He did not speak – he just took her hand and led her to the river.

"You see," he said softly, indicating their surroundings, "It is beautiful here – there is peace – everywhere – always – the stillness of each moment – each breath."

But now there was no peace within her – this was the river of her vision – the river that flowed with Teilo's blood – the river that divided him and Romarrah.

"Are you asking me to turn against Romarrah?" she asked.

He shook his head. "I ask you to turn against no one – only to find your freedom. Every link of the chain you carry has the name Romarrah upon it – not the person, Syrath – the ideal. Break it – go – go now – walk away."

He watched the training of a lifetime rise up against what he knew to be in her heart and he wished he could hold her. Her anguish was pleading with him. "Take back your power," he urged. "I entreat you – do not stay – if you want this to end – claim what you have lost."

"The warriors..," she began.

"I will look after them." He refused to let her squirm away with an excuse of responsibility. His hand tightened around hers. She felt his strength.

At first the child in her swam determinedly against its current – then suddenly surrendered.

"I do not know where to go," was her tremulous response.

"But you do – follow your heart – be guided by it – it does not lie – let it take you home."

He let go of her hand.

"Do I stand so far from the truth?" she smiled at him sadly.

"You stand so close, Syrath, you stand in its shadow."

These were his final words to her and it took all her courage to walk away from him although she knew she must. If she stayed she would see that which he did not want her to witness. If she stayed the anger she had harboured towards him since his return would erupt and stand between them. It would attempt to carve a different path for them both. If she stayed he would not only be lost to her, she would be lost to herself.

The truth of his words became stronger with each step she took and her heart guided her straight towards Maurapin.

He watched her leave, sending with her a prayer for her safety. Nevertheless, he was relieved.

As he took up his place of watchfulness, he felt an easiness within him. The churning was forever present – it alerted him to what was almost upon them, but for himself he was at peace – the waiting would be as still and quiet as any other time.

It was Cencian who brought him food, bowing respectfully as he placed the bowl before him.

Teilo smiled at him.

"I cannot find Master Syrath," the young warrior spoke still looking around him.

"She has gone," Teilo replied quietly. "My gratitude for the food son."

Cencian bowed again and turned to leave. Although puzzled by Syrath's absence, he did not question it.

"Stay with me, Cencian," Teilo requested.

They sat in silence for a time. To Cencian it was a silence that carried a burden. He observed the food remained untouched – the Master had placed it to one side.

Finally Teilo spoke. "It will be a long night."

His words were calm but the chill of their message could not be mistaken.

"What am I to do with you – whether I send you away or keep you close, I cannot guarantee your safety. Do you feel ready for battle, son?"

Cencian felt his heart beat quicken and an instant dryness in his mouth.

"I do not know, Teilo, but if battle is upon us should you not prepare the warriors?"

"Not yet – let them be rested in peace. I wish so much to avoid this war but I must seek our opponent's measure. If there be a path around the conflict, be assured I will take it."

"But you can offer the warriors protection can you not?" the young man's faith was solid.

"Cencian, I protect no one from death if it be their time – that is not my right. I can offer protection to their being – to bring them steadiness and strengthen their hearts and this in turn fuels their will. I protect them in that they do not succumb to their own base desires. I protect their souls that they stay in peace – this is from where true power comes."

Cencian was silent – feeling these words carefully.

"Has Master Syrath left to alert Romarrah?" he asked.

"I do not wish to alert Romarrah. I know what he will do. It is for this reason I risk all our lives – forgive me son. I trust you not to speak of this as you must trust me to deal with it. When I give you a sign leave immediately for Yeshotruen. Tell Jemai to bring the warriors to Manon. They must go by the way of the Longing of Tharseywon – it is by far the shortest path – I have left marks that will guide him. If, when they arrive, I still live, I may need them to stand with me. If I am dead they will have to choose whether to walk away, or stand with Romarrah and destroy Manon again. But that is not now – it has yet no substance – the important thing is that you do as I ask. Travel to Yeshotruen by the forest paths – have no fear – if battle comes to you – honour your opponent – keep the dance alive and steady within you and do not kill with disdain or pleasure. It grieves me to ask this of you but there is no other here who can carry it without compromise."

They both stood then and embraced. Teilo touched the young warrior's cheek

"When you return to Yeshotruen, Allencia will indeed find joy in the man you have become, as I do now. It is a deep pleasure in me to call you son. Go back to your companions now and rest well – do not let your mind play in the future. I will come for you when it is time."

Cencian turned to go back to the camp but hesitated.

"Teilo," he began, looking at this man before him – feeling the power which emanated from that form. There was so much he wanted to say but his mind was tight with too many thoughts.

"I cannot help but think of what you told me – of Apheilio's death – and your love for him," he said at last. "Know that I love you in the same way – that you have taken me soaring from the first time you sang that song to me. It does not matter what happens does it? Nothing can take away the good of us and you have never failed any of us."

He walked away then before his feelings took hold and stood between him and the steadiness now required of him.

Teilo wrapped himself in his blanket and the kindness of Cencian's words. The night had settled and the fires from the camp spoke their own comfort to the darkness. Soon a full moon would bless the sky – its light dancing upon the wandering surface of the river. He could sense Syrath's presence getting further and further away.

As was his custom, he closed his eyes and let the images come. First was the beggar woman and he held her – there was something more he wished to see of this woman. He probed each detail – the hooded cloak – dark and stained – the ragged clothes beneath. All spoke of age – even in poverty they were not the clothes of youth. But the hesitant hand that reached out to take the coins – that was the hand of a young woman – beneath the crust of dirt were long, fine fingers. This beggar woman liked to create illusions and he would like to hold that hand and read the story in the pulse of her blood.

♋

Syrath walked blindly through the night. Sometimes she ran – pushed forward by an urgency which pounded in each footstep. The tide of her emotion burst as she stumbled into the clearing of Maraka and she fell weeping, beside the ancient pit. All her anguish – even that which, for so long, she did not know she held – poured from her – faded images of the past – this life she had led with such reverence – honouring the Great Wisdom – giving of herself in the teaching of others. When had it become the web that ensnared her when once it had been that which sustained the very goodness of her? When had the beauty of her peaceful life grown spurs of discontent? They probed her flesh with an undeniable longing. Part of that longing was for Teilo – she could not bear to think of her life without him.

"Do not weep, Master Syrath," a soft voice spoke from the shadows, startling her. At first she could see nothing then slowly his form appeared.

"It is sad when we lose our faith, good warrior, for the heart breaks with the weight of our loss. All we have lived for becomes dry in our heart and tasteless on our lips. I nursed him through his doubt – so hard to keep him still – his purpose is always strong. He wept when he saw himself – how imperfect the vision when the surface is disturbed – how can the reflection be true? You will become cold there in the dark – let me find warmth for you."

She said not a word – she just stared at the tree man as he gathered wood and started a small fire. Who was this creature? He spoke with such eloquence yet sometimes so incoherently that his words rambled on, caught in a dust storm of their own.

"Of course I will help her – do not fear – she is of his heart – I promised – he would want it – she has such goodness."

The more she watched him the more she saw him – what she had missed in their first meeting so long ago.

"Tree man, it is you – is it not? You are the wisdom of Maurapin – the spirit – that which has been written and speaks to us from this sacred, ancient place."

He shook his head. "The wisdom is already here, Master Syrath – it is not from my self it comes – but I hear it. I feel it in my brothers and sisters – I know the language of the earth and I can speak it for you – I can place it in your own tongue."

So quickly had he brought the fire into being that already its warmth touched her.

"I cannot bear it if he dies, tree man – he brings such joy to life – I feel so safe when he is here."

He put his head to one side and looked at her with his fierce intensity.

"That is why, good warrior, he keeps pushing you away. There is something you are not seeing – it is in your heart but you have not yet named it."

She frowned at him then looked into the flames.

"What is in your heart, warrior? Whisper it now – give it to this earth."

Again the tears spilled down her cheeks.

"That – that which you weep – what is its name?"

"It is too many things – it is freedom – it is to be the one who holds the lamp – it is to open my arms and embrace all that needs to be held – it is to love and know fully that love – to know fully myself – unshackled and unknown. Forgive me, tree man – I make no sense."

"Sense is not what you make, Master – it is what you feel. You want everything that you think Master Teilo is and he asks you to find it in yourself. It must be yours in your own right – it cannot come from him."

He came to her side. She felt the tenderness of his heart. When he spoke his voice was like a caress.

"What you are asking for is the wisdom of mother earth – the wisdom of woman – that which Shimmera gave to Teilo. It is that which Master Tharease also longed to embrace. She brought you here so you would feel it in the earth – hoping that you would one day have the courage to take that which you have been denied. You see warrior - only woman can hold the lamp – do you understand – only she can shed the sweetness of that light. Find what has been stolen from you, Master Syrath – from the earth – from the mother – that is what he wants you to do."

His words changed, again becoming erratic. He spoke as if to the shadows. "Does the good warrior know where she will find it? Is it beneath the earth? Tell her – no it is not my place to tell her."

"Hush," she said kindly, "this part I know – my answer lies in Manon – that is where my journey takes me."

The little man nodded vigorously. For a time there were no words between them then she spoke again. "What is his plan, tree man?"

"The secrets he does not give me I will not take."

She nodded and smiled at him. "In my heart I pray he does not suffer. If Shimmera was indeed from Avarinsa, then perhaps, like her, he too need not know death."

The tree man looked at her – searching her face to find the source of her words.

"Shimmera died," he stated abruptly. "I watched her – even as the last breath left her crumpled body."

He saw the disbelief on the warrior's face.

"It is true. She came because Apheilio called her – she heard his longing and that of the world. She came to birth the son who would feed us all. She knew the price she would pay. You cannot take this form, Master Syrath and escape the death of it – it does not matter from where you came. The sadness of her leaving groaned in my brothers and sisters – they had known the love of her hands. She knew I watched her. She knew my promise was steady – that I held her in my heart. She gave herself up to those men. They drove her off the edge of the land and I saw her fall to the earth – her body shattered – only then did the mist scatter her spirit."

"But why, tree man – why did not Apheilio stop them – why did he not take her and Teilo with him to Imoshtan?"

"Understand, Master – it was her choice – to take the shadows away from the one she must protect. Romarrah would not have welcomed her – have no doubt of that – but the child he would honour."

Syrath let go – she did not wish her curiosity sated. What the tree man had already recounted troubled her enough.

"What was your promise?" she asked

"To watch over him – now yet another he has drawn from my lips."

"My gratitude to you, dear friend," she gently touched his shoulder. "I must continue my journey – in this way I will honour him."

He watched her as she stood to leave.

"Do not carry your sword to Manon, Master – you must go in peace."

She was uncertain of this caution. Nevertheless she unsheathed her sword and handed it to him.

"Take only the forest paths," he warned, "until the land rises to Manon."

Syrath nodded and walked into the shadows.

A cool wind rustled the leaves beside him.

"Why do you not show yourself?" Teilo asked.

His voice was barely audible but he knew he would be heard. As he slowly opened his eyes, she stepped forth – her hood still drawn forward – her face hidden. He sighed and stood to face her.

"What is your purpose here, beggar woman?"

As he spoke she bent to pick up a stick from the ground. Without warning, she threw it towards him. It became a writhing serpent, its scales shining in the moonlight.

His reaction was fast and instinctive – the sword was in his hand and the creature lay in two parts upon the earth.

"Do you not see what you have done, warrior?" she spoke. "You have slain an innocent creature."

He kept his eyes steadily upon her – not looking at the ground.

"You created it for your own purpose," he said, "the illusion of the serpent is yours, not mine."

"It is not to the serpent that you should direct your attention – it is to your self and you, warrior, reached for your sword – it has become your instinct. Do you really think you can lay yourself bare?"

The thrust of her words was sure and sharp. He blinked at their impact. Pauroseng could very well have uttered them, he thought and smiled somewhat ruefully.

"You have not answered my question," his tone was softer.

"When the moon is in its eleventh hour you will be attacked," she answered. "Of this you are already aware. Your attackers easily outnumber your warriors – coming here, to this place, gains you but little advantage. My path is not one of war but one of healing and, like death, I hover awaiting to be summoned. I can turn them away if that be your wish."

"I did not summon you healer, nor will I. Stand aside and let this day be done. I do not need to be tested thus – my path is set – not you or any other will hinder me now, unless of course you know a better way. If you – a healer – have the knowing you appear to have, you will see this to be so. I will ask you but one more time – what is it you want?"

"We are here for the one purpose, my friend – it was you who summoned me – with your song. You wait for death and I await my birth and neither of us knows the surety of our purpose. Your heart longs for the peace that comes when it is all over and mine longs for the beginning – to see the mystery in the new-born's eyes – yet I remain dependant on you for my freedom. I am no stranger to you Master Teilo – you have met me again and again – you already know the fullness of who I am."

He tasted her words then – and also the tears that rushed to his eyes. Each one held an image – that of Shimmera dancing towards the light – Pauroseng patiently holding the lamp – Syrath in her tower – the lonely prisoner. He saw Allencia – the silent agony of her years with Mercenta – and Edora, quietly gathering the broken pieces of her woman into her strength – mending her fractured soul.

He turned to the beggar woman but she was gone. The mystery still surrounded her but now he knew something of who she was. He bowed to the darkness. There was a comfort in knowing she was there.

He waited until the moon was high in the heavens then roused the warriors one by one – giving them directions – letting them feel his steadiness, his confidence. He instructed them so that, regardless of what befell him, they would carry through.

They moved noiselessly while he watched, touched by their courage and the trust they placed in him. It was without question – a loyalty that went beyond mere camaraderie. They have been taught and cared for so well, he thought – Romarrah has been a good leader.

With that thought, his doubt surfaced. It was not too late to change this – he could still raise the alarm – send the smoke towards the heavens and once again wipe this threat from the earth with the might of Romarrah's entire force. He cast his doubt aside.

The warriors had taken up their positions – the more experienced to the fore, the remainder to the rear – Cencian where he could see him at all times. He nodded to them and they became invisible among the shadows.

Taking the pouches of sand and kneeling in the centre of the clearing, he began the chief warrior's ritual of protection. When it was done, he blessed it with the golden circle.

We will see how well these warriors of Manon have been trained, he thought. He took up his own place among the shadows.

5

Syrath was the first to see them in the valley below her. They moved in unison – a silent, dark shape. She could almost smell the battle lust upon them. Her every instinct urged her to run back to the warriors – to Teilo – to stand by his side, but the voice in her bid her to be still and wait.

It was a large army, easily outnumbering the warriors in the clearing by the river. Protect them Teilo, she prayed. Cautiously she left the path and made her way slowly through the thick forest.

Light did not penetrate into Maurapin except for rare slivers and they created a mystical beauty – illuminating narrow bands with soft moonlight. Syrath was marvelling at this exquisite display when she stepped into empty space and disappeared into the earth.

The warriors of Manon arrived at the clearing only to find nothing. It was quiet and still – not even a leaf stirred. There was no evidence that, only hours before, it had been host to a great legion. The hushed voices of the invading army could be heard clearly in the stillness.

"We have been fooled," one muttered

Others murmured their assent.

"Wait." Their leader spoke calmly as he kneeled to touch the ground. "The smell of their fires lingers – the earth is still warm – they cannot be far."

At that point the moon emerged from behind clouds, bathing the landscape in its soft glow.

"Over there," called another in a loud whisper, his attention drawn to the golden circle glistening in the moonlight. In unison the leading warriors moved closer to view the mysterious patterns that evoked in them a sense of nervous awe.

"It is the mark of a chief warrior," said a young man, "they have unearthly powers – the land is under their spell."

"Do not give your thoughts to such superstitions," snapped their leader, grabbing the man's arm. "I know these warriors – believe me they have no wondrous powers – they are but flesh and blood – they die."

Before he could finish speaking, there came a soft humming sound. They turned to find themselves surrounded. It was difficult to ascertain the numbers of the warriors who suddenly appeared, or to determine what was shadow and what was flesh. The moonlight tipped their swords – their confidence and might was unnerving. A quiet rush of unspoken panic broke like a light sweat across the army of Manon though no man moved.

"Stand firm," their leader urged seeking to reclaim their focus. Silently he cursed himself for his lack of foresight. Of course the warriors of Romarrah would have been in readiness – that was their way – he had been fooled by an empty space.

"We have no wish to spill your blood upon this earth," Teilo said stepping from the shadows so close to these warriors that some visibly reacted to the sound of his voice. "What is it you want that you come prepared for battle?"

The leader faced the chief warrior and moved towards him.

"We come to take back what has been denied us for so long – our land, our dignity, our power."

Teilo had been carefully studying this army, and especially its leader, from the moment they arrived at the clearing. He had felt their confusion and uncertainty. It had many different levels. He knew the origins of their unrest and his heart was heavy. He wanted to take each and every one of them and release that uncertainty – to show them their true nature and let them weep with realization.

"What is your name?" he asked, still appraising the man before him. He was neither young nor too old. His frame was indeed powerful but his face spoke of trial and loss – a time perhaps forgotten by others but forever present in him.

"My name matters not," he said flatly. "To you I am no one."

Teilo stepped closer. "To me you can never be no one. Nor can you reclaim your dignity or power through brutality friend – you will only succeed in spreading more fear and sadness, breeding more hatred. I honour the strength and courage of you and your men but without understanding know that you are weak and cannot be victorious – either within yourself or in your quests. Do not do this for I can see in your heart you do not truly want such an end."

For a moment the leader looked confused. This warrior before him spoke with such gentleness. It had been a long time since he had felt the genuine love of another and now it came to him from his sworn enemy. He glanced at his men. They were waiting – dependent on him for guidance – there was no other way for them now.

Teilo saw his thoughts. "Did you not see how easy it was to infect these men with uncertainty?" he said. "It lives just below the surface in their minds – given fuel it becomes fear and its infection races like a fire in them. If you choose this battle, I know my warriors will win. They have something these men do not – they know from where their power comes. So once did you, good man – of that I am certain. Why did you forsake your knowing?"

The leader did not want to listen. It would be dangerous to allow these words a place in his thoughts.

"I will not surrender to you," he growled. He could not back down – there was no where to go – there was nothing else to hold them and they were too weary of the world to go back.

Again Teilo responded, speaking louder this time so that the warriors of Manon would hear his words. "If you lay down your weapons and surrender to me now, I promise no retribution. I will offer every one of you the opportunity to train with me – to have a new life – one of freedom and understanding."

Even as he spoke, he realized his words would find no place in their hearts. So clearly he saw their longing but they themselves no longer recognized its source. It was as he suspected it would be.

"We reject your offer," the leader was steadfast in his refusal. Teilo almost glimpsed the apology in his eyes.

"Then give me the name of your Master and your intent in being here."

The chief warrior's words drew a line between them.

"We fight for Master Amis of Manon," came the reply, "and our intent I have already stated. Perhaps I should make the same offer to your warriors for our numbers are far greater and without you, Master Teilo, they will no doubt be lost. Our orders are to see you dead."

"You cannot destroy me," the chief warrior smiled, staring into his opponent's eyes. "If you take my life, that which you wish to destroy will always remain – it will rise up within you again and again until you surrender to it. Ask yourself this good warrior – why does your Master not come to do this deed? Let me tell you now – he cannot face his own treachery."

It was then, without warning, the leader raised his sword. With eyes that begged his own death, he lunged at the chief warrior.

To Cencian, watching from the shadows, it was as if Teilo willingly gave himself to that sword. Not one part of him offered defence. It was inconceivable that the Master had not anticipated the attack, yet he made no attempt to counter it. His opponent was strong. The chief warrior stumbled with the force of the thrust. He felt the blade enter his body – the sickening numbness that accompanied its probing – the hatred and anger that tore his flesh apart – the shock of violation as the sword was ripped from him and the mind raced to recognize its injury.

The struggle began – the pulsing of the blood, the cold heat, the weakness, the nausea – he could feel his body beginning to crumple beneath its conflict.

No one moved. The disbelief hung in tatters on every breath. There would be those who later swore, that at that moment, the earth groaned beneath their feet and in the silence that followed came the wailing of its unified voices.

Teilo blinked – he could see the earth spirits gathering around him – just as they had gathered all those years ago at Maraka – fragments of light like those from his childhood – reaching out from the mist – soft and comforting – he could surrender to their care.

But the voice also came – clear and commanding. *'Behold what you do!'*

He heard them all then – a thousand voices clamouring for understanding – imploring him to listen.

'Give back what you have taken – back to the source!'

He could see Orphaele – why was she here still?

"Teilo," she implored, reaching out her hand. He tried to touch her.

Cencian could not bear it any longer. He stepped towards the Master.

The movement broke the spell. Teilo's assailant turned to the young warrior.

"Take one more step, boy, and I will finish him now."

Then he addressed his own warriors. "See – he bleeds – he has no powers – he is no different to any of us – how easy it is to defeat him. Be assured, his warriors will fall the same way. Take your place to claim victory. Take your place for battle."

His words rekindled the men's fervour. With their intent clearly visible, they faced the warriors of Romarrah.

As this man had been speaking, Cencian saw Teilo slowly reach inside his coat. The young warrior was aware that something had changed in the Master and he took a deep breath – almost as if he breathed for him. He was not the only one who sensed the change but by the time his opponent spun around, Teilo stood straight – his sword in his hand, his eyes unwavering.

"This cannot be," the leader hissed, unwilling to share his disbelief with his men. "Your blood is still on my sword – I can see the stain of your wound and I know the weight I gave to my blade."

"Then stop now," Teilo urged, "ask yourself why you do this. Does your Master truly see you, because I do. You were not meant for this. Does Amis inspire you with his wisdom and understanding – do you want to die for him or do you want to live for your freedom? Once more I offer you this choice but before you raise your sword again, know that I am ready for you this time and I will weep to take your life."

The warrior's stone was in his hand – he could feel the strength flowing into him but his heart was chilled with the thought that this war was upon them – he knew he had failed to turn it away. Briefly he glanced at Cencian and nodded. The young warrior slipped into the shadows.

♋

Cencian encountered no difficulty stepping quietly into the bushes – all attention was on Teilo and the leader of the Manon warriors. He did not wish to leave. The disbelief of what had just taken place still echoed in his thoughts, begging answers. He had seen that blade enter Teilo's side and the warrior's reaction was what one would expect – his body reeled from the impact – the blood gushed forth as soon as the sword was ripped from him. The blow may not have been fatal but no one could have rallied from it as Teilo had done. Cencian wanted to have one more look – to make sure he had truly witnessed such a transformation.

Suddenly the stillness behind him erupted with the cries of war and the clash of swords. The sounds sickened him to his core. How many warriors whom he now called his friends would be slain by the time the sun broke over the land? And Teilo – for how long could he stand in battle – his body already weakened? The young warrior wished only to go back – to face death with those he knew would fight so honourably. Why had Teilo elicited such a promise from him? His footsteps faltered. By the time he reached Yeshotruen, the battle would be long finished. If the outcome was unfavourable, Romarrah would learn of it and Cencian pitied those of Manon – retribution would be swift and powerful. What could those of Yeshotruen offer to the outcome? Did Teilo only then wish to spare him – to keep him safe? That was unfair.

The battle sounds had become feverish – a constant pandemonium of voices and striking metal – an explosion of violence. He knew the warriors of Romarrah would utter not a sound – they would waste nothing of their energy. He stopped. Forgive me Teilo, he thought – I cannot walk away.

Before he could turn around and retrace his steps, he experienced the uneasy feeling that he was being watched but all around him the shadows were unmoving. It was something in that distraction which created another space in his anxious thinking and in that space was Teilo's voice. *"Know that I love you, Cencian, as I would my own son.'* The Master's faith in him felt warm in his blood – it banished the wavering of his doubt, calmed his resolve. He set off again towards Yeshotruen at a steady trot.

♋

Syrath felt the pain rip through her body. Like an animal she was curled in an earthen burrow. Her sanctuary was warm and protective. The smell and quiet murmurings of the earth were comforting. It was an untroubled womb.

But now her comfort was shattered. "What has he done?" she groaned.

She prayed – releasing her prayers on her breath – knowing they would gather around him. It was then she saw them – the others who came to him. A young woman warrior singing sweetly in a room that nursed an ancient song – an unknown woman, tending the sick. Her head was bowed in prayer and she held the hand of one who suffered. It was Teilo.

They are holding him, Syrath thought – just as I hold him. Then the old warrior appeared and handed her the lamp that she might keep it steady for him. In its flame, she could see Shimmera. She knew it was Shimmera – reaching out to her son. In death or in life, they all held him.

"Syrath, Syrath."

It was his voice. She lifted the lamp, peering into the dark. The pain in her side was constant now. She could not see.

"Teilo – where are you? What has happened?"

He was crying – she could hear him. Every part of him was crying.

"It was a long battle. I am so tired, Syrath – I have sent the warriors home."

She called out but he did not answer. Then she felt him walk away.

As she awoke, her dream remained fresh before her – it panicked inside her. The pain still throbbed in her side. Steadying her breath, she listened to her visions. The battle was over – of that she was certain. Of Teilo, she saw nothing.

6

Teilo reached the gates of Manon late in the afternoon. He sat on a large rock trying to steady his breath. The clothing he wore, his hands, were splattered with blood – his own and that of others. His body was wracked with pain – the heat of infection already smouldered beneath his skin.

Overcome by nausea he suddenly retched and vomited – a mixture of bile, water and blood – then rested his head in his hands. Again he tried to steady his breath and the quivering of his body. His mind almost desperately wanted to play through the visions of the battle but he refused them access. He must stay firm for just a little longer – there must be no reflection, no recrimination, no anticipation. He had not the strength to wander.

Staring without seeing into the forest below him, he could still hear the sounds of the day – the slamming of steel, the groans of torn flesh, the gasping gurgle of death. All remained – as if the air held them trapped – reluctant to spread their sorrow throughout the land.

His numbness was such that the world around him held no life, no reflection – a painted canvas wherein he no longer existed.

He roused himself – his movements slow and disconnected – his body now functioning without him, knowing what it must do. Walking through the large stone gateway, he made no attempt to conceal himself but followed the path down towards the walled city.

There was a part of him that registered his surroundings – that knew he was being watched. A chief warrior of Romarrah walking alone in the Land of Manon would no doubt cause an excitement. At times a crouching form scuttled from one rocky outcrop to the next and word of his approach spread among the cave dwellers.

Gradually the buildings became clearer, the movement around them ceased and the hush that followed told that all eyes were now upon him.

When he was within shouting distance, a voice rang out, asking the stranger to identify himself. He made no reply.

A small group of warriors left the compound and came to confront him, swords drawn.

"What is it you want?" he asked – his voice was weary but it remained firm. They hesitated. This man spoke without fear but it was his eyes that unnerved them. He looked at them with such sympathy – as though he saw in them some deep sorrow.

Subdued, one of the men removed Teilo's sword. The warrior made no attempt to resist. He was led, as a prisoner, into what appeared to be a hall – a long rectangular room without decoration made entirely of stone. Even the seats down each side were carved from rock. None of the warriors spoke – they just left him there – closing the heavy doors and securing the bolts.

Removing his coat, Teilo spread it on the floor and lay down. No longer able to hold himself present, he surrendered his consciousness and entered a world of darkness and dreams.

♋

Night had turned to day and back to night again and still Cencian travelled. At times he felt his aloneness so acutely. It was hard not to give way to the fear that every now and then shivered through him – not fear for his own safety but for Teilo and the other warriors.

When he was well clear of Maurapin, he rested at last beside a small stream. Being too tired to make a fire and prepare food, he wrapped himself in his blanket and slept.

What awakened him he could not say but he could have sworn that he heard a voice warning him of danger and felt an invisible hand shaking him. He woke with a start and leapt to his feet, sword drawn.

"Show your self," he commanded.

A warrior of Romarrah stepped forward. Cencian smiled.

"Was it you who awakened me?" he asked relieved. "What is your purpose here?"

"I am seeking Master Syrath," the other replied. "Do you know where I might find her?"

"That I do not," Cencian responded genially but something in the other's manner disturbed him. "Why do you seek her?"

"She is wanted at the compound," the warrior's reply was abrupt.

"You are not who you say you are," Cencian was sure now. The man before him knew nothing of how a warrior of Romarrah behaved. He did not meet Cencian's eyes when he spoke – his speech was not careful or confident.

"What is it you want?" he asked again, his voice now strong and direct.

"I have already said – we seek Master Syrath."

As the man uttered these words, two more warriors came forward. Cencian felt a tightening in his stomach. His sword skills were good, though they were not yet refined. He knew it was more than unlikely that he could match those of three men. Teilo could – but Teilo was not here. His first taste of battle and he was alone.

What would Teilo do, he thought, and in that thought there was strength.

"Look at what is before you – Cencian – what do you see?"

The Master's words were strong in him. He looked clearly at the men and they shifted uneasily on their feet. They had heard rumours of these warriors. This one seemed little more than a boy but did he have powers? He read their doubt and smiled.

"I tell you no lies – I do not know where Master Syrath has gone nor do I wish to engage in combat with you. I would ask that you leave me to my sleep and be on your way."

He might have got away with it except these men had trained for one purpose – to defeat the warriors of Romarrah. This desire in them was well entrenched.

One of them smirked. "You're very sure of yourself for one so young but what brings you here alone – that is my question. I can think of several reasons. One is that you deserted your patrol when it was attacked by the river – or perhaps you left with Master Syrath and you lie with ease. The other is that you carry a message – that I think is closer to the truth and if that be so, I will tell you now warrior – that message will never be uttered by your lips."

Cencian's face remained impassive. He felt a deep sense of calm and quiet that came as a surprise to him, quelling all fear. Watching these men he suddenly saw, not their ignorance and contempt, but their goodness. They became as Teilo himself – standing before him. He laughed then as the understanding became firm – without question. It was a riddle just as Teilo had said – the riddle of separation. He felt the moment expand into an ecstasy within him.

"You speak to me with scorn, yet I have done you no injury. If you wish to take my life I will do my best to protect myself but my sadness lies with you. As I face death, I know the truth of what my Master has told me. It does not matter what you know or don't know, my friends – what belief you hold to – it only matters that you give yourself fully to life with joy and love in your heart. That is why my sadness rests with you, for you do not know this to be so. No – more than that – I feel the enormity of that which I am – of who you are – that which my Master spoke of so often – this you cannot kill. My gratitude to you – through you, my enemies, this truth comes to me now."

Momentarily the men were stunned by this speech – the passion of his words – the radiance the young warrior exuded as he spoke. Yet, it did not prevent what Cencian knew would happen. When they came at him, he stood ready.

♋

Syrath crawled through the tunnel hoping to encounter no one. Obviously this vein in the earth allowed people out of Manon and into Maurapin undetected. She had known the moment she entered it that Teilo had been here before her, but when she arrived at the point where she dropped down into the next shaft, she felt a sudden pang like an old treasured memory, too faded to recall.

When at last she emerged into the morning light and beheld for the first time the mystery that was Manon, she knew it – its smell – the sound of the earth – the hollow wind that wept across the hills.

It was a vast and lonely place but not without beauty. She did not find it oppressive as she had so often heard it described by others – to the contrary, she found it welcomed her.

"I am of Manon," she said aloud. With that realization came many emotions – those of loss – those of fear and those of possibility. She saw as Teilo had done the stone buildings that now were seething with warriors. She could feel the quiet panic alive in their movements. They are preparing for invasion, she thought.

For a time she just sat – watching her feelings – letting them come and go. The one thing that stirred in her more than anything else was the vision Teilo had given her in the forest at Imoshtan – that of the mountain of bare stone on which she stood and the immense freedom that soared like an ecstasy within her.

When she realized she was being watched it was too late to hide. The beggar woman stood on the ridge above her. Syrath was being summoned.

Without hesitation she began the ascent.

♋

Teilo's dream was vividly graphic as his mind allowed the anguish of the battle to spew forth unchecked. The horror of what had occurred could be encapsulated in the conflict between himself and the leader of the Manon warriors and that was the part he now relived.

The man was a giant and he fought with an aggression that did not seem congruent with the soft sadness of his presence. Teilo's eyes never left his opponent's face and there developed between them an unspoken dialogue. One told a story of hopelessness – of feeling the pain of every waking sunrise and the loneliness of each setting sun. The other offered hope and purpose. One unleashed a lifetime of hurt and his grief accompanied the swaying of his sword. The other attempted to coax the sadness into surrender. The conflict seemed endless. Teilo was loathe to take the man's life but nor could he disarm him - his grip on the sword was welded solid – his strength unwavering. At last, the chief warrior had no choice and his blade sank into the other's flesh. There came those few seconds of disbelief as the giant refused to fall, then his legs buckled beneath him and he sank to the ground.

Ignoring the combat around them, Teilo knelt beside the man and put his arms around him as one would a child. "Tell me your name, good man," he said, "that I may honour you."

The eyes that looked at him were already claiming death.

"I am Vulone," he whispered, "forgive me, Teilo, for the wretch I have become." He looked at the warrior's tears and smiled. Then he was gone but his words stayed. They became the clashing of the swords – the cries of the dying until the battlefield was a waste of bloodied bodies and the sobbing of the earth finally drowned out the pain of that one lonely voice.

The dream changed then. He was in a cave – facing the beggar woman. She threw stick after stick at him and each one became a squirming serpent whose head he severed with his sword. Still he could not kill them – they would join themselves together again and again until he was surrounded by the angry, slithering creatures. In desperation he threw his sword to the ground and caught the next snake with his bare hands.

In an instant he was standing on a rocky mountainside. He could see the barren, desolate land stretching out before him. In the distance was the Land of Romarrah – the forest of Maurapin. He could see Yeshotruen weaving its new life into a fertile path across the land. He looked at the snake in his hands only to find it was once more a small branch – leaves were shooting from its stem – roots spreading from its base.

When he placed it on a rock beside him, the roots immediately clung to the surface and began to expand. They split the rock in two and spread deeper and further. The mountain began to crack – the ground rumbled with moving rock, pieces of which bounced down the mountainside and into the valley below. Still the roots did not stop. They moved like the serpents themselves – slithering throughout the Land of Manon – reducing rocks, hills and mountains to rubble. The sound was deafening and chaotic.

Then as quickly as it had started, everything became still and silent. Where the tree roots had penetrated deep into the earth, small trees began to appear. They moved as if in a dance.

Again the beggar woman stood before him. She removed her tattered and stained old cloak. He beheld a beautiful young woman.

"Who are you?" he asked.

"I am Lethayelling," she replied. "I will heal you Teilo."

Stretching out her arms, she herself became the tree he had seen in Yeshotruen so long ago – spreading a golden shadow upon the earth. The peace of that shadow just touched his face when the dream ended abruptly.

The warrior became aware of the hard stone floor and the pain in his body. He groaned. There was something else – he was no longer alone. Opening his eyes, he beheld Amis standing over him, with the chief warrior's own sword in his hand.

♋

When Cencian fell, he knew it was all over. He waited for the final blow that would take the colours of the world away from him. He could sense his blood draining from his body and he let his awareness reach for a vision to guide him through death. Then something happened – an unexpected cry of pain and a frenzied medley of raised voices and combat.

"What creature is this?" he heard one voice shout.

He wanted to see what was happening and he made an attempt to raise himself. A body fell across him - he had not the strength to push it away. The young warrior knew he had slain one man and perhaps wounded another but now a second warrior had fallen. Who had come to fight for him? He could hear the sound of an animal – grunting and hissing – perhaps it was his mind playing with the confusion of death but he no longer cared – he could simply sink into peace – the struggle faded.

"No warrior," a voice close to him spat its words anxiously, "you are not done yet."

The weight was being lifted off him. Cencian opened his eyes. There was a creature staring at him – or was it a man – old and weathered – like a tree, he thought hazily. The creature kept talking – an incessant babble that made no sense.

"It's a mess – he cannot do it – I cannot leave him – they'll eat him – someone has to go. He will not like it if you die warrior. Is it my fault – did I fail you?"

This creature was ministering to his wounds.

"Who are you?" Cencian forced himself to stay present.

"You see – it does not matter – they have nearly taken your life – so much blood but you must be safe – forgive me."

Suddenly the creature rolled him onto his blanket and the young warrior groaned in pain.

"It has to be this way," the tree man whispered. "Pray warrior – pray for your heart to stay strong."

Hasty hands wrapped the blanket around his body – he was being trussed in a cocoon. He could feel himself being dragged but it was too much to find the sense of it all and he let it all fall away.

7

Syrath was intrigued by the beggar woman's clear, hypnotic eyes. "What is it you want?" she asked.

"I have no need, Syrath, it is you who has summoned me. Why have you come?"

"I want to know my story," the chief warrior answered, "and I feel you can tell it." There was something so familiar about this mysterious woman and yet, at the same time, Syrath still felt uneasy in her presence.

"What is your name?" she asked.

"I am Lethayelling. It is true warrior, I can tell your story. You are a child of Manon – you were born here. I will give you the knowledge of the land to which you belong."

She closed her eyes as if she was reading the words in her mind. She spoke fluently, without faltering.

"In the beginning Manon did not exist – nor did the Land of Romarrah. It was simply The Land. The people who lived on this land were the Manon tribe – Manon was a people, not a place. They were an enlightened people with great healing skills. They understood light and darkness and the power contained therein. The Manon lived in complete harmony with each other and with the land for a great passing of time. They knew there were other tribes beyond their borders much different from their own but they remained unaffected for their land was, as you would know, protected by mountains and almost inaccessible. They developed a law that if one of their tribe should choose to leave they could not return, lest they bring back the wrong knowledge. Nor were they permitted to divulge knowledge of their land to others.

Although it was very rare, there were, from time to time, ones who left never to be seen again until the one did return. His name was Tharseywon. He left seeking adventure and discovery but what he found were lands where people fought for wealth and supremacy – he saw war and the sadness it left in its wake. He longed to come home. No sooner had he returned than his attitude towards his people altered. Their simplicity and gentleness caused him aggravation. Their life lacked the colour he had seen in other places. His discontent soon became contempt. Tharseywon began to infect other young men with his longing for power.

When he again left the land of his birth, he took others with him. To them he showed the rulers he wished to emulate. His ambition grew and gathered more followers, seduced by his talk of a beautiful land beyond the mountains where they could create their own domain.

In time, the deluded young man led an army against his own tribe. The horror of that attack was shameful – these humble Manon people did not prepare for war. Tharseywon could not control his army once the battle lust was upon them. His intent was never to slay his own people, only to rule them. But slain they were.

One young man who witnessed the destruction was a boy named Romarrah. He saw the death of his own parents – the humiliation of his people. He vowed one day to avenge their suffering.

But Tharseywon's reign had begun. The stone fortress you see here today – the walled city – these he ordered built to form the foundation of his empire. In time he became a tyrant – leading his armies beyond the land - raging wars to gain wealth – leaving entire tribes desolate and bereft.

The Manon people who remained gradually became cave dwellers – living in the rock cliffs – tunnelling into the earth.

Tharseywon regularly sent his men into their caves to take the older boys. They too were trained as warriors. The young Romarrah was one of these boys. He became a favourite with his Master who had no idea of the dream the boy harboured in his heart.

Of an evening, Romarrah would secretly leave the fortress and seek out other young men who shared his desire for revenge. These he helped escape to the far edge of the land. In time young women also joined their ranks. Romarrah recruited yet more followers in what is now the Land of Romarrah. Many willingly united to his cause because they lived in fear of Tharseywon.

It took him years – past his own youth, until Romarrah was ready. Then one night he led his army to destroy the tyrant's rule. Not knowing an attack was imminent and having become complacent through their indulgence, Tharseywon's army believed they were invincible. Their defeat screamed in numb disbelief.

At first the Manon people rejoiced, believing they would again live in peace, but the cycle of vengeance had commenced. It was like a force within itself. Romarrah gathered all the people and decreed that he would annihilate this place completely – it now held only sorrow – it was tainted with the blood of so many. The Manon people could not deter him from this path. He was adamant that they follow him to the land beyond the mountains where he promised to build a city of great peace and beauty.

Although many did leave, there were those who chose to stay and continue the way of life of the Manon.

True to his word, Romarrah razed the land. The fires burned for years. When the deed was finished, he ordered the stone gateway to be erected above which were written the words – *'for those who seek to destroy, who hold animus in their hearts, let this be their home – the place of destruction'.*"

Lethayelling paused for a moment to let Syrath reflect on her words. At last the warrior spoke.

"How is it that I am from Manon?"

The healer smiled and continued with her tale.

"When Romarrah chose to destroy this land, he decided to leave the fortress and the walled city intact as a stark reminder of the delusion of wealth and power. It was when he strode through the deserted rooms that he came upon a small child cowering in a corner. This was a daughter of Tharseywon – orphaned by the war. Romarrah was not without feeling – he would never have harmed a child and so he took the girl with him.

As sometimes happens, such actions take on an almost mystical symbolism. They become woven into legends – they develop into traditions. There have been many Romarrahs since that time, Syrath. Each one has come to this land and taken a female child – a direct descendant from the line of Tharseywon. This child is raised to rule the land with the next Romarrah. You were taken from your parents as was Tharease. Your birth father is a descendant of Tharseywon and your mother also is of the Manon people. They still live here as cave people – waiting for the land to be healed – waiting for Teilo to come."

Syrath frowned. "So it is true – Teilo is the one who comes to destroy the Land of Romarrah."

"No Syrath – Teilo comes to heal and at this moment not one of us knows if he will live to do so. His life is dependant on the mercy of Master Amis. He could heal himself but he does not wish to do so."

"Can you not heal him?" the warrior almost pleaded.

"Only if I am summoned to do so will I heal him."

"I will go to him immediately." Syrath made to leave.

Lethayelling shook her head.

"Do you not yet know this is not your battle? Master Amis will soon be aware you are here. He will send guards for you. Romarrah is already gathering his warriors to descend on Manon. You must leave Teilo to his own destiny. However apprehensive you may be, you must meet with your parents. It is time you came home."

8

"Would you really kill an unarmed sleeping man, Amis?" Teilo asked. Before the other could respond, the warrior continued. "I think not."

He forced himself into a sitting position then, feeling the weakness of his body, reached out his hand to Amis. The Master of Manon was speechless at this gesture of complete defencelessness but instinctively he too reached out to help the ailing man stand. Realizing what he had done, he quickly brushed the other aside. Teilo smiled his gratitude.

"I can see you are already doomed," Amis spoke curtly, "there is no need to kill you. It is obvious you did not come here to challenge me."

"Oh but I did, Amis," Teilo leant against the stone wall. "You avoid addressing me by my name – does it pain you to do so? Does it remind you we are of the one tribe – we were children together? Have you paced outside this room deliberating whether or not to kill me? No doubt you had hoped the deed already done – that you would be spared the weight of that decision. You had planned an unsuspected attack, intending the warriors with me would all be slain. Your identity and that of your men could remain unknown. But I had more warriors than you expected and your men were not ready." His breathing was difficult and he paused to bring it to steadiness.

Amis sneered. "We were never of the same tribe – be silent or I will cut you down where you stand. It would be an act of mercy – look at you – you are nothing. Why have you surrendered yourself to me? Why did you not limp home to Romarrah – surely he would have embraced the return of his most famous chief warrior."

Teilo's head was spinning. For the briefest moment he felt he could not go on. He knew Cencian had fallen and that the young warrior's life force was no longer strong. He wished only to be with him. Again a shadow of doubt reached out almost like a comfort – let Romarrah take his revenge, it whispered. He shook his head and looked at the other man.

"I came because I do have the power to make that choice," he said. "I came because of Vulone and all the others who, like him, lived the agony of walking death."

'Vulone," Amis spat the name, "did you seduce him with your words also? Did he too lay down his sword like so many others and run off into the night? I am the one who gave his miserable life purpose."

He stopped, somehow silenced by the look on Teilo's face.

"Vulone was true to what you asked of him, Amis – to his last breath he honoured his commitment to you and I could not turn him away from it. It cost him his life. Is this how you repay him – with contempt? You gave to him the deed you could not do yourself and you were not there to hold him in death – I was. Let me tell you his dying words – *'forgive me, Teilo, for the wretch I have become'*. Does his death rest heavily on your heart because that is where it belongs."

Amis was dark with rage and his grip on the sword tightened. Although he saw the instability of the man, Teilo continued. "You could so easily have given him another way – you could have given all these people another way." His voice was little more than a whisper - tears spilled down his cheeks. "Romarrah was wrong to leave a people without hope – but you – you could have given them that hope – instead you fed their wretchedness with your own vengeful purpose. I have only come to give you back your debt." He could feel the mist taking his sight.

"I am done," he groaned, "do what you will."

He fell then and again, instinctively, Amis reached out to hold him.

"Summon the healer!" he snapped at the guard.

Teilo knew precisely where he was going. Unencumbered by his body, he drifted in that first place of peace but his purpose propelled him to where time was light and the strands played their dance through the ether. He grasped one strand only and waited for the voice to forbid he take this burden but the only sound was the rushing of creation.

Cencian was where the tree-man had left him – still trussed in his blanket inside a small cave. Outside an enormous fire had burned down to hot coals that would pulse with the breeze for days to come.

The young warrior opened his eyes. "Teilo – I knew you would come – I have waited for you – I wanted to tell you..." his words became lost in the struggle of his breath.

He heard Teilo's soothing voice. "I am here Cencian – I will not let you die."

Cencian smiled. "That may be your power," he said weakly, "But it is not your right. You yourself told me that. It is my choice."

He listened to Teilo's sadness as it fell about him – sadness for Cencian, this beautiful young man he had sent to his death – sadness for Allencia and the loss of her last child.

"Do not be sad for me, Teilo – I have seen who I am. I have never known such joy. I ask for nothing else – it is my freedom – it is love in me. You did not send me to die – you sent me to my understanding. Is that not what you have always wanted for me – that which I have now been given? Were not all your words preparing me for this moment? And you will tell Allencia of my love – you will tell her of whom I have become. I could never be greater than who I am – you know this – can you not rejoice in my freedom? I no longer need this body – this earthly bind."

Teilo released the strand and its light became stronger.

"Hold me," Cencian spoke again, "while I take these steps."

He held the boy tightly as the strand spread through time – a spiral of light that opened an ecstasy between two realities and he would have stayed with him forever had not a voice from afar called him back.

♋

Deshan could not breathe – it was no dream – someone was holding a hand over his mouth and another over his nose. His eyes opened in fear and he stared into the crazy face of the tree man – so close to his own that the features were blurred. Those fiery eyes were telling him to make no sound. Desperate for air he nodded and the hands left his face. He could smell the not unpleasant odour of earth and wood and resin.

Indicating for Deshan to follow him, the tree man disappeared quickly from the room and into the night. The warrior caught up with his visitor among the young forest trees within the compound. He knew whatever had brought this old man to Yeshotruen it was not good and he prepared himself for words he did not want to hear.

The tree man was distressed. "Do not ask me – I do not know – they both play with death. I come only to tell you the words the Master gave the boy." In a rush he related Cencian's message for Jemai.

Deshan nodded and listened carefully to the confusing directions that would lead them to Cencian. Somehow he knew they would be too late. Then the tree man astonished him by repeating every word Cencian had said to his attackers.

"These words are his legacy, warrior – you must know everyone of them so that, if he dies, you can tell those who love him. They are powerful – they set his spirit free from this world – they leave his goodness in place upon the earth. Master Teilo saw what I did not see – I waited too long to save him – forgive me."

He was whimpering now. "You have never betrayed me, warrior – he gave you your goodness too. That was the part I did not want to see – my words stripped you of worth and his gave you sight. I did not want to be part of this – if I must die now, it is with joy I die for that boy."

It was then Deshan saw the tree-man was covered in blood.

"Let me help you," he said gently touching the gnarled old hand.

"You already have, warrior – it is time for me to go my own way." The little man turned to leave.

"How did you find me, tree man – here among so many?"

"I know your smell, warrior – it is not beautiful but it has its own kindness."

Deshan smiled at these words – they were a heartfelt compliment – an honour.

"I do not know if your Master will live," the tree man looked at him sadly. "He has taken another's debt to the world unto himself. No more will he heal by his own hand. I have no place now." He kissed the warrior. "You are not a curse – this was my blindness – your spirit is strong. May it guide you well."

He was gone so quickly – lost among the trees. Deshan briefly watched the darkness before he made his way in haste to the Master's chambers.

♋

Syrath at last beheld her family – her mother and father – her younger sister. They lived in one of the many caves of Manon – it contained their peace and patience – the stillness of their sanctuary.

The chief warrior felt a lonely awkwardness as she beheld these strangers. They were linked to her by blood but not by a memory of their knowing of each other. Their lives could not have been more different. In a glance she saw the women's clothes made from skins and coarse fabric – most likely that of the grain sacks that came from Imoshtan.

Her father Rassein sat gazing into the fire. He had a strong countenance and his silence spoke not of discomfort, but of calm. Her heart ached for them – living in poverty and exclusion while she had wanted for nothing.

"Do not feel sorry for us, daughter," Assara her mother spoke. "We are rich in our way of being – connected to our earth and each other. We have suffered no separation for we live with peace in our hearts."

Syrath bowed her head. How quickly she had judged them. When had she allowed this separate state to become part of her living?

"Forgive me," she said, taking her mother's hands in her own – feeling the loss of their holding in her life.

"Come," the older woman spoke, "sit with us – let us find our path to each other."

They sat around the fire – studying each others expressions and gestures – feeling each others words and laughter. Parts of their lives reached out, as spiders cast their threads between two anchors, and sought a common foundation.

Syrath was aware of a new, hidden corner of her being tentatively opening. Something was moving closer – something that was softer and more yielding in her.

Sarena, her sister, suddenly seized her hand and broke the comfort that was gathering.

"But surely you cannot stay here. Master Amis desires your capture and Romarrah also seeks you – both have anger in their hearts."

"Romarrah will not harm you," Syrath quickly defended the man who stood as her father. "I have only known him to be a fair and kind man. Why do you fear him?"

Rassein looked up from the fire and smiled at his daughter.

"No doubt he has been a good father to you, child – your love for him is true. I take nothing from him for his intentions have always been good but you are more than a daughter to this man. You are a belief to which his very existence is bound – it is his purpose. He will stop at nothing to guarantee your safe return."

Suddenly he changed the subject of their talk. "What of your young friend, Master Teilo, whom I have met not so many weeks past?"

Syrath did not expect the tears that came so readily to her eyes. She shook her head.

"I no longer feel him," she said. "All our lives together we have held each other as we promised. I know his joy, his pain, his triumphs and struggles but now I feel him not."

Distracting herself, she took the reading stones from inside her coat and handed them to her mother.

Assara smiled as she felt the weight of them in her hand.

"His touch is strong upon these stones," she murmured.

Without speaking further she cast the stones on the floor and ran her hands over them. "Ask your wisdom, daughter – which would you take?"

Syrath closed her eyes. She could feel the stones and the life that moved from one to the other. Reaching out her hand, she touched the smoothness of one and opened her eyes. It was the fifth stone. *"This is your stone, Syrath,"* he had written to her. The tears slipped down her cheeks – a lifetime of tears.

Assara hesitated for a moment. A flicker of sadness passed through her as she knew more of her daughter's life.

"Discipline has been your way," she began, "but it will not see you through – discipline alone is not enough. Your grace and lightness have always carried you but beneath them lies your unmet destiny. You must taste your fate alone Syrath. Not as a warrior – but as yourself. You have never surrendered yourself to that which is. You dare not break the glass that reflects for you all that is good – all that you love. If you would have this change, know that first illusion must shatter and be released. Go without sight and trust, daughter. Be in your gratitude for the love that awaits you."

Syrath looked into her mother's eyes. She saw the deep love and wisdom therein and she knew then that it had always been with her.

"What do the stones say for Teilo?" she asked softly.

Assara's eyes challenged her daughter. "Would you dare ask of another's fate? The stones will speak only if your destinies be linked."

Once more she cast them upon the floor. Syrath watched her close her eyes and reach out to take one – it was the seventh stone. For some time she did not speak.

"His hands are soft and gentle," she sighed. "They weave all life's colours – not one slips from him unknown. He holds forgiveness. He holds that which we only glimpse from afar and yet he is lost – in a spiral between the two ends of existence. I cannot read his destiny for he has taken it beyond this realm." Assara looked to Rassein and said quietly. "He carries the warrior's stone."

Rassein nodded, as if already he knew of this secret.

"What is the warrior's stone?" Syrath asked.

"It is the stone of ultimate power – that of death and destruction but also of healing and creation. It gives and it takes away and this daughter you must tell no one – only his hands are to hold that stone. It is of the same ilk as these reading stones, except all power is given to the one of deepest red. It is the bleeding of the unspeakable – the one heart. Pray this warrior knows what he is doing."

"He does," Rassein began but he said no more.

The warriors of Manon came into the cave, their swords drawn, seeking the daughter of Romarrah.

※

Romarrah had gathered the full might of his army and was marching to Manon vowing to tear it apart had Teilo or Syrath been harmed in any way. He put aside the questions that had troubled him ever since his warriors returned. Why had his daughter deserted them? It was incomprehensible that she would do so. That Teilo had left them did not come as a surprise – the man was unfathomable.

It was clear to the Great Master that his chief warrior had known an attack was imminent and yet he had not sent word to Imoshtan. He had taken on the might of this rebel army and put all the warriors in his care at risk. Despite their being victorious in that encounter, the losses had been great. Teilo had made a grave error and he would have to answer for it – if he still lived. But as puzzling as these circumstances were, Romarrah let his mind be untroubled. His resolve was evident in his stride. His answers would come because he would demand them.

※

Amis knew of the Great Master's advance just as he knew of Syrath's arrival in Manon. His men were seeking her out with orders to bring her to him. She and Teilo were now perhaps his only chance of freedom. The remaining army of Manon would be powerless against the sheer strength of Romarrah's. Amis would be forced to bargain for his own life. Yet there was something else that had become the greatest irritation in his thoughts – the story Teilo had related of Vulone's death. It would give him no peace. Such was its persistence, that it gave rise in him to a nervous sickness. When he tried to block it out, he saw Teilo's eyes – his tears – and although Amis feigned contempt for those tears, he could not despise them. They did not speak of fear – they did not spring from weakness or even pain. They spoke of deep compassion. They were tears of greatness. Teilo was everything Amis longed to be.

How simple had been their lives as children, he thought bitterly – but that time was lost. The least he could do was summon the healer to save the chief warrior's life but even then, he would use it to his own advantage.

♋

The tree man stood beside the Pit of Maraka. He smiled at the memory of the warrior dropping into its icy water. The Master would not have done so perhaps if he had known it really was a bottomless pit.

The old man stared at the forest where he had so surely belonged. Here there were no secrets hidden from his knowing. He had played life among these – his brothers and sisters. He had seemed forever young – so close to the earth spirits he knew their voices inside his own being.

It was over now. His belonging was spreading – he could feel it leaving him. He turned back to the Pit. It would take him so that he left no trace – nothing to mark his being there. No longer was it his place to stand upon this earth. He was losing his familiar as all around became blurred.

When he sensed the warrior's presence he did not turn around.

"Why have you come?" he asked

"You called me, tree man," Teilo replied, at once by his side.

"If I did it was only a wisp of longing that escaped, warrior – just to see you one last time – to tell you I could not save him. I was not meant for this play of men – why did you give me that task? Can you now not let me go in peace?"

"Hush friend – forgive me." Those strong arms wrapped around him. He could feel the warm balm of their holding.

"We will go together," the warrior soothed, "as I promised. The choice was not yours to save him, tree man – come – come with me – I will see to your wounds."

The old man let himself sink into that comfort for a moment – just long enough to know it then he drew away.

"You cannot come with me, Master – you are not finished. Why do you linger here, beyond the curtain? You should not be here seeking redemption when you have been given the task to redeem. Ah – I see it now – how are you to exist without an existence – to see yourself dispersed. You forget I have lived thus until I became known to you. Perhaps I did call you back, warrior – we both needed to release that boy – you could take him no further, just as I could not save him. He came to show me it was my time also. You cannot protect a destiny that has already set its course. Nor can you stay with me, my beautiful child. Go – I want no witness to my death

– it is a silent thing, between myself, the earth and the heavens. Go before you leave it too late for your own return – perhaps it is so already. You will see – you have no need of me – my love is yours for eternity – they hold it – my brothers and sisters - go."

Teilo kissed him. They held each other until the tree man released him and the warrior was gone.

When he was sure he was alone, the tree man kissed the ground beneath him, raised his eyes to the heavens and dropped out of sight into the Pit of Maraka. The forest became silent and unmoving.

9

Lethayelling had watched him, day and night. Her vigil had entered its fourth day. Although her power as a healer was great, she could not hold this man's spirit steady long enough to spread a warm, healing fire through his body. Already she had lost him once – she had felt the spiralling of his being as it fell through time and she called him back in a voice she knew he loved. Now once more he had gone. The heart beneath her hand held no life – no passion smouldered in his blood.

"I will not call you back again, warrior," she whispered, "for that appears not to be your choice. And yet I know your destiny upon this earth – it is that which gave me to this realm also. I am not sure that you are finished here and if your purpose is incomplete, so too will be the healing that was to be your gift to us all. Be that as it may – your body grows cold beneath my hand – I fear you are done."

She was loathe to leave and tell Amis that she could not save this man. Through the window she could see the Master of Manon moving among his men and she smiled. If only he could see that of his own heart, she thought – but the one who would show him that picture had, for whatever reason, chosen to leave them. The healer sighed. She glanced at Teilo's peaceful face. His expression was one of utter surrender – so touching – like that of the most perfect innocence. It was difficult to let him go – the sad beauty of that face was compelling. She reached out to touch it.

There came the smallest flicker of his eyelids. Again she placed her hand upon his chest – she could feel life – however faint, and with every second it became a deeper pulse in his body. She let her hands reach into that pulse and coax it to steadiness while her own joy beat a rhythm between them.

Teilo felt the heaviness of his body and with it the solid realization that Cencian and the tree man were gone from this earth. This knowing added to the weight of his encumberment and again he made to turn away from his earth bound form. But the hand on his chest was insistent. It rested there so lightly – barely touching – yet he knew the strength of it – the heat of it. Images began to clutter his mind. It scrambled to grasp an understanding of what had transpired since he had come to Manon. He watched, letting questions find answers and become quiet. Inside, his body was groaning – he could hear its lament, but he could also hear the heart song of Lethayelling spreading a blanket over its moaning.

She did not take her eyes off the warrior's face. She saw a solitary tear escape his eyelids – a shadow of a frown crease his forehead. She watched a soft stain of colour slowly touch his skin. When she knew he would not be leaving her again, she gave her attention to healing his body – listening to the sound of his ailing and matching it with the clear sound of wellness. Her heart soared in her for this was her purpose above all else.

All the questions in him had found a home except one.

Slowly he opened his eyes letting the light steal his images until they were replaced by the beautiful face of the healer. It held a stillness he had not seen in another face. What he read in her eyes was unmistakeable, yet it puzzled him – he did not know this woman while her knowing of him was clearly discernable. She returned to him his own gaze. To speak would require too much strength so he closed his eyes again and waited. There was a conversation in him somewhere that he couldn't quite hear, then all became quiet and he let himself drift.

When next he awoke, the same gentle face was watching him.

He smiled. "I am not dreaming now, am I – you have no serpents to cast at me? Or perhaps this is but a beautiful vision of death."

"I am not death," she returned his smile, "though I fear you have walked close in death's company these past days."

The warrior glanced at his surroundings. He was in Amis' own chambers.

"Who are you, Lethayelling?" he asked, turning his attention back to the healer. "Tease me no more with your riddles for I am far too weary of words."

Without warning his hand reached out and grabbed her wrist. "Why is it I feel light and dark in these veins? As great as is your power to heal so also is your power to destroy. You are not of this land – what then is your truth and purpose?"

Neither spoke for a moment and when at last she did reply, it came not as an answer, but as a soft command.

"Close your eyes, warrior – I will show you."

He hesitated. She spoke as he did – her knowing as surefooted as a forest creature in the dark. He heard the voice speak. *In everything there must be the marriage of the two before there can be the one.* He let go then. The sense of release was like the snapping of a taut wire. He gave her everything – every step he had taken upon the earth – the weight of every decision he had ever made. He was as sure as she was.

"Go back to the mist, Teilo."

It was the first time she had said his name and it fell from her lips as if it had been there a thousand times.

He did not have to search for the mist – it was instantly before him – the beloved mystery of his childhood.

"Look well," her voice reminded him.

He stared into the thick veil. Again he saw the flashes of light – he heard the muffled sounds – just as he had as a child. Now those flashes swirled into a pattern – the same pattern his mother had embroidered on the cloth he always carried, wrapped around the warrior's stone. Now he could really see and recognize them – the strands of creation moving in a dance – never still – reaching out – falling back – weaving together like lovers – drifting apart – exploring separation until it too became a freedom to dance in.

The warrior's stone appeared in the centre of the mist. Its light burned a hole through the curtain. At first he could not see her, but he knew she was there. When Shimmera came to him it was as if a strand of creation had taken form. Her eyes looked straight into his. He saw she cradled in her arms the body of Apheilio. When he looked more closely, it became Orphaele – then Pauroseng. She held Cencian and the tree man. She held them all – all those he had loved and more. She held Tharease and Vulone. She held Mercenta. Shimmera was the eternal mother – giving of herself again and again – to life and death – cradling the tragedy of a world unfulfilled. A world that inflicted sorrow upon itself time after time. He knew she was the essence that once more needed to flow like a stream through the land.

"You were the sword I gave to the world," she spoke to him.

His understanding of her words was instantaneous. The illusion was shattered forever for he would indeed destroy it. He need not ask Lethayelling of her origins – she came from that same essence and just as Apheilio had done before him, he had summoned her. He became aware of her so close to him.

"I will wait for you," she whispered. He felt her ease her hand from beneath his own. "Sleep well, dearest Teilo – the dreamless sleep – that which heals."

Drawing her hood over her face, she touched the warrior's hand lightly, then walked to the door and knocked quietly. It was Master Amis who opened it and not the guard.

"Is it done then?" he asked.

"The warrior sleeps," she replied. "When he awakens his healing will be complete."

"Then you may go, healer – I am sure your skills will be required by many before this dark day is done."

♋

It was many hours later that Teilo awakened from his sleep. By that time Romarrah and his warriors were nearing the Gates of Manon. They had shortened their journey by going through Maurapin rather than around it. The earth there had shuddered beneath their weight not willing to take the burden of their purpose.

Amis stood at the window watching for their arrival. His mind would not hold its quiet. He so longed for a different ending to this story. Gladly would he be anywhere than where he now stood – among the ruin of his distorted dreams, awaiting humiliation and defeat. His only hope lay in using his captives to buy his freedom but even that hope was eroding with each passing minute. Besides, what would his freedom be worth? Like stale bread in his mouth – a banished warrior – without honour – a man to be scorned, or even worse, pitied.

"Where is your power at this moment, Amis? Do not waste it on self-pity – the day is not yet over."

When Teilo spoke, Amis startled – he had forgotten he was not alone. He turned sharply, his resentment evident.

"My gratitude to you," Teilo said quickly before the other could speak, "for summoning the healer."

"It is better for me that you are alive," his captor responded sourly.

Teilo sighed. "Amis do not do this. Turn your predicament to your advantage – think as a warrior. Defeat is not possible. You can surrender with an honour that will ensure your warriors are not harmed. Do not wait for Romarrah – you will find no mercy there – surrender to me now. He cannot harm you if you have already begged my forgiveness."

"Your forgiveness! Why should I do so? And do you think that Romarrah will respect what transpires between us? Let me tell you now he will not! All those years ago when I made that grave mistake on our path through Maurapin, and I own that it was a mistake, I went back to Romarrah just as

Syrath had bid me. I told him of what I had done – I asked his forgiveness. In his mercy, he banished me here and ordered me to stay until I was sent for. He has never sent for me nor did he intend to. Have you any concept of what Manon was like then, Teilo?"

A faint smile touched Teilo's lips as Amis spoke his name. He shook his head. "No, I have not – tell me."

"It was a place of ugliness and emptiness. There were two kinds of people living here. The real Manon people – they lived underground like burrowing animals – and those who had been left here to rot and be forgotten. Sometimes entire families were sent to this heartless place and left to fend for themselves. Sacks of grain – that is all Romarrah sent. People hunted outside the gates – forever fearful of what might occur should they be discovered. The Manon people in some ways fared better. They understood the land – they had their own ways and they kept to themselves. Often they would be attacked by those in exile who were driven by need or simply madness. It was a life of misery. I saw a way to bring Manon back to life and so I trained warriors. I encouraged people to make weapons. At night I led patrols to steal from the villages for there was no other way to obtain what we needed."

Teilo knew very well those raiding parties wore the same attire as the warriors of Romarrah. It was they who caused the unrest in the villages and the animosity that had so troubled Syrath.

"I gave these people a purpose," Amis continued. "I gave them discipline and we both know discipline is the key to overcoming fear."

Watching this man before him, Teilo saw glimpses of his childhood companion in the expressions and gestures.

"I applaud your commitment, Amis, but I cannot concur with your reasoning. Without understanding and compassion, discipline ultimately creates more suppression. The purpose you gave them is the same as the one you so detested in others. It is one of revenge and loathing – you repeat that for which you cry vengeance."

"Do not preach to me!" Amis punched his fist into the timber panel beside the window. "It was never Syrath I wanted to kill – it was always you. You talk of compassion – can you so easily forget what happened to the people of Athanan because of you and your wretched parents?"

The chief warrior said nothing. Amis turned back to the window but he could not let the matter rest. He continued to vent his long held bitterness while watching the distant horizon.

"It was a simple happy life in Athanan. In our own way we were prosperous – we lived without interference. We saw little of the warriors except when they passed through our village and they brought with them a ripple of excitement – they were good to us. Sometimes they would camp nearby and their talk around their fires was lively and passionate. It is one of the happiest memories of my childhood. You and I both tried to emulate them with our wooden swords and ambitious dreams. The elders of our village knew your mother came from Avarinsa. They knew the prophecies of the ancients. She was shunned because they feared what she would do and because of her, and your father, our village was destroyed – our people were scattered – families were separated – sent to places where they were not welcome. There is no one left in Athanan except for the ghosts. I have wept for our people. Romarrah killed no one but he robbed them all of their lives. I hated your mother – and your father. When he was killed, I rejoiced. As a young warrior when I trained beside you, I realized how alike we had become – lost and lonely on the inside – angry and fearless on the outside – and we were being trained in the art of peace and compassion! Does not that seem strange to you?" He glared at the chief warrior.

"What is it you want me to say? I have no power to change what is past." Teilo had slowly cast off the bedcovers and was sitting on the edge of the bed. "Forgive me, Amis, but my knowledge of those events of course differs from your own, but it is all too old. Why keep living that which is already dead – why keep living that hatred which feeds upon itself and tortures all that is good in you and others?"

"Spare me your sermons, Teilo – words are hollow when they come from your lips."

Amis closed the conversation.

Teilo let the silence take hold before he spoke again. He knew there was but little time to reach this man. He could feel the rhythm of the hundreds of softly treading feet that made their way towards the gates.

"What happened to your family, Amis?" He was careful that his words held not even a flutter of imposition that might tear this fragile moment away.

Amis responded automatically.

"My parents were sent to a village at the most south western point of the land. They had no place there – no point at which to rebuild their lives. Any children from Athanan who were of age were sent to Imoshtan to train as warriors. In his anger, my father vowed this would not happen to his daughters and so one night he took my sisters away. I never saw them again. I watched my mother slowly shrivel inside herself until she died.

Then I too left to become a warrior. I have no idea of my sisters' fate."

"Allencia I assure you is alive and in good health. She lives at the compound in Yeshotruen."

Though Teilo's voice was quiet and even, the words cut into Amis like a knife.

"Do not tell me she willingly stayed at the compound under your rule for I will not believe that could be so," he snapped.

"Your sister came to me seeking refuge at a time when her life was not bearable. There she tends the ill and dying and cares for the children." Teilo noted the bewilderment on his companion's face.

"The compound at Yeshotruen is far different to that in Imoshtan, Amis. But we have both added deep suffering to Allencia's life. I sent her only son, Cencian – a young man of seventeen years – whom she trusted to my care – to deliver a message to those at Yeshotruen. Your warriors took his life Amis – one so young – your own blood. Where is your war now?"

"How do you know of this?"

Teilo had kept his voice soft, without emotion. He could hear the doubt in Amis' words.

"I know of it – that is all that needs to be said." As he finished speaking, he quietly began dressing while Amis wrestled with his own thoughts.

"We all have the power to heal or destroy," the chief warrior broke their silence as he strapped his coat firmly over his bandaged wound. "That is the power of all beings – it is your power also."

"I too have read the prophecy, Teilo," Amis retorted. *"The one who comes out of the mist – beneath the beating heart – there is the one who will destroy the reign of Romarrah forever.* Your mother was with child when she came from Avarinsa – you were beneath the beating heart. The one who was sent to destroy."

Inwardly Teilo groaned to hear these words yet again.

"That is but myth. One does not need to have hatred in their heart to destroy that which is already finished. You do not understand destruction – you see it only as violence."

To Amis' surprise, the warrior sat down on the bed and rested his head in his hands.

"Has the healer not done the work?" he asked. "Are you still ailing?"

The warrior looked at him. "I do not want this which is before me, Amis – how does one stand against a father?"

"Romarrah is not your father!" The response was curt with barely concealed disgust.

"We are all that which breathes on this earth – there is no separation." The chief warrior countered but there was a touch of defeat in his reply.

The Master of Manon saw it then. What he and most others before him failed to see – the frailty of this man. This one who most thought to be indestructible – who appeared undefeatable – tireless – forever strong, vibrant and sure. At this moment his strength was wavering and Amis saw a gleam of hope.

"You cannot destroy Romarrah and all his army alone, Teilo, but perhaps with my warriors and those of Yeshotruen…"

"Do you not yet understand," Teilo's voice was sharp with impatience. "I do not seek to destroy Romarrah – my love for the man is strong. There will be no more of this waste if I can prevent it."

Amis raised his hands - a gesture of exasperation. "Then why did you send for the warriors of Yeshotruen – that was the message you gave to the boy was it not?"

"The boy's name was Cencian," Teilo reminded him pointedly. "In the event of my death, I wished for the warriors to protect the people of Manon if that was the only course left, but even then, understand, it would be their choice whether or not to do so. And, if I am to be honest," he continued staring at his hands, "I needed them. I needed to feel the strength of their presence – I did not wish to stand alone."

Amis did not conceal his bewilderment. "You could have saved your self - that is true is it not? You did not need the healer woman."

Teilo smiled. "It takes time and patience to heal, Amis – one has to know oneself already healed."

"But why the heroic stand on the battlefield? My warriors returned babbling of your immortality – I do not understand you – for what purpose did you take that blade?"

It was Teilo's turn to look away. He need not be reminded again of that battle.

"It does not matter anymore," he sighed. "I wished to make Vulone and his men back down. It was a mistake. I should have known they had nowhere to go. Take away the purpose you gave them and still they had nothing in their hearts to sustain them – they were already lost. Do not torment me with this anymore – it is done."

Teilo stood and crossed the room to face the other man. "I do not know how this day will end," he said, "but if you surrender to me, upon my life, I swear you shall keep yours."

The Master of Manon smirked.

"A rash promise, my friend – one I can not conceive you will be able to uphold. You are one man against a multitude – what can you hope to achieve?"

"I am not alone – what have you done with Syrath? I know in my heart that she is close and you have not harmed her in any way."

"I would never harm Syrath!" Amis all but snapped turning his back on the warrior. "It was never my intention to do her any harm – far from it."

He went back to the window.

Suddenly Teilo laughed. "I do believe that your feelings for Syrath are much deeper than I would have considered possible – can this be true?"

At once Amis appeared awkward. He gave his words, not to the space between them, but to that beyond the window, unwilling to share them with another.

"I have thought of little else since that night I left you in Maurapin – her strength – her softness and beauty. You may laugh – my feelings will mean little to you and what does it matter – the world knows Syrath will one day be your wife. Romarrah will decree it to be so. Do not mock me, Teilo, for what I feel or I might wish I had let you die."

"I do not mock you, Amis," Teilo responded then laughed again.

A shadow of a smile softened Amis' face. For a moment the tension between the two men dissipated. They were boys again – their swords and voices ringing in the forest.

"I simply cannot believe," Teilo continued, "that you would plan to capture someone like Syrath and force her to be your companion – it shows me how little you really know her. Do not be deceived by softness and beauty my friend – her will is cast in iron – you cannot bend her to your own."

"But to you she will gladly give her affections," came the acrid response.

"You pay too much attention to idle talk. I love Syrath – that is no secret – we are one in our knowing of each other's moods and feelings. Gladly would I give my life for her as she would for myself. Our bond is such there is none can break it – no friendship could be greater, but she will not be my wife – of this I am certain. We know too much of each other. If Syrath would choose a companion – which she may or may not wish to do – it would be someone with whom she could share the joy of her mystery."

Amis said nothing. He looked out the window.

"They have come," he muttered indicating the dark line across the horizon. Romarrah had reached the Gates of Manon.

10

Jemai turned to Edora. "What do you feel now?" he asked.

The warriors of Yeshotruen had just crossed Tharseywon's Longing and entered Manon. They experienced little trouble in finding their way. Teilo had notched clear markings into the stone. As always he had been meticulous in his planning, but it had been a long and hazardous process.

"He lives," Edora said simply, "but we must not linger, Jemai."

The Master nodded and called the warriors from their rest. He had felt pangs of anxiety for Master Teilo. He understood him well. He knew what Cencian's death would have cost him and he was also aware that something far greater than this play of earthly beings was taking place throughout the land. But above all, he knew Teilo was not invincible and that when he had asked Jemai to be there for him, he was asking for them to hold him when he feared his own strength may give way.

Edora's hand touching his arm steadied him. "We will be there soon, Jemai – be still."

They walked in calm silence. The warriors numbered close to three hundred – a small army – a pittance against the strength of Imoshtan but this was of no concern. Their aim was to stand with Master Teilo no matter what that commitment entailed. They moved steadily towards their destination not knowing yet what awaited them.

Syrath had for some time paced her room – the motion of her steps keeping time with her thoughts. It was a very beautiful room. The furnishings obviously had been chosen with care for their richness and comfort - so alien to this place of banishment.

She had no idea what was happening beyond this sanctuary. There was part of her that did not want to know. Of Teilo's presence she was very aware and that he was close – her sense of him had grown strong again and that knowing itself warmed her thoughts. Romarrah also was near.

She knew his resolve. If Amis had not escaped by now it would be too late. He had committed the worst crime against the land – it was doubtful if his life would be spared and it was this that most troubled her – this and the fact she did not want to be found. She did not wish to be reclaimed and she stumbled over this knowing as if the ground beneath her was unsteady.

Her meeting with Amis was not what she had anticipated. Instead of the superiority and contempt she expected from him, he treated her with the most courteous respect. There were times when he appeared uncomfortable but he was at pains to assure her he would cause her no harm and that Teilo was being cared for. Before he had left her he said words she did not at first understand – *'I am not that which you think of me, Syrath. Understand that my intent was never to harm you. I would have given you what has never been your right – that which you have always been denied. I beg forgiveness for causing you pain.'*

He had left her then and he had not returned. She smiled now as his words found a home within her. This room had been her refuge for the past days and in that time she had contemplated all that had occurred since she left Teilo by the river. She recalled him as she had last seen him – the love in his eyes as he watched her struggle with her feelings – the distance he placed between them as he refused to take her burden from her and unravel its confusion. Bless you Teilo, she thought and with that came the longing to see his face again – to hear his laughter – to let him see her own visions.

But she must also meet with Romarrah. She could not avoid causing him grief – it was impossible. He had always been so strong and calm. It was often difficult to fathom what he was thinking, but she loved him – dearly. She of all people knew the goodness of the man.

She closed her eyes. The first image that came to her was the painting Teilo had sent her with the fourth stone. A man and a woman – between them the stream and at their feet, the ruins of a city – the water washing over it as if to cleanse away the sorrow. The child was joyfully filling a cup – sitting contentedly among death and destruction. At the time this painting had moved her deeply. Again it evoked the same emotions. What were the words he had written – *'there are choices you will make to find freedom'*. She knew she had already made those choices.

Deliberately she removed her garments – those of a warrior of Romarrah. There was clothing prepared for her and she chose the simplest – that which carried no identification. Then she sat in the softness of her new being feeling at once exposed but sure.

♋

Teilo placed his hand on Amis' shoulder prompting him to turn and face him. "There is no time left for you, my friend," he said. "If Romarrah is at the gate, believe me, he will have warriors even closer. Do not let Vulone's death be in vain. Can you not honour this man who gave his life for you? Do not die as he did – wishing his life could have been different. Amis, hear me. You have let your heart become cold and yet I still know the warm goodness of you – I know you long for that which you think lost."

Suddenly he took the other man's face in his hands. Amis flinched.

"No – do not turn away from me." Teilo would not release him. "Give me your trust – let there be love between us as there was in the past. Embrace your self once more and you will move closer to your freedom. It is yourself you must forgive for losing sight of your love – surrender to me now."

He took his hands away but his eyes remained steadily fixed. Amis could feel them compelling him to go deeper into a place he dare not enter, yet he could not look away. He was clutching for an escape but there was no edge to which he could cling. He fought against his welling tears and the longing to feel this man's love. He fought against the words that rushed to his lips.

"I give you my life, Teilo." Amis bowed his head – he could fight no more. It was as if something had left him. Something that carried no life of its own – lonely, dusty – devoid of colour – it simply crumbled.

But Teilo knew they were not done. Amis still held himself hidden – like a sad secret beneath his honesty but time was against them. He embraced the other man warmly. "My gratitude to you, Amis."

As the Master of Manon unsheathed his sword in order to complete his surrender, the door burst open. Romarrah's warriors had seized him within seconds.

"I ask you to release this man," Teilo requested. "He has done me no harm and now this minute has he surrendered to me."

The warriors hesitated, but only momentarily.

"Master Teilo," one bowed and addressed the chief warrior. "We are acting on Romarrah's instructions.

Amis smiled. "You see my friend – Romarrah is still in command."

He held Teilo's gaze. "What you seek is beneath you," he added quietly as he was led away.

Teilo waited. He knew Romarrah would expect him to accompany them

– to account for his actions – but to go to the Master now would be futile. It was Syrath from whom he must seek counsel and Amis had just told him where to find her.

♋

Romarrah stood at the Gates of Manon, flanked by his warriors, waiting. His face showed nothing – impassive as always, he watched the land below him.

A lone warrior had made his way from the rear of the compound – out of sight – to where the Great Master stood and now informed him of the capture of Amis. Of Master Teilo he said little except that he appeared unharmed.

The warriors of Manon were unaware of what had taken place. They stood resolutely awaiting orders.

Romarrah's frustration was not evident but it rose in him like a quiet heat. Where was Teilo, he thought. Why did that man leave so many unanswered questions? Why had he, wounded and ailing, left his warriors and gone to Manon? Could he not face the mistake he had made? If he had gone to find Syrath, why not take others with him?

Romarrah's warriors had stealthily searched the compound. He knew any resistance would have been dealt with silently and lethally – there was no choice now. This was war and not of his making. But Syrath had not been found. Did Teilo know of her fate? That harm might have befallen his daughter was a flickering possibility in his thoughts but he would give it no space.

The Great Master was tired of waiting. He turned to the warriors on his left and motioned for them to descend with him towards the compound. Then he indicated to those on his right to encircle the city. Satisfied, he strode boldly towards the waiting army.

Halfway down the slope, he stopped. To the north he could make out the approach of another small army. He knew instantly it could be no other than the warriors of Yeshotruen. For what purpose had they come to Manon? A shadow of unease passed through him. He released it but it was followed immediately by a wave of seething anger and a quiet almost weeping despair. He breathed deeply – there was nothing he could do but continue.

♋

Teilo had not gone far when he came upon the first of Amis' men to be felled by Romarrah's warriors.

"No more, Romarrah," he whispered. "I beg you wait."

As he made to step over the crumpled bodies, one of the men groaned. The chief warrior knelt beside him, gently turning him over to see his face. He was but a boy – not much more than thirteen years, soft and fair, his eyes holding death within their glassy vision. Teilo knew this boy would have made the first move – never would Romarrah's warriors inflict a fatal wound on one so young. Why was this child made to carry the sword? Why was he so armed?

"Master," the young warrior mumbled – his words barely audible.

Teilo placed his hand on the boy's chest. "What is your name son?" he asked.

"Olio," the boy replied.

"Where are you from Olio?"

"I am of Manon, Master." The response was weak – a mere whisper. "I have..."

"Hush," Teilo interrupted, "say no more – be still."

He studied the boy's face for a few seconds then lifted him and carried him back to Amis' chambers, laying him gently on the bed. He felt sickened to his core and his mission began to fall about him in tatters. How could he leave this child?

"Are you fearful of death, Olio?" he asked softly and watched as the young apprentice warrior weakly shook his head.

"What claims your heart right now, boy – death or life?" As he spoke he gently prised the clothing away from the seeping wounds. Olio's eyes opened. A brief flicker of light touched their sadness. "To walk beside you, Master," he answered.

Instinctively Teilo unfastened his coat and drew out the folded cloth containing the warrior's stone. He noticed his hand was shaking.

"Hold this tightly, Olio," he said placing it in the boy's palm, "and you will walk with me – give your thoughts to nothing else – promise me."

The boy nodded. Teilo dressed the wounds as best he could. When he finished, the young warrior was no longer conscious.

"Sleep well," he bid. "I will be back for you."

Once more he left to find Syrath.

Romarrah stopped his advance when he was within hailing distance of Amis' army. No one challenged him. It was obvious they were awaiting an order from their Master. Romarrah could not help being impressed with the warriors confronting him. That Amis had been able to unite these men to a common cause and train them to a level of adeptness was commendable – that he had chosen to attack the warriors of Romarrah showed his inexperience and foolishness.

The Great Master was aware that his presence alone was intimidating and that he brought with him a reputation for leadership that was unequalled, but the sight of him surrounded by the might of his warriors – men and women who stood with confidence and ease, that would put fear in the heart of any army. He could sense that fear in the men before him now. Their hearts would be beating faster and louder as that fear rushed through their blood. He wished to end their torment.

Still he hesitated. Where was Teilo – why had he not come? Must I capture my own chief warrior, he thought grimly – no, he could wait no longer.

"Warriors of Manon," his voice rang out clear and powerful – it echoed in the surrounding hills. "I will harm no one if you lay down your weapons. Your master is now my captive. All I require is your surrender and the release of Master Syrath. If you refuse, then you leave me no choice but to wage war against you. Make no mistake – I will be relentless. I expect your answer before the sun reaches its descent."

He watched the confusion among the opposing army. Leaving them to their deliberation he turned his attention to the approaching army from Yeshotruen.

♋

Edora was aware Jemai felt compromised and uncomfortable. He was, after all, a warrior of Imoshtan – the Great Master himself had often been his teacher. She stepped forward beside him to meet Romarrah.

"Why have you come, Jemai?" the Great Master did not waste words on polite salutations.

"We are here at Master Teilo's request, Romarrah," Jemai bowed his respect.

Edora could feel the anger of the great man – concealed though it was, she knew it in him.

"For what purpose has he summoned you?"

There was no hint of emotion in his voice but again she heard the threat his words carried. She had only met this man once before. She had considered him kind and thoughtful but reserved in a way that protected him and held him separate. She saw Jemai's hesitation.

"We come to stand with Master Teilo," she replied openly. "I am chief warrior Edora, Master."

"I know who you are, Edora." It was a blunt dismissal.

"As you can see, Jemai," he turned his focus back to the young Master of Yeshotruen, "there is no need for your warriors, but since you are here, you may join those of Imoshtan."

This time Jemai did not hesitate. Romarrah could see the pair were as one – both so strongly independent in character yet they blended with malleable ease. Teilo knew precisely what he was doing when he left them to govern Yeshotruen.

"I beg forgiveness, Master," Jemai's respect was evident in his manner and his words but he did not falter. "We came not to stand with the warriors of Imoshtan – we came to stand with Master Teilo and we stand without aggression toward any party."

"Do you fully understand what you are saying?" The Master's stare was unnerving but his young counterpart would not flinch.

"I do," he replied simply.

"Very well." The Great Master was finished with this discourse. "I am sure you then realize the consequence of such actions. You stand in defiance of the Law of the Land. It is with deep regret Jemai that I renounce you as a warrior of Romarrah."

To his irritation, it was again Edora who replied.

"Then you will have to renounce us all, Romarrah, for we are as one in this decision – of that I am certain. We are warriors of our own conscience – each of us is here on our own account. We simply wish to care for the one who gave us life and honour all others – we stand against no one."

"Do as you will," Romarrah would give no more time to their exchange but it was clear it was not over. He glimpsed the faces of these warriors from Yeshotruen. There was something different about them and at first he could not grasp what it was. Then he saw it. They might be united in their stance only they stood, not as one, but as themselves. Inwardly he sighed. He had always been prepared for invasions and dissent within the land but never would he have expected it from his own warriors. He suddenly felt old. Teilo had much to answer for – he had insidiously eroded the strength of their teachings.

Jemai watched the Great Master as he turned and walked away and for the first time he recognized what Teilo had known for a very long time. It was all so perfect – the warriors of Imoshtan lived an enlightened life by the Law of the Land but it was so clouded – a thick veil. It made him want to weep because what they perceived as their goodness, was part of the veil.

♋

Teilo made his way into the underground maze of tunnels and rooms beneath the compound. He moved without haste even though the lives of so many depended on the timing of his actions. Although he had found the bodies of more warriors slain by those of Imoshtan, he could not allow that urgency a pathway in his thoughts, reminding himself as he so often did, that he had no power in the past or the future.

It was almost impossible to have any true awareness of his location among this myriad of possibilities and he let his senses guide him. When he realized Syrath was in none of the rooms before him, he gave his thoughts to Amis – how the man functioned and reasoned. He surely would have chosen somewhere perhaps known only to him. He would have had no need of guards so confident would he have been that no one would find this secret – especially the warriors of Romarrah.

There were shafts at intervals along the tunnels – obviously they had been dug for ventilation. When he had looked into these shafts, Teilo had seen the small circle of light that marked their origin. Certain these entrances would be around the outside of the compound, he used them to gauge his whereabouts. Now in his mind he saw one shaft that had seemed different to the others in that it was slightly wider. Retracing his steps, he had no difficulty in locating it. He reached his hands up inside and felt the notches in the earth – this one was meant to be climbed and he pulled himself into its narrow opening. His body only just fitted with barely enough room to manoeuvre. Slowly the warrior inched his way upwards from one foothold to the next. Sometimes it felt as if he would become wedged there and he smiled at his discomfort. *'You will not like the place warrior,'* Once again he heard the tree man's words.

Halfway up his right hand felt nothing when he reached out – there was a tunnel off to one side and he crawled into its blackness. To his relief, he could now stand upright. Feeling with hands and feet, he made his way forward. He had covered only a very short distance when, stretching out his hands, there were suddenly no walls to guide him – the tunnel had opened into a void.

Prising a piece of stone from the earth, he dropped it into the empty space, relieved when it hit something hollow not far below him. He sprang lightly onto strong wooden boards and ran his hands over the surface. His fingers hooked around an iron ring. Pulling the trapdoor open, he lowered himself into the light below.

Lit by a single torch, the room was quite splendid – adorned with many rich fabrics – so incongruent with the starkness of Manon. That Syrath had been there was a certainty in him but she was there no longer. For the first time in his life, frustration suddenly consumed him and became rage – it came from him in a roar and he plucked a wooden seat off the floor as if it was a mere twig and hurled it against the wall.

As quickly as it had arisen, the rage subsided. He stared at the broken seat where it had fallen – misshapen – its purpose lost in an instant – a picture of his own helplessness. He had so needed to speak with Syrath that he left a boy alone to face his death or continue a painful struggle for life. So too had he deserted Amis to the same fate after vowing to protect him.

Teilo's peace was shattered by the force of his feelings. He stayed unmoving until he again became aware of the quiet beauty of the room in which he stood. Calmly he sat on a large rug and closed his eyes. Everything was as it should be – no matter what was taking place beyond this room – for whatever purpose – known or unknown.

'One day you will know the greatness of who you are,' Shimmera had told him. He felt so far from greatness. Like the broken chair, that which had been so strong in him, seemed shattered. Greatness had been so simple in Yeshotruen - applying will and effort to love and heal a place and its people into new life – but this – this was fighting a battle of a different kind – where love was not enough and his will and effort were slowly breaking. He smiled at his thoughts and the sudden warmth of the air around him.

"I thought you were no longer here," he spoke as she entered the room.

At first Syrath did not answer. She was so moved by what she saw in him – the weariness – the sadness – all hovered around him like a shadow.

"I have so longed to see your face Teilo, and now I ache with the sadness in you – what is it, for it is more than I know?"

He opened his eyes then. She stood before him and her love flowed through him like a warm current and now her eyes sought nothing from him. Syrath had at last come home in herself.

"I believed you would be imprisoned here," he said.

"So too did I," came her reply, "yet here in this room I have, perhaps for the first time in my life, felt that I could walk away from all I have been chosen to be. Amis said he wished to give me that which I had always been denied – he meant of course my freedom. How is it he knew that which I did not? There are no locked doors – I could walk away whenever I chose. There is a vein that leads from this room to the far side of the compound walls. I had made the decision to leave when I felt you calling me back. Teilo, there is so much I want to share with you," she looked at the broken chair then back at his face, "but now is not the time – what is it you have come to tell me?"

He smiled at her. There were some things about Syrath that would never change – her meandering words had always delighted him – from their very first meeting as children he had loved watching those words bubble from her lips.

Standing, he took her hand. "Syrath – I came to tell you who I am and what I know in my heart I must do. I seek your counsel and forgiveness for the grief my actions may cause you."

He told her then as simply as he could. She listened intently, as always, and although he knew his words pained her deeply, she shed no tears.

When he was done, she simply folded her hands around his. He could feel the new vitality in her – one that she held quietly as someone who knows, without doubt, that they hold the lamp. He let it flow into him.

"Come," she said, "we will go together."

♋

The warriors of Manon had made no move to surrender. Uncertain of their fate – not willing to trust the man who had been their nemesis – they remained steadfast in their defiance.

"Bring me their leader," Romarrah spoke to chief warrior Prisheed. Amis was brought before the Great Master.

"Tell your men to surrender," Romarrah commanded him.

"And I have your word they will not be harmed?" Amis responded.

"They will never return to the land beyond Manon," Romarrah replied, "but they will not meet with violence."

Amis shook his head. "There is violence that does not result in physical harm – is that not the type of violence you sanction?"

Romarrah held the man's eyes briefly, then dismissed him by averting his gaze. "You have your choice," he said quietly. "And you may tell me where you have taken my daughter, Syrath. Your life is already lost but if you would value the lives of these men, you will do as I request."

"Why would you punish these men for what I have done? Not one of them knows where Master Syrath is – there is no one in Manon who knows that place except for my self. Surely Romarrah you would not kill these men for what they do not know. Nor is your daughter captive. You must ask yourself why she has not come to you."

He then turned to his warriors. "I am no longer your Master," he said. "I have surrendered to Master Teilo – a man I trust and honour – but I will not surrender to Romarrah. You must make your own choice but to resist the might of this army would be to face death. There is no escape. I urge you to surrender. Forgive me that I have led you to even greater suffering."

"Then let us face death," one of the men stated boldly. "What is a life without honour? Master Amis – you gave us purpose. If we have failed in that purpose so be it, but I for one will not lay down my weapon – to do so would be to admit that I am worthless." His companions showed their allegiance by holding their swords before them.

"We shall prepare for combat," Romarrah replied, "but you fight without your leader for he will face death first. What will your purpose be without him? It was not your purpose for which you fought – it was his. You are in Manon by your own choice. I have no desire to do you harm but I will command my warriors to take up arms against you if you do not stand down. I will wait no longer."

As he finished speaking the warriors of Yeshotruen calmly filed in front of those of Manon. It was only then that Romarrah noticed they wore no swords. The significance of this gesture was not lost on him. He could not allow such defiance. To condone this conduct would be to corrode the order and peace of the land. It would only lead to more uprisings – tribe against tribe, until once more the land would fracture beneath its conflict.

The Great Master motioned to chief warrior Prisheed to take up his sword. Another warrior firmly pushed Amis to his knees.

"Do you wish to ask for forgiveness?" Romarrah asked quietly.

"Of whom do you ask forgiveness?" was the bitter reply.

The cave people of Manon left their underground sanctuaries and now stood watching the proceedings below them. It was obvious they were there, not merely to witness this event unfold, but to honour the man who, for a time, had been the self-appointed leader of Manon. In his own misguided way, he had attempted to improve the lives of these people.

Still Romarrah vowed to show no leniency. Amis closed his eyes. Again he felt the warmth of Teilo's embrace and heard his words – *'it is yourself you must forgive'*. It all seemed so long ago. He saw the face of Syrath – looking at him – wondering why he had taken such pains to capture her and then set her free. His only sadness was that he had not told her. He asked for a vision to take him through his dying. Immediately he beheld a tall bush covered in the palest pink flowers. It had grown in the centre of Athanan – such a strange vision with which to face death. Yet, as he looked deep into its blossoms, he saw the soft, aching beauty of life. Somewhere within him an understanding opened. He was free – free to die.

It was Syrath's voice that broke the silence. "Romarrah – I beg you – do not take such action. This man is not guilty of doing me harm – now or ever – I am in Manon by my own choice."

Romarrah looked up. Signalling to Prisheed to stay his sword, he turned to Syrath and Teilo as they made their way towards him. He could see and feel the difference in them and the distance between them and himself quickly lost its understanding and became estranged. There was a beauty to Syrath he had never seen. She looked as a mother of a new born – quietly in love with a song that no one else can hear. His eyes moistened with a mixture of relief and sadness. He knew her love for him was strong only now it held a faint thread of something else – he prayed it wasn't pity.

But it was Teilo's appearance that set the Great Master on edge. That the young man's inexhaustible energy and vitality had been sapped, replaced by a weariness, was easily discernable but it was when Teilo raised his head slightly and looked directly at him, that Romarrah reeled with the full force of this man's power and intent. He was looking at what he had seen on the day of the Great Battle and it quaked in him.

"You ask for this man's life to be spared?" he questioned Syrath but it was Teilo who stepped forward. He bowed respectfully to Romarrah and kept his voice low and calm so as not to give his dissension to those around him.

"I am not asking, Romarrah – I am insisting this man's life be spared and not one more drop of blood be shed on this land."

"It is not your place to insist, Teilo," Romarrah frowned. "You may request leniency and as always I will listen, but in this instance – I tell you now – I will not grant it. How many of our warriors died because of this man?"

Although he did not say as much it was clear he also held Teilo responsible for those deaths.

"He has surrendered to me," Teilo persisted. "He asked my forgiveness which I have given – what then would be your reason for this execution?"

"I will not be questioned thus," Romarrah raised his voice that his authority be heard. "This man has forfeited his life. His debt to the world will give him no peace – not even in death."

Teilo lowered his tone even more but his words were intense. "He has no debt Romarrah – I have burned it in my own flesh – at this moment he is more free of debt than you or I."

From where he knelt on the earth, Amis heard these words. Their meaning left him no doubt as to why he had faced death with such freedom.

Romarrah shook his head.

"He will die for his disdain toward the Land and its people," he said. "I have made my decision."

Teilo stepped closer. "And I have made mine – you will have to take my life also."

Romarrah could feel the growing tension among his warriors. This was Teilo – the one they held in the highest esteem – their champion. He could not allow the situation to continue. He nodded to Prisheed to lower his sword.

"What is it you want?' Romarrah asked.

Surprisingly, Teilo hesitated. What did he want at this moment? There were so many possible outcomes that could determine how this day would end. But there was something else – it was not yet clear to him and briefly he closed his eyes – searching for that clarity. Romarrah, watching him closely, mistook the silence for uncertainty – a weakening of intent.

"You do not know do you?" he spoke softly – almost soothingly. "I can feel your weariness, Teilo – stand aside and let this be finished. Return with your warriors – you have suffered enough."

Still Teilo waited – watching the missing piece fall like a leaf – that which had always eluded him was spiralling so fast that its pattern remained blurred. Romarrah sighed – he looked to Prisheed.

The leaf had stopped twirling – its colours became still.

The Great Master gave an almost imperceptible nod to Prisheed indicating the execution should proceed. At the same moment, Teilo opened his eyes and witnessed the unspoken command.

No one expected what happened next. As he spun around, the sound that came from Teilo's lips was not human – it arose from the bowels of the earth and pierced the ether with its agony. It froze in the air and on the faces of those watching. His sword was instantly in his hands. His feet sprang from the earth to cover the distance between himself and Prisheed. He slammed the blade from the chief warrior's grasp with a might that made the mountains ring. Prisheed fell back and toppled to the ground. Such was the force behind the blow the impact did nothing to impede Teilo's speed. One foot had lightly touched the earth and the contact only added to his momentum as he turned back towards Romarrah. Every part of his body seemed to accompany the weapon. He flew towards the Great Master – one arm outreaching – guiding the blade with deadly accuracy. Watching from the ranks of warriors, Deshan closed his eyes – not willing to witness again what he had seen in the early morning light of Yeshotruen many years before.

Voices broke through the silent tunnel of Teilo's flight. *'The warrior's stone is nothing – it is your power you fear'*. *'Do not use it, warrior, unless you ask their permission'*. *'Did you use it to destroy Mercenta?' 'Who am I to have this power?' 'Were you without aggression when you killed my father?' 'Can you really lay yourself bare?'*

They all tried to still that hand but it was Syrath who gently held him. Syrath who stood unflinching as the sword whined past so close to her face. No longer did she stand in contest. She lent her quiet purpose to that of his own. It was enough.

He used every muscle in his body to halt the force he had given that blade and it came to rest abruptly against Romarrah's throat as the warrior let his feet again find their balance on the earth.

The stillness was pounding with the rush of emotion from all those around him. A soft southerly breeze played quietly through the space. They all breathed of its freshness as it courted that moment of relief.

Romarrah was staring into Teilo's eyes – so close their colours danced but they offered him no reflection.

In haste Prisheed grabbed his sword from the ground.

"Do not, Prisheed!' Teilo snapped at the warrior behind him without turning his head. No one else dared move and Teilo did not lower his sword. To the Great Master he whispered "Come with me, Romarrah – let us speak alone." His hand rested briefly on Amis' shoulder. "You have your freedom, Amis, but I must ask you to summon the healer."

The Master of Manon bowed. Teilo led Romarrah towards the compound.

The warriors of Yeshotruen and Manon parted to let them through. Briefly Teilo looked at Jemai and Edora and acknowledged them without word or gesture. It was then he noticed that Rassein, Syrath's father, and many others of the Manon people had joined the warriors of Yeshotruen in their peaceful stance. Rassein nodded slightly to Teilo. The warrior again felt the steadiness of this man.

Syrath watched them go. She wanted to run to Romarrah – to reassure him of her love, but she knew she could not take this burden from him. Instead she addressed the warriors of Imoshtan. Although they appeared, as always, calm and focused, she knew their confusion.

"Do not fear," she spoke with quiet confidence. "All is as it should be. There will be no more blood shed – lay down your weapons and be in accord with Master Teilo's wishes. Know that he will not harm Romarrah."

These warriors had not before been asked to discard their weapons but they complied without dissent. Never had they seen Master Syrath command such power. To Amis she said nothing but he too bid his men to do the same. They hesitated.

"If it is honour and worthiness you seek," he told them, "then be without fear."

As they placed their swords on the ground, Syrath knelt to the earth, placing the pouches of sand before her. She began a ritual – not of protection but of healing. The land of Manon was waiting.

11

Once inside, Romarrah spoke, again assuming his authority. "You may lower your sword, Teilo. If this be your wish to take me as your prisoner, then so be it."

Without replying Teilo lowered his sword, but not before he had taken Romarrah's from its sheath and placed it on the floor.

Romarrah raised his eyebrows. "You do not trust me? Do you think I will not honour my word?"

Teilo looked at him then. How well he knew this face – this man who had bestowed on him such kindness and who had most emulated for him the unhurried pace of a warrior.

"Forgive me, Romarrah – but at this moment I do not know if I trust myself."

The Great Master frowned. "And do you still not know what it is you want? There is an unease about you that is not common to your way of being. Why are we here – what is your purpose?"

Teilo's only response was to motion to Romarrah to continue down the hall to Amis' chambers where the warrior went straight to the boy. Laying his hand upon Olio's chest he felt the thread of life beneath – not vibrant but at least steady. His relief was evident by the softening of his features.

"Do you know this boy?" he asked the Master.

Romarrah glanced briefly at Olio, shook his head then turned his attention back to the warrior.

"Your anger is visible, Teilo – it accompanies your words – it betrays weakness in you."

"You are right, Romarrah, this anger seethes in me but it does not arise from my own feeble frustration – it comes of its own accord for this sickening disdain I see for life. This anger is a force in me - I need it and I will use it to see me through, but it will not dictate my actions or my behaviour. I will ask you one more time – do you know this boy – look carefully."

Once more the Master looked at the fresh faced youth. He saw the soft, fair curls damp with sweat. The dream from so long ago, when he was first given the title of Romarrah, again became vividly present. This boy was older than the child of his dream but the face was unmistakeably the same.

Teilo saw the older man's expression change. He waited.

"The one who comes to destroy the mountain," Romarrah mumbled, as if to himself.

"He is my son, Romarrah. And it is true – indirectly he has come to destroy the reign of Romarrah."

"I do not understand," Romarrah began, but Teilo interrupted him.

"No you do not, do you? I myself have only just grasped this awareness – but you will remember Orphaele because it was you who sent her here – to Manon. Why? We were not much more than children ourselves – what had she ever done to cause harm?"

Romarrah looked away for a moment before he spoke. "Teilo, I had watched you every day – you were lost to us all. When I sent you to Maraka – I prayed you would not fail, for already I knew you could very well be the next Romarrah. Think what your life might have become had I not intervened. Orphaele had come from Manon – her parents were of the Manon tribe. I merely sent her home."

"But you knew she was with child – she confided in you did she not?" The words were quiet but leaden with the weight of their accusation. "To what life did you condemn that girl? To what life did you condemn this boy?"

Teilo turned his back on the Great Master and stared out the window at the warriors – patiently waiting. He watched Syrath weaving the sands through her fingers.

Romarrah again tried to justify his actions.

"Teilo, had I not intervened would you ever have known such greatness? You may have lived as a simple villager but look at what you achieved in Yeshotruen – it would have been unrealized." He saw the unmistakeable look in the other man's eyes that told him to go no further.

"Greatness is not measured by achievement," the warrior stated bluntly. "If no part of me is closed, Romarrah – that is greatness. When I am to the world all that I am – that is greatness. If I live this state of openness as a hermit or as a mighty leader, the greatness I give to life – to the world remains the same. Make no mistake – greatness has nothing to do with prominence. What we do in this world is but part of our illusion."

Romarrah sighed. "What of Orphaele?" he asked quietly.

"She is dead," Teilo again turned to watch Syrath – as if mesmerised by the dance of her hands. "I felt her story in her bones. She died brutally – viciously – a gentle victim – violated by the culture of this man-made wasteland."

He looked back to the Great Master. "My lowest instinct would urge me to make you kneel and beg forgiveness before I take your life with my sword. Is that not what you would have done to Amis? Where is the difference in your crimes?"

"Teilo, that is absurd. I have never sought revenge – I have sought order. This you must know. Look at the warriors of Imoshtan – they have understanding – they have been taught the Great Wisdom. They never seek to destroy, but to protect. A leader must make decisions so that order prevails. As Master of Yeshotruen did you not consider how best to act for the welfare of all? Does one not have to make sacrifices for the good of the whole?"

Teilo struggled with his impatience. "Your order and the revenge of Amis carry the same aggression and if I make a sacrifice, Romarrah, it is my choice. If I ask others to make a sacrifice it too must ultimately be their choice but I will not sacrifice others to achieve an ideal. Where was Orphaele's choice? Where was Syrath's choice when she was taken from her parents? Where was Tharease's choice to follow her own heart? Even Pauroseng – where was her choice at Yeshotruen to live as her heart dictated? Because of her strength she claimed her right and by that decision she was abandoned. Those women were all denied their freedom and that denial is the suppression of love. That is what ails this land Romarrah – the denial of that eternal mother. You talk to me of these warriors and their training – you speak of the Great Wisdom but your words are flawed and tainted because the Great Wisdom cannot be taught – it doesn't exist. There is no Great Wisdom. One cannot interpret for another that which is. Once your own ideal is imposed on any teaching, understanding is already limited and you separate people from their own wisdom. Do not delude yourself, Romarrah – you create that separation for your own desire. Clarity can only arise from a needless state. Once you bring your own need into the play you immediately colour what should be clear. Where then is that which you call the Great Wisdom?"

He stopped, returning his attention to the scene outside. Syrath was intent in her ritual. The warriors of Yeshotruen were moving aside, adopting a contemplative posture. Their song began quietly – a rustling of sounds, like leaves moving against each other. Then it explored the space around them – reaching out its peace in waves to the land of Manon. But not yet did its blessing reach the room wherein these two men stood.

"What then of the lives you sacrificed?" Romarrah spoke at last. "What of the warriors who died fighting beside you against those of Manon? You knew you would be attacked and yet you did not guide them away from that conflict. Instead you led them into it. Where was their choice? Had you told me what was to come that battle need not have taken place. The loss of those lives is on your hands – even worse because you sent the one you loved, Cencian, to safety."

He watched the pain his words inflicted – he knew it ripped through the other man's body although it was only visible in the slightest tightening of his jaw.

He waited for Teilo's response.

It was not defensive. The tone of the younger man's voice was one of sad resignation. "Cencian is dead – he died on the way to Yeshotruen. It was not Cencian I sent to safety – it was Syrath. And I gave your warriors the choice, Romarrah. They chose to stand with me. Change always involves sacrifice. It is the reason it is so feared."

Offering no further explanation, he faced the Great Master.

"If you had known of the threat that Manon posed, the loss of life would have been far greater and let me tell you now – and think very clearly on this – Syrath would have perished in that conflict. I know because it was given to me in a vision long ago. You are correct – I made an error in thinking I could avert the course of that conflict. It was not in my power to do so for the same reason you would have slain every last warrior of Manon. Those men would not lay down their swords. In their hearts their life was already over. Let me ask you, Romarrah – is Amis indeed a great leader because he took the ones you deemed unworthy and he saw worthiness in them? No his warriors do not have understanding. Their discipline is but a shallow law but before Amis came here, they were a people scorned."

He paused again as if uncertain whether or not to continue.

"The first life I took in that wretched conflict," he said at last, taking a deep breath, "was that of Vulone – a sorrowful, empty shell of a life that begged forgiveness and release."

At the mention of Vulone, for once, Romarrah's face betrayed emotion. Teilo continued.

"Why was he ever made to carry the entire weight of the Great Battle? You could have helped him redeem himself. Like Orphaele – what was his crime – to love? Was it not your own personal grief – that which you could not acknowledge – that condemned this man? Did you not send Orphaele to Manon because you saw Syrath's love for me? You wished to give your daughter that for which she longed – that which you yourself had lost. And again, was that not to quell your own sorrow and guilt and keep her love close to you? Did you not in some part of you keep me close because you feared who I might be – that part of me you could not see? And were you not surprised when Syrath and I chose, not the path which you thought would be our destiny, but our own? Why then did you not send for Orphaele, knowing the mistake you had made? Yet all these transgressions – and make no mistake, Romarrah, they are transgressions – are but born of your own longing to give the best you could. We can never really ask forgiveness until we forgive ourself and that we cannot do until we truly own our intent and the actions arising from it."

The mention of Vulone had left Romarrah torn.

"What is it you want, Teilo?" His voice almost wept its sadness. "You confront me with what is past but you still have not stated your purpose now. Are you asking me to surrender my title to you – that you may take the lead? Is that what you wish? Or is it my life you would take – retribution for the crimes of which you have pronounced me guilty?"

"Why would I desire to perpetuate this endless cycle of vengeance so mistakenly called justice?" Teilo again sat beside Olio and placed his hand on the boy's chest. His anger had left him and he wished this exchange to be over.

"It is for you to decide your fate, Romarrah. For myself I will never again take another life nor will I train any man or woman to fight for an ideal. Do you not yet know that there will be no more Romarrahs? Until I found this boy, I struggled with that decision – should the reign of Romarrah be over? Now there is no doubt in me. The minute the first Romarrah laid claim to one land and destroyed another, the damage was done. But you – you have been a great leader and teacher. My love and honour for you remain as strong as ever."

He was watching the older man. He saw him take the burden of his suffering and place it between them.

"Do you not think, Teilo that I have always known in my heart who you really are? Do you not think that I have wept for my own ignorance and seen that you are far greater than I? It was that greatness I feared for I could never match it. You have my surrender – do as you will."

Teilo shook his head. He would not leave this man stripped bare. He stood to face him.

"No, it was your own greatness you feared – that which has been buried beneath your beliefs and duties. Be very clear on this, Romarrah – I am no greater or better than you – I do not exist above you or below you. I am you. We are the Great Wisdom – all of us without exception – even those you have banished to Manon – they too are that which is. The part of me you could not see – that was your self – that was your own greatness."

He placed his hand upon the Great Master's chest. The shock that moved through Romarrah's body caused the man to gasp. What he had always seen in Teilo was the capacity to destroy – to take away. But what he now felt was his capacity to give – to love. Even love, as Romarrah understood it, could not describe this feeling. This was a power that could heal the rift between the soul and the stumbling of the earth bound form. It was a moment of clarity – when all clamour within him ceased and he reached perfect understanding.

Then the warrior took his hand away. Romarrah witnessed the haze of his confusion again come between himself and this blissful void. But one thing was different – he was not diminished.

"Go home, Romarrah," Teilo said softly. "Go home and make your own prayer. Not the prayer of another but your own – that which is true in your heart – that which all people must honour and be allowed to honour."

Lethayelling quietly entered the room to tend to the young Olio.

The last shafts of sunlight tipped the bare mountains of Manon as Teilo and the Great Master emerged from the building. Romarrah spoke first to his beloved warriors. His voice held no trace of bitterness as he delivered a simple statement of surrender.

"Warriors of Romarrah – this day I have relinquished my command to Master Teilo. The reign of Romarrah is over. Give no anxiety to this circumstance – it is as it will be. I understand your confusion but be clear – there is no animosity between Master Teilo and myself. It is time. I honour you all for the brave men and women you are – for your discipline and loyalty – for your strength and compassion."

The Great Master then turned to the warriors and people of Manon. The expressions on the faces before him openly displaying surprise and, for some, barely contained relief.

"People of Manon," he continued, "I seek your forgiveness that I and all those before me, betrayed you to suffering." He said no more.

A Manon warrior, unable to check his long held anguish, seized his sword from the ground and rushed towards the Great Master. He must have known the futility and foolishness of this action yet he propelled himself forward in a desperate bid to claim his retribution. In the space of his short flight, hundreds of hands reached for their swords – the fragile thread of peace already fraying. Teilo's hand grabbed the warrior's wrist before he could inflict injury. The blade clattered onto the stone. Defeated, the man folded to his knees.

When Teilo spoke, he did so quietly, without spectacle.

"What is it you wish to kill? This man before you or the pain in your self? You kill for something that can never be changed except within you. Do you desire to keep opening the sadness of your wounds or would you rather they be healed?"

Helping the warrior to his feet, Teilo handed him his own sword.

"If killing this man will change that which you feel – will heal your suffering and that of all these people – if it will heal the weeping of the earth – then I will lend my own sword to your deed but ask yourself this. What courage does it take for a man such as the Great Master to surrender, not only the flesh and blood of his life, but that which is his very foundation, when he could, so easily, have destroyed every living soul in the Land of Manon. Now the choice is yours and it also belongs to every one of us here this day. Choose well, my friend – do you want this to be over?"

And it was over. Still no one moved.

Teilo took back his sword and for a moment stared at its blade, seeing the lives it had taken – the lives it had saved – the world it symbolised – the illusion it honoured.

"Forget who I am," he spoke to those watching in silence, "for that is not what I am. Let this illusion be no more."

He placed the sword on the ground and without another word, removed his warrior's coat. He did not claim victory or sovereignty – he simply walked away.

♋

The five warriors sat around a stone table. Instinctively Syrath placed the reading stones in the centre. No one spoke. Soon they were joined by Rassein and their numbers were complete. The atmosphere was one of easy calm but a small current of expectation was at play among them. They were all waiting for Teilo to speak but it was Rassein who opened the conversation.

"I am uncertain of where to begin," he said. "In my heart I know where the Manon people seek to be and that is here – where our memories and voices still live in the earth. Yet this land is struggling to hold us – it has nothing left to give."

Still Teilo did not speak but his eyes moved to Jemai. The Master of Yeshotruen responded.

"Rassein, this land can be healed – of that I hold no doubt. Just as the land of Yeshotruen was healed, so too can Manon be given life. For the most part, it will be a far easier task."

"Why do you say that?" Amis spoke - a slight obstinacy evident in his tone.

"We have more people who are willing to bear the burden of such an undertaking," Jemai replied calmly.

"And what of those who are not of the Manon tribe – those who were sent here as punishment? Are they to remain banished to this place?" Amis posed the question looking at Teilo.

Edora's eyes met Teilo's. She smiled.

In the twenty four hours since Romarrah had left, Teilo had requested everyone to remain except for the warriors who had also returned to Imoshtan and Yeshotruen. All in all, several hundred warriors stayed to enable this tentative peace to become firm.

"They will be given that choice, Amis," Edora spoke, "but only when they are also aware of the many possibilities that will now open for them. If they find their freedom first in their banishment and pain, their choice will be all the sweeter."

Teilo returned her smile.

Amis remained doubtful. He could not conceive the success of this transition.

"Why do you believe Romarrah will allow us to determine the path we must take? He has returned to Imoshtan – what is to stop him assuming his former position and control?"

"Romarrah has given his word. It would benefit you, Amis, to hold with at least a little faith in the goodness of others."

Syrath's words were calm and strong and Teilo's sudden response of surprised laughter immediately altered the sober mood. It linked them all – these five strong people – it cut away the hesitancy. They were no longer treading new ground – they were at home – they were at play. The seriousness of their undertaking need not smother the love and joy that would give life back to this earth.

Their conversation flowed without restraint. Plans were formed and the bonds of understanding grew strong. It was Syrath who first noticed that Teilo had quietly left the room. He had placed the seventh stone – that of completion – in his place.

12

Romarrah stood, as always, on the balcony absorbing the settling tide of this late afternoon. He felt a curious sense of peace and freedom within him – much like the first quiet breeze of spring lends a fresh curiosity to life. It was a long time since he had known such harmony.

When he had returned to Imoshtan his grief had been intense but surprisingly brief. Before leaving Manon, he and Syrath had talked as they had never done before. His hidden fear of losing her was at last laid bare. To not have her physical presence close did not pain him as he thought it would and where that fear had made its nest in him there was now a quiet contentment.

He saw the man walk through the gates and across the courtyard – slow measured steps that bore no questions. Romarrah smiled – he had been waiting for him to come. He went indoors to prepare a warming drink.

"You have had a long journey I feel," he said as Teilo entered his chambers. He went to the younger man and embraced him. Both men held the warmth between them. There were no ghosts – no shades of coolness.

"We have much to discuss, Teilo," Romarrah smiled. "I see you are strong and well again."

At first Teilo seemed reluctant to respond. He had spoken little since leaving Manon, except for the short time he had spent with Allencia in Yeshotruen. They had given each other the sadness and joy of Cencian's death. Their words and tears held a beauty only they could see. They were gentle with each other. Yeshotruen reached out to Teilo like a treasured gift that does not need to be unwrapped and savoured yet again.

He had spent time in solitude in the cave where his spirit had held Cencian and stroked his dying form. So too had he sat beside the Pit of Maraka listening to the crazy babble of the water that now trickled into its depths.

"I am well, Romarrah." he replied at last.

"And your son?"

"When I left him, Olio's strength and spirit were very steady," Teilo smiled.

"You need no longer call me by my title, Teilo – I am preparing for my return to the village of my birth and have again adopted my birth name Ahmeron. When will you be ready to take your place here?"

As soon as he had spoken these words, Romarrah sensed he had missed something in the other man's presence.

"I will not live in Imoshtan, Ahmeron – I have no purpose here. I came only to ask you to stay. It needs your wisdom and stability – it needs your love."

The Master was stunned by these words – a multitude of thoughts and feelings leapt forward in him as if grasping this chance to be seen. Teilo rested his hand on Romarrah's.

"Did you think I would not know you?" he said. "Your passion beats in your veins, Ahmeron, and your passion is here. Tell me – what will you now offer these men and women?"

He did not need the other man's answer – he had seen it already.

When he returned to Manon, the restoration was already well underway. He felt in the land the same tremor of anticipation he had known in the earth of Yeshotruen many years before.

Jemai watched his beloved Master carefully. Teilo spent most of his time walking among the people – talking to them – hearing their stories. Jemai felt his own sadness. He knew Teilo would not stay – nor would he return to Yeshotruen. But how could he leave? These people longed to be close to him.

As was his custom of an early morning, Teilo gave his time to dance. At first only the remaining warriors of Yeshotruen joined him. Gradually many more were drawn to the practice. Deshan and Kesten revelled in being with their Master again and their laughter was like an inspiration to the warriors of Manon.

The long hall became a sanctuary and the song of the warriors gave its reverence to every heart.

Jemai observed that Teilo spent much time with Rassein. The two men seemed to have a strong bond as if they shared a common knowing of the earth and each other. And of course, he gave of himself to Olio. At first the boy displayed a mixture of adoration and awe for his father and Jemai witnessed that slowly settle into a more familiar pattern of love. He himself remembered what it had felt like to stand it that man's shadow.

One afternoon as he stood quietly reflecting on the day's work, he sensed Teilo behind him. As he turned the latter gave him a quizzical look.

"You know me too well, Jemai, and your eyes have probed my every move these past days – what is it you wish to say?"

Jemai laughed. "Forgive me for my intrusion." He then spoke earnestly. "I do not understand why you are leaving. Although it is not my concern, I do not know where you will go for neither Imoshtan nor Yeshotruen claim your heart. I see these people of Manon turn to you as leaves to the sun – instinctively they know that which you give. They expect you to lead them and yet, you will walk away."

Teilo looked at this young man for a few seconds before he spoke.

"Do you not see that you ask nothing of me, Jemai? Nor does Syrath, or Edora. Rassein also is without need. Deshan and Kesten will soon be fully awake within themselves and when Amis has shed all the scales of his grasping and surrendered unto himself, he too will stand alone. I have no purpose being here – there is no need in me to repeat what is already done. Tell me what you know for yourself."

"I will return to Yeshotruen as soon as the healing here is complete – when I feel the land of Manon breathe again."

"And what of Yeshotruen?"

"It is in accord with itself. Edora and I, and all those at the compound, seek only to maintain its steadiness.

"And you will maintain it through the joy of your own being and not the expectations placed upon you," Teilo replied. "So too will Romarrah – or Ahmeron as he now prefers to be called – do the same in Imoshtan. Jemai, you have my gratitude for your presence here when my need was greatest. You came to this place without violence. We are both aware of how you knew what your actions must be. I can give you nothing that you do not already have."

There was no more to be said – the love between them needed no words.

We have become that which he is, Jemai thought. He lives in all of us and he keeps spreading only now he himself no longer needs to be part of the play – and yet, how I still love to stand in this man's shadow.

Syrath too sensed Teilo's withdrawal. "Why must you leave us again?" she asked. The thought of Shimmera's death as told to her by the tree man cast a shiver of apprehension in her.

He felt it and laughed. "It is not yet my time, Syrath. There are other paths before me still. Did you think I would simply disappear into the mist – throw myself off the edge of the land?"

They had walked to the top of a hill overlooking the city. Manon no longer seemed a stark landscape. There was now a boldness to it. A new character was being formed from its ancient foundations – a child joyously filling a cup from the ruins.

"Can you feel which way the wind is blowing?" he asked.

She frowned. "It comes from the south."

He watched the realization slowly reach her eyes.

"Teilo, how can this be?"

"It is because there is no mist at the edge of the land, Syrath – only an ocean that stretches as far as one can see. The mist is again settling on the mountains and in the valleys. As we speak it drapes its whispers in the darkness of Maurapin. Avarinsa is once more among us."

They stood in silence for a long time – just watching – the years of their friendship moving quietly between them. She knew so well where this man had gently led her – every footstep she had taken, he had walked beside her and there was still no part of him hidden from her. She knew where he was going and why for every footstep he had ever taken, she had walked by his side also. They had indeed held each other as they had first held each other in Maurapin a long time ago. She turned to face him.

"Will I see you again?" She searched his face to assure herself of his next words.

"We will meet again, Syrath," he answered, gently wiping a tear from her cheek. "Of that you can be sure."

She slipped her hand into his.

♋

"You always knew Olio was my son."

It was not a question – it was a statement. Amis felt his flesh cringe beneath the weight of it. He had avoided this conversation – he should have known better. Teilo waited. "Why are you fearful, Amis," he spoke at last. "You have my gratitude. You cared for him as any father would – and more than that – you loved him."

"I cannot feel within me enough worthiness to ask your forgiveness, Teilo." The torment of the man's misery was apparent in his voice. "Had Vulone succeeded you would not be here now – my intent was to take your life. I have contemplated taking my own since then but I will suffer nothing for what I have done – you have removed that burden also. I did not face death staring at my own delusions – I was ready – I was open. Nor have you stripped anything from me. I do not know what to say to you. In my heart I knew you were not aware Orphaele was here but I blamed you for that also. I knew who she was – I watched her from a distance. It was her death that spurred me to create an army to destroy Romarrah."

He stopped, silenced by the look Teilo gave him.

"Let me tell you, Amis, and be very clear on this, Orphaele did not ask for vengeance – only for love and understanding."

He watched as his words found their home.

"And so did you," he added quietly, "only you did not listen. There is no place here for your guilt – it serves no one – least of all you. I told you I came to give you back your debt. You may no longer carry it but you can live your life as if you do.

"Would you be so willing to forgive me if you knew it was I who betrayed your mother? That is the guilt I have carried most of my life. Whatever I have done since pales beside that one despicable act. I told my father of the red dove – that Shimmera had the power to summon death – I had witnessed it. That was all the provocation the elders needed to condemn her to death. Now is your heart so forgiving?

Having listened to the other's confession, Teilo took his time to respond. "Do you not know the legend of the red dove? Let me tell you. In the beginning the wandering dove's feathers were of purest white. It carried the earth spirits – it bore the joyful tidings of creation's heart beat. At that time earth spirits were visible to the eyes of the men and women who walked the earth. To find by chance a feather of the Wandering Dove was the highest honour – it signified one who had attained pure knowledge. There was one man who discovered, by way of his own nature, the taste of desire and he longed for one such feather above all else so that others would praise him and see him as greater than themselves. He hunted the dove relentlessly yet always it would elude him. He began to loathe the bird and his desire and loathing become as one – they gathered intensity and lingered as shadows on the earth. Finally, blinded by his obsession and the loss of himself, the man felled the beautiful creature with a stone. When he held the injured body, the blood was staining the white feathers yet he could find no tear in the flesh. Still the dove bled until not one white feather remained. '*Where is your desire now?*' the earth spirits whispered. '*This bird bleeds that you may see the nature of your true being.*' The earth spirits were never seen again and the man wept as understanding once more filled his sight.

"Shimmera was the dove, Amis," he said softly. "The one who bleeds for the world that we may see our true nature. Be at peace, my friend – it is done as it would be done." Teilo smiled at the other man. "There is an irony in the parallel paths our lives have taken."

"Where will you go?" Amis raised his eyes to meet those of his childhood friend.

"I wish to be at peace for a time in the place of my birth and that land too must be healed."

Teilo read one final question in the other man's eyes. "It is his choice, Amis," he answered, "but nothing separates love."

♋

He made his way up the slope towards the Gates of Manon. The calm peace of his soul was like a quiet unbroken melody. There was no rending, no severance, no grieving to be done. There were only his footsteps on the earth – falling lightly – each step knowing fully that which held him in place.

"Master Teilo," said a voice beside him.

He stopped and looked at the soft, stainless face – so open – so easy to read. It reflected a gentle soul but the will that ran through its core, though not yet tempered, was like a thread of steel.

"I still have your stone," the boy opened his hand. In his palm was the dark red warrior's stone.

Teilo smiled at him.

"Do not call me Master, Olio," he said kindly. "You are your master – now and always. Trust your own wisdom, son – it comes to you untarnished. The warrior's stone is yours – I no longer wish to hold it. One day you will know its power."

Olio looked at the stone. At once the mystery intrigued him.

"It has a power of its own?"

"It has," his father replied aware that this young man's destiny was already reaching out to him. "Pray you will never have to use it except to heal and that by the time you know its power, you will also know your own."

Olio hesitated then looked at his father.

"My mother always said you would come. She told me your destiny would keep you from us – that you were called to greater things – and I must speak of you to no one. She said you often sang to her in her dreams."

It was as if he had waited until they were completely alone to share this secret.

"My gratitude, son – your words have put to rest an old sadness in me."

When they reached the Gates, Lethayelling was waiting. Teilo extended his hand to her.

"Come, let us go home."

♋

"You ask of me that which I cannot give – that which always eludes you. You wish for me to give you peace. It is for you to live your own peace, but begin by understanding what it means to cause injury. When you are violent to life – no matter what form that violence takes – you reject the very essence that holds you and you leave it weeping your denial into the world around you.

For centuries you have looked to teachers for the wisdom that cannot be heard, only known within you – it is unspeakable. Do not wait for the teachers – listen – listen to the wisdom in your own heart. Hatred and loathing – those which arise from your fear – do not come from your heart. They are born in your mind.

The love and mercy – the joy – these that are undying – that ask for nothing – these come to you from the place of wisdom within you, for if they are born in the mind, they carry with them conditions and claims and are but a fleeting mimicry of that which truly elevates you. It is your heart that beats the passion of your truth – your wisdom – through your veins. That which in time becomes your knowing. When you seek to create that which already exists of its own accord in you, it is the mind but speaking its desire and you create illusion.

Be very clear on this – understand it fully. It is the uncreatedness in you that truly creates – that which cannot be named. Yet, in our smallness, we seek to give it titles such as the Great Wisdom. We seek to hold it and claim it so as to make it ours. We seek to harness it so as to give us dominance over others – over life – and in doing so, it splinters into a thousand fragments of separation within us. If you would have peace, know then its nothingness and let that be at home within you without the shackles of your intellect. For it is the mind that wishes to clothe it in preordained teachings and robes, monuments and rituals, that serve only to take away from its nothingness.

I cannot give you anything that you do not already hold in your hearts. Let that speak to you and when at last you truly listen, you will see its reflection in everything – no matter how small or even how abhorrent a thing is to you – there is no exception – it is there. And that my friends will be your peace.

When you know beyond any uncertainty that the child within every womb is the same child – is your child – peace will hold you in its womb also.

This world lives and breathes for you. Live in it then with wisdom and understanding. Live in it as you would have it be."

For those of the land, the words and laughter the warrior had given them became the soil that covered the naked earth.

They became the rain that healed and soothed and coaxed new life.

They became the stories people wove for their children.

Like Shimmera's dance and Pauroseng's song, they lived among them – in every touch of life.

They whispered the love and joy of the eternal mother who cradled them all.

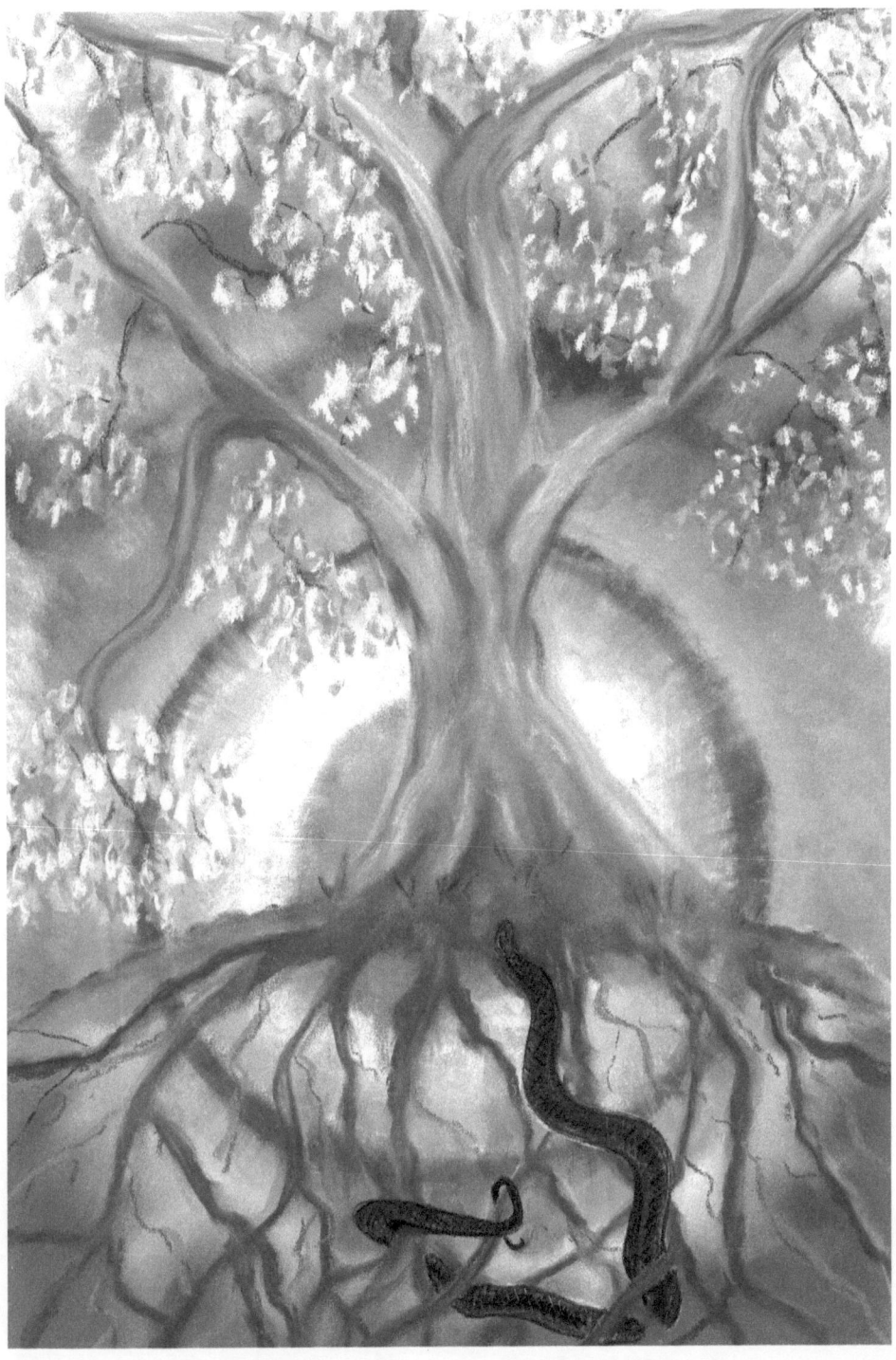

EPILOGUE

Allencia closed the door of the hospice behind her. The afternoon was unusually quiet – the last rays of sun filtered through the groves of fruit trees and the contentment of such stillness gave her reason to pause and breathe the peace with a prayer of gratitude.

The spirits and wisdom of Mealle and Cencian were forever present in her joy and the time spent with those for whom she cared. The life and death of Mercenta was now the blanket of love and compassion she spread around her. Amis had come to her. She had held the last of his anger and pain just long enough to test the weight of its lonely misery then she let it melt. It was something old and dead and although she recognized it, she no longer knew it in herself. It was this knowing that released her brother also.

It was now, as she stood, that she saw the young woman waiting at the gates, babe in her arms. She sighed. Another lost soul, no doubt – seeking refuge.

She noticed the warrior standing to one side as one who offers courage and support. She frowned. Perhaps this woman wished to visit someone in the hospice, she thought but her heart began to beat a faster rhythm.

By the time the stranger had walked halfway along the path towards Allencia, she was no longer a stranger.

Mericia placed the baby in her mother's arms.

"This is my son," she said and raised her eyes to meet those of the woman who had given her life. "I have been well cared for."

The voice was like a familiar song.

"I have suffered little – only an unknown aching somewhere that I did not understand. Master Teilo sought me out and told me of its source. He let me know my story – he let me feel the lives of my brothers."

Again she looked at the babe in her mother's arms.

"I have named him Mealle. His father, Rolande is a warrior. We have come to stay in Yeshotruen." A lonely tear slipped down her cheek. "We have come home, Allencia."

ABOUT THE AUTHOR

Gerry Hillier lives her dreams among the passing seasons – watching the expressions of the world around her – weaving her tapestry of colours and patterns through yoga, meditation and creative expression. Service is her creed, divine love her inspiration and fulfilment, storytelling a chosen vehicle to reach out to inspire and enable others to heal.

Gerry has taught yoga for thirty years and is the proprietor and coordinator of the Yoga & Relaxation Centre in Gympie, Australia where she conducts classes, counselling and healing sessions, workshops, and training. Gerry is also a drama teacher, writer, stage director and published author who combines her understanding of creative expression with the philosophy of yogic tradition to facilitate self-inquiry and healing.

Gerry lives on a property in the beautiful Noosa Hinterland, Australia. It is her sanctuary and a place of peace and tranquillity.

If you enjoyed reading this book and would like to receive a newsletter or find out about the Red Dove Teachings please contact:

gerry_hillier@yogahouse.com.au
or go to
http://www.yogahouse.com.au/totouchtheworld/the-red-dove/

www.ingramcontent.com/pod-product-compliance
Lightning Source LLC
Chambersburg PA
CBHW032026290426
44110CB00012B/697